POLIO GIRL
IT ONLY TAKES ONE

By

Susan L. Schoenbeck, MSN, RN

Also by Susan L. Schoenbeck, MSN, RN:

The Final Entrance: Journeys Beyond Life

Near-Death Experiences: Visits to the Other

Good Grief: Daily Meditations

Zen & the Art of Nursing

Heaven and Angels

Praise for POLIO GIRL

POLIO GIRL brings the everyday reader into the lives of polio survivors each of whom experienced poliomyelitis in a unique way. The book takes us on a journey through family members' reactions to polio in their midst, community fear, quarantines, and the disparities in treatment between the wealthy, poor and racial groups.

Struck by polio at age seven months, Susie and her family grappled not only with the unmistakable physical aspects of the disease but also the uncertainty and stigma spawned by societal norms. Schoenbeck's vivid descriptions of the distinct reactions of her parents and brother, extended family, friends, and teachers throughout her childhood and into adulthood provide insight into not only the devastating acute aspects of polio but also the long-term complications of this illness heretofore not openly discussed.

Schoenbeck's book, including the extensive well-researched information about polio the disease, is also a very important resource for healthcare professionals most of whom have had little or no exposure to polio survivors. POLIO GIRL is a helpful stockpile of information for the over 300,000 people in the United States and 15 million polio survivors worldwide who continue to deal with the long-haul symptoms of polio.

Polio continues to step its footprint in other countries. This book shouts the message that viruses can damage more than is visible.

—Marny Eulberg, M.D. family physician, polio survivor, and educator serving on the board of directors of Post-Polio Health International. Eulberg founded the Mountain & Plains Post-Polio Clinic and the Human Gait Institute.

People across our planet need this book. It is touching, informational, and inspirational.

POLIO GIRL reflects how many of us feel when facing seemingly overwhelming circumstances. In challenging, traumatic conditions we can choose to be angry and vengeful, or to be decent and kind.

As I read, my heart and eyes opened further and further to what it means to live with daily pain and disability. The stories help the reader understand the separateness and fear of a child alone without a voice. As a victim of childhood trauma, I heard my own cries. An advocate can make a difference. For polio survivors, that champion could be a nurse, a doctor, a family member, teacher, me, or you.

Information about the sequelae of polio and how to address a polio survivor in a person-centered way, using the tools outlined in the "Toolbox" section, mean this book is an ideal text for nurses, doctors, and ancillary healthcare staff. Professors across the healthcare spectrum will find in POLIO GIRL an understanding of the needs of people who carry with them the burden of viral disease damage.

I will integrate its content into psychology courses I teach and recommend it to professors of other disciplines.

—Tess Yevka, Professor of Psychology, Clark College, Vancouver, Washington

******

This book is a dynamic fusion of a survivor's resilience and an artful approach to care delivery. A powerful lesson of understanding wholistic care extends beyond the physical.

—Roda McLees, RN, BSN

As an internal medicine physician, I urge doctors to read POLIO GIRL. It is a treasure trove of information that may surprise you and help you understand and help polio survivors.

—Dr. Fred Mendoza, RN, MD, Diplomate on American Board of Internal Medicine, Hospitalist.

******

POLIO GIRL is a must read. This book brings the reader a heartfelt family story revealing the physical, psychological, and emotional challenges a poliomyelitis survivor has faced. It also will educate healthcare providers who care for polio patients.

—Tim Martinez, PA-C, MPH

******

POLIO GIRL provides physical therapists with a resource which will increase their understanding of the multifactorial issues polio survivors face. Physical therapists are vital practitioners in helping the 15,000,000 people worldwide who face the long-haul symptoms of suffering poliomyelitis many decades before.

—Kristi Carriere, PT, DPT

Compelling and thought-provoking personal story about a time in our history that has been all but erased by the success of the polio vaccine. The historical information interspersed throughout the story is particularly enlightening.

—Jessica Beach, MSW

Copyright © 2022 Susan L. Schoenbeck, MSN, RN

All rights reserved.

ISBN: 9798533926980

Springwater Press • Silverton, Oregon
springwaterpress.com

CONTENTS

Praise for Polio Girl iii
Dedication ix
Special Thanks xi
Overview 1
Stories 3
Foreshadow 5
Al • 1933 7
Marjorie Clare • 1940 13
Al • 1941 21
Marjorie Clare • 1941 23
Marjorie Clare • 1945-1946 31
Al • 1946 37
Susie • 1946 39
Marjorie Clare • 1946 51
Al • 1947 55
Marjorie Clare • 1947 63
Susie • 1947 69
Susie • 1948 73
Al • 1948 79
Marjorie Clare • 1949 83
Marjorie Clare • 1950s 87
Susie • 1950s 95
Al • 1950s 99
Susie • 1952 103
Susie • 1953 111
Susie • 1954 125
Marjorie Clare • 1955 139
Susie • 1955 141
Susie • 1956 159
Marjorie Clare • 1959 165

Susie • 1961-1964	169
Al • 1962	187
Susie • 1964	189
Susie • 1968	199
Susie • 1984	211
Marjorie Clare • 1984	217
Susie • 1990 Awful	229
Susie • 1990s-2000s	231
Al • 1997	251
Marjorie Clare • 2000	255
Marjorie Clare • 2001	259
Al • 2001	263
Susie • September 15, 2001	267
Al • 2012	269
Susie • 2012	273
Susie • 2022	275
It Only Takes One	277
After the Fact: The Sequelae of Polio, Dealing with the Long-Haul Symptoms	283
General Index	362
Name Index	365
Family Tree	367
Bibliography	369
About Susan L. Schoenbeck, MSN, RN	417

Dedication

For David
who cracked my heart wide open
and caught the pieces in his loving arms

Special Thanks

With gratitude for editing and caring support of polio survivors.

Karen Tetz, RN, PhD, Professor, Walla Walla University School of Nursing, Editor

Overview

POLIO GIRL presents the history of polio amidst the backdrop of World War II, and the March of Dimes vaccination campaign. The world stage finds Franklin Delano Roosevelt and Adolf Hitler's right hand propagandist Joseph Goebbels displaying disparate views for treatment of people with disabilities.

Fear, shame, blame, and the stigma of polio cut razor sharp through people's lives. Families fractured. Isolation hospitals filled with nurses pumping bellows of iron lungs, scrubbing their hands raw, and wearing masks put together by volunteers using gauze and string.

Children grouped in iron lungs and on wards ceased crying when their pleas to see their parents went unmet. Parents of children wrested from their arms set up ladders reaching to the higher floors of hospitals to catch a glimpse of their child. The lives of people who realized they may have been the one to transmit the polio virus and cripple a child became haunted by guilt.

America today has only a handful of doctors educated about polio to serve the Christopher & Dana Reeve Foundation estimate of 300,000 polio survivors now living in the United States. POLIO GIRL contains a wealth of information for doctors, nurses and other healthcare professionals who may have an opportunity to treat one of the 15,000,000 polio survivors worldwide.

Polio's damaging effects on the body did not end at the time of infection. Survivors went on to deal daily with long-haul symptoms for the rest of their lives. Polio did not just paralyze its victims. Speeding along the neurological tract chewing up neurons, the virus spread its destruction throughout the body. By outlining the polio virus' pathway, the book methodically presents what is often hidden from the onlooker's view. The everyday maladies of polio survivors will surprise you.

A quick-guide TOOLBOX compendium gives the polio survivor, healthcare professionals, family and friends information about common problems polio survivors face and *conversation starters* for engaging in dialogue to address polio survivors' deficits thereby improving quality of life. An extensive list of resources provides references (hyperlinked URLs in the eBook edition).

Stories

We tend to believe the story of our life begins with our birth and ends with our death. *First, there was nothing, then I was born. When I die, I no longer exist.* This is not so.

Human lives are not pieces of string that can be separated out from the lives of others. We are woven together…like it or not.

Families are like chemical reactions in a test tube. It is impossible for one family member to touch another family member without stimulating a reaction.

It is impossible to understand oneself completely without having a sense of the tribe from which we come. Everybody has an individual story. But that story is part of a bigger one.

You may drift apart from family members, but their stories still affect you. You might turn your back on family, but that does not mean others do not feel your presence even in your absence.

Our life stories are not static. People go in and out of them. Even when we leave this earth, we are remembered in the hearts and minds of others.

There is a beginning and end to everyone's time on earth. But what happens in between the beginning and the end is oftentimes the most interesting. For that middle place between birth and death shapes each one of us into the unique beings we are and always will be. This is wherein the real story lies.

Some of us recall details. Others do not. The particular of events vary with the eye of the beholder. People and events influenced us. Achievements that mom and dad had in mind for each of us. Graduations. Vacations. Marriages. Divorces, Wars. Depressions and Recessions. Storms of epic proportions: fires, floods and winds that swept with fury everything in sight away. Funerals—the crying mostly.

Muddling up the details of our middle story is natural. It is soothing to forget some events and people. What would it be like—*just ask yourself*—if you could remember everything that ever happened in your life story? *Better to not know your life by heart. Someone much smarter thought forgetting can be kinder.*

This story is a reflection on life with polio. The author presents one person's recollection along with the writings, photos, historical references, and first-hand conversations with the characters involved.

What is past is prologue.

William Shakespeare

The Tempest

Foreshadow

Holding his baby tightly against his chest, Al runs into the darkness to reach the car parked in an alley behind the house. Rain pelts him and he places his jacket over his child to protect her from the sudden downpour on this muggy day. The doctor told Margie to get Susie to the isolation hospital as soon as possible. Oh my God, I'd better hurry. This cannot be happening.

He lays his daughter on the car's front seat and then worries she might roll off. He scrunches up an old tarp and stuffs it snugly against her body, so she does not fall over the seat's edge.

It's not a traffic jam that has slowed him down. Rather, he misses a turn because his heart and mind are burdened with fear and the ponderous possibility that Susie could have polio. He wants to disbelieve what he knows could be true. Trembling with dread, he must loop back.

The sky darkens as rain intersperses with occasional flashes of lightning when Al arrives at the medical center grounds. A bright lamp illuminates a sign reading Southview Hospital. Shadows made by a canvas canopy overhanging the walkway shade the entrance door from view. He reaches for the doorknob. The latch clicks but does not move. Locked.

Al pounds on the weathered wood. Please, please open up. His sweat, born of the humid day mixed with copious tears, pours off his head and onto his child. He smears his nose onto her hair matting the blonde curls. She feels so warm. She screams which makes him squeeze her more tightly.

Susie coughs and chokes between breaths. Accustomed to the cadence of Al rocking her gently while singing softly, she is frightened by his jerky movements which feel foreign to her.

Alerted by the sound of repeated striking on the door, a tall man dressed in white opens it and beckons Al in with a wave of his hand to a corridor with benches. A stern-faced woman wearing a nurse's starched white hat puts out her arms in expectation of taking Susie. Al looks up at the people, but he cannot let go of his precious daughter. He is bewildered. Tapping on Al's shoulder, the man in white says, "You must give her up."

Shaken and scared, Al hesitates. The man repeats his direction this time spacing his words deliberately, more slowly. "You must…let us…take her." He places one arm around Al's shoulder in a gesture meant to be reassuring. The man knows giving up your child to people you do not know is not easy. He says, "Give me… your child." Dozens of times, he has opened the hospital door to parents seeking help but not wanting to let their children go. Al wonders: *If I give her to you, what will happen? Where will you take her?* Riveted to the ground, he weeps.

The woman wearing the nurse's hat steps up and lifts his baby into her arms. The tall man and the nurse nod at him but do not smile. "Take a seat. We will take good care of her."

Al looks around. His arms and heart are empty. Standing in the corridor, he takes in the sounds and peculiar smells. Out of the corner of his eye he catches sight of a man and woman nestled in each other's arms. They are crying. Although they hide their faces on each other's shoulders, Al recognizes their feelings. Oh my God. This cannot be happening.

Al • 1933

Life for Al, as a young boy, centered about fifty miles west of Milwaukee, Wisconsin on the family farm. Farm chores consisted of caring for Holsteins, hayfields, and crops that rotated in the fields through Spring, Summer, and early Fall.

The land was fertile in part due to ditch drainage from the Rock River. Known by Native American Sauk and Fox as the Sinnissippi, it was a 299-mile-long tributary of the mighty Mississippi. On days others might find too inclement, you could find Al catching bass and walleye off the side of a rowboat floating down an offshoot stream.

The roads twisted with weathered red barns and houses snuggled in and around each bend. This was home.

Al was precocious learning to play the fiddle standing on his head by mimicking his grandfather doing the same. Never had a lesson. Just watched and played by ear. After chores on the farm, he often sat on the farmhouse porch rail and entertained the family. Al got everyone singing and swaying. A natural entertainer with a full-on toothy smile, he made the crowd beam and clap.

Ten students occupied the one-story wood frame Eagle school. A pump stood ready for young hands to help the teacher gather water. A bell fastened in a tower atop the roof reminded students when school was starting. A merry-go-round, two slides and two swings were set off to the building's side. The rain puddled in

Spring. Winter brought with it a slippery, musty-smelling classroom floor.

Students lined up in a straight line to enter school when the bell rang. On festival days, parades of students wearing paper crowns on their heads marched around the building banging on boards and pots. Kids had little of material value but could make a lot of noise.

A lone teacher taught all subjects except industrial arts. Her job also included making sure kids got breaks, lunch, snacks and the classroom was swept of outside debris dragged in on soggy shoes and boots. A fellow whose arm had become caught and injured in a farm machine accident came to the school once a week to teach children industrial arts: how to build doll beds, small wooden racing cars, planters, and such.

Al's ready smile vanished when the teacher walked up to begin morning lessons. After giving instructions, the teacher sidled up to Al's desk and looped a piece of rope around his left arm. Writing left-handed was prohibited. The fellow helping teach carpentry had placed a steel bolt on the back of the desk. The teacher tied Al's arm to it while telling him he must write using his right hand. "I will," he whispered with his head looking down at the blank paper in front of him. The teacher's power etched into his heart how it felt to be looked down upon.

Every school day the teacher tethered his arm. Al said nothing. He grew up in a German household where kids were expected to be quiet and do as they were told. Al learned when young to follow rules. He managed to print right-handed. Al did not stay in school long enough to learn to write in cursive.

Men lost to WWI made his family desperately need more hands milking cows and harvesting crops in the fields. When his family grew short of men to tend the crops and milk the cows, Al's schooling was done. He stopped attending at the end of eighth grade. His family needed him to help on the farm.

World War I brought anti-German sentiment and alongside that was a ban on beer. Bootlegging was commonplace. It was not unusual in these times to have a child or teen transport the beer. Al's swiftness running made him a natural choice to be the family moonshiner. He not only had musical genius, but his cleverness also made him the family secret in avoiding the law set out to catch those involved in brewing, storing, and transporting beer.

Running for beer was one of his favorite things to do as a kid. Al would take a bucket just before eleven in the morning, run a mile over fields and fences to get beer for the men who were coming in for the big meal of the day—farm lunch. Getting there was not hard. Al could be trusted to run and climb fast and not get caught. More challenging was keeping the beer from spilling on his way back. This counted. The farm crew always checked his bucket upon return and chided him if it was not full.

No law enforcement caught Al carrying beer. Federal agents were after the bigger fish like Al Capone who owned a home in the Milwaukee suburbs. His gang made moonshine during the Prohibition.

The thirties brought layoffs to Milwaukee. Over 51,000 Milwaukeeans lost jobs by the end of 1933. Too proud to take public assistance, more family members moved onto the Schoenbeck family farmland. It became a temporary home to unmarried uncles. Crops and milk had to stretch further to feed the extended family and in mild weather some men slept outdoors, in the toolshed or in the barn. The kitchen table seating was elbow-to-elbow.

All men shot game. Al learned to gun down ducks, pheasants, and rabbits by age 11. Pots of hassenpfeffer were boiled with onions and potatoes grown on the farm. The smell of garlic and bits of bacon thrown into the stew welcomed workers in from the fields.

The Great Depression had dawned and shadowed Al throughout his life. Knowing to be polite and not eat too much so all could be fed, sharing a bed with more than one kid, lights out when the sun went down, hand-me-down, mended clothes and shoes, and prayers that a better life would come eventually were all part of Al's every day.

Socialist politics called for reform as many families were in dire straits with county relief given to 2,000 Milwaukee County individuals in 1929 and 34,000 in 1933. In 1932, Milwaukeeans elected a socialist Mayor, City Attorney and City Treasurer along with capturing fourteen of the twenty-seven City Council seats. Times were changing.

Farm life was tough, but Al had family ties that meant everything to him. He loved helping others including in the evenings providing the music for them to sing and dance a little when the world was falling apart. Cheerfulness was ingrained in him. Determination and thankfulness grew to become Al's strengths.

Getting through challenging times, using his body to run miles for beer and helping with adult farm chores, putting aside being mocked for his left-handedness and not wasting his time fighting back against something he could not change—these were traits Al incorporated into his personality. He would use these characteristics: helpfulness, toughness, and hopefulness later in life more than he imagined at the time. Al's motto became: *No matter how hard it gets, you will survive. Feel sorrow and let it go. Keep reaching for your goal.*

Left-Handedness

Why did teachers in the 20th Century attempt to change the handedness of children displaying left- handedness? There are a couple of reasons.

Bias against left-handedness stems from the common notion that someone who is not like us is less than us. Left-handers comprise

10% of the world's population. Twice as many men are left-handed as women.

Dominance rules. Difference is beaten down. Since the majority of people are right-handed, movements from the left side of the body may appear strange to the majority of people. People fear the unfamiliar.

This concept is not something new. Left handers have faced stigma since Medieval times. The Latin word "sinister" defined as "evil" means "on the left side." Lefthanders were called witches. The mothers of left-handers were labeled as "stressed."

The Latin word for "right" means "dexterous or adept." Biblical references place those people saved by God on the right hand.

Cultural perceptions about use of the left hand often note that the right hand is used for clean tasks such as eating and shaking hands. In other words: Do not extend your left hand to shake mine.

Research findings show that left-handers are more imaginative and creative with higher scores for complex reasoning. Left-handers are better at using their right hand than right-handers at using their left.

Left-handers are more likely to have an IQ above 131. This is advantageous when needing to adapt with medical conditions such as stroke.

Being left-handed in a right-handed dominated world can have its consequences. Left-handed males serving in WWI had a higher mortality rate. This higher death toll is thought to have been associated with using right-handed equipment.

Similarly, left-handers are more likely to have accidents because many everyday tools and household items are made for right-handers. Not all left-handed surgeons may be given left-handed instruments.

Marjorie Clare • 1940

Called "the pretty one" by everyone who met her, people were taken in by the brunette whose eye-catching gaze would attract the attention of men even across the room. She graduated at the top of her high school class in 1940. Friends and family called her Margie.

Margie was part of the twenty percent of women welcomed into Milwaukee's work force as the city became a major manufacturer of products aimed at winning the war. Being smart was paying off. She now could earn steady money at a time when her family needed it.

She was proficient at writing and stenography. Margie took correspondence, organized files, and did bookkeeping at a factory supplying radar systems for military aircraft.

Margie, keenly aware of anti-German sentiment, lost the German accent her parents handed down to her from their immigrant parents. Although forty to fifty percent of the area population was second or third generation German, the family tried to hide their heritage.

Speaking German—other than short phrases—like "gesundheit" was forbidden at home. Margie's mother and father broke ties to "the old country" and considered themselves Americans not Germans.

Being intelligent kept her mainly inside the office, rather than on the factory floor but this did not stop guys from approaching

Margie in the cafeteria. Always taking the approach that you can get more flies with honey than a swatter, she cast a radiant smile while her mind cautioned her, "Be careful."

When the end-of-the-day whistle blew, Margie's younger sister, Mary grabbed her arm as they left the factory and tucked it tightly around her own. "You are not going straight home tonight. You are coming with me. War time. Party time!"

Margie pulled back and almost fell trying to loosen Mary's grasp while yelling, "I'll be in trouble with Ma (Margie's mother) if I go with you." "So, what," replied her sister. "If I can get in trouble, you—Miss Goody Two Shoes—can too." Freeing herself, Margie turned and ran to catch the trolley home.

One year younger than Margie, Mary was not about to lose this argument. "Come on, Margie, just this one time. Promise, the dancing will be grand. I am meeting Clarence and he said to bring a friend. Sister, you are that friend tonight!"

"Oh, darn it, I can't get this lit with you pulling on me," moaned Margie when she struck the match to light one of the three-in-a-pack cigarettes given out to women who poured out of downtown buildings to take advantage of free smokes provided by companies with mottos such as "Lucky Strike green has gone to war!"

Pa, their father, was a hooked chain smoker after he was given cigarettes in rations when he fought with U.S. forces in WWI in France. She knew her parents would not detect her new smoking habit because her father was always creating billows of smoke over the dinner table where he squatted on a chair, drank booze, and took a drag.

The Navy's strength in Milwaukee grew during the war. One million sailors were trained on ships near the Great Lakes. Sailors swarmed the city. Clarence, originally from Virginia, had debarked in Chicago and took the 95-mile train ride from Great

Lakes Naval Base in Chicago to a depot near the Milwaukee Lakefront.

Two weeks before, Clarence met Mary dancing downtown at the Eagles Club. Designed by a student of Frank Lloyd Wright, the dance hall was known as the most beautiful Milwaukee ballroom. The rotating big bands played the jazz of the Woody Herman band and Chicago's Les Paul performed Ragtime on his electric guitar. Couples met at the club and danced the night away.

Young men and women held each other closely in public and no one interfered. The wartime feeling that life could pass one by and be blown up and forever gone was ever on the mind. The pace of romance grew with each war year.

While Margie was exhausted from her day, Mary felt she was falling in love with the Virginia sailor she had promised to meet. "We will be home by ten, "Onward, let's light up this town!" she promised her sister. Margie stared at Mary's pleading face. She was always giving into her younger siblings' needs.

Mary's arms were wrapped around Clarence's neck, their hips touching and their feet shuffling together. Margie looked at her watch. It was getting late, and Ma would be expecting her help at home. Staying out any longer could be met with repercussions from Ma.

A tall, dark-haired, handsome man stared at her as he walked over. She had danced with him once before. He had an Italian accent.

No sense, she thought, getting mixed up with him. Pa would have a conniption fit. We may be trying to blend in, she thought, but he had limits to his acceptance of newcomers from other places. Margie knew his rules. She would not disobey Pa.

Margie turned and tapped Mary's shoulder, "I have to get home. Ma will be steaming mad if I'm not there to get the little ones to bed. Got to go. I'm off. I won't tell you are here."

Marjorie Clare • 1940

Rushing from the creaky trolley, Margie flew up the stairs, through the living room, dining room and hallway and into the kitchen. Wrapping herself in an old apron that was too big for her (but fit Ma fine), she began pouring milk and arranging cookies on a platter for the kids' bedtime snack.

Margie was oldest of seven—five girls and two boys until the birth of the youngest who were twins, bulging the family number up to nine. The family was one of the fortunate ones because Emil, her father had a steady job as an engineer for The Milwaukee Road railway.

The growth in large-scale defense production meant railways were in demand for transport of Midwest goods. A railroad job was prized. The number of locomotives, passenger cars and freight cars increased dramatically since World War I. There were now 25 percent more freight and 30 percent more passenger cars, along with 32 percent more locomotives. By 1944, the railroad system carried almost twice as much intercity freight as it now had in 1940. Margie's Pa had a secure and esteemed career.

Whenever she could get one of her older girls to watch after the younger children, Ma dressed up to go out and volunteer at a charity sorting donations. Charities had lots of work for idle women during the depression.

This "job" gave her first-buyer access to boxes of hand-me-down outfits for all the children in the family in exchange for the hours she put in helping with donations. She was valued in part because she was a big, strong woman who could lift heavy boxes and unwieldly piles of garments and shoes with ease.

When Ma's charity work took her away from the household, life at home was more calm thought Margie. Ma constantly argued with Pa over his drinking and shooting off his gun to kill squirrels in the backyard and alley where neighbor kids played.

All this scared Margie. But she could not say anything. Whenever Margie tried to intervene between Ma and Pa's harsh words and repeated throwing of dishes and empty beer and booze bottles at each other, her mother would shush her.

Margie learned to shut her feelings inside. Margie figured out that speaking up only escalated Ma and Pa's yelling. *Not using her voice became her way of being safe* and keeping the younger ones secure too.

The littlest kids in the family would stand and cry as they watched Ma and Pa argue. A back arm across the face was Ma's way of quickly getting older children like Margie out of the way. For the younger kids, punishments for interfering were being shut in a closet or locked out of the house—at times in the cold.

Margie often put her finger to her lips cautioning the little ones to be quiet. She waved them away with her arms. Margie had to protect them. *Being voiceless was the safest maneuver.*

The family home was big and on the valued East side of Milwaukee near the lakefront. A porch with wicker chairs and a rocker adorned the front of the house. The first floor contained the main quarters with a spacious living room and dining area. There were three bedrooms, a large bath and huge kitchen area.

A poorly lit, creaky, back staircase wound up to a second-floor apartment and atop that a third-floor attic space where homemade curtains separated a sleeping quarter used by the older children. The basement had a wringer washer and clothes lines along with Pa's woodworking tools and hunting equipment. Blood stains on the floor were a sign of recent killing of chickens or cleaning of freshly shot game.

The backyard abutted an alley where garbage cans rested until racoons and squirrels upended them. Pa would sit for hours with the basement window ajar, rifle cocked, picking off squirrels and stray rabbits which were considered edible.

As a railroad engineer, Pa made friends in the places he went and often came home with live chickens he kept in the basement until "showtime" when, gathering the younger children in a circle around him, he wrung the chickens' necks, watched them run around and then fall over before he handed them over to Ma for plucking and boiling for dinners.

When Elisabeth walked in, arms loaded with "new" clothing, Margie usually had supper ready. Everyone sat around a large dining table while dishes were passed. The older siblings helped the younger ones by spooning out and cutting their food.

Squawking and griping here and there were met by Pa's command to be quiet and eat. Children were to be in their assigned spots and quiet. That was a household rule. "*MargieMaryEmilyRichardBarbaraJimmyCarol*" shouted Pa as he called the family to mealtime prayer. A Lutheran Bible in his hand, he read a verse without comment, mostly he said because he didn't understand how so many wars there could be in one book. One war's worth of killing, he said, is enough to know people should have figured out better ways to live side by side.

Pa did not believe in attending church. His religion was spelled out in the way he lived his life. He taught his children that being a good person was all about helping people and being decent to others. Religion, he told his family, sometimes walled off beliefs that did not allow for people to openly talk things through with each other. Churches were for baptisms, weddings, and funerals he said. Besides these events, Pa had no use for churches.

Pa and Ma bickered constantly in front of their kids as was their habit. Fueled by liquor consumption, the conversation sometimes caterwauled off the walls. Maria Callas opera recordings often blared loudly from the next house adding to cacophony that surrounded mealtime.

The younger ones didn't always understand the commotions and arguments that developed between their parents especially after the twins' birth. When the two youngest of the nine children were born, Emil moved his bed to a backroom off the kitchen. This bedroom was more like a porch which had been added onto the original structure. Its windows on three sides enabled Pa to see the outdoors, which calmed him.

Margie knew the history of Pa's drinking. On April 6, 1917, the U. S. declared war on Germany. On August 5, he was called up to military service. On January 13, he sailed for France.

Pa fought with the **32nd Infantry Division** at Alsace in May 1918. His troop was part of the first American troops to fight on German soil. They advanced to the city of Fismes on the Vesle River and an important ridgeline surrounding Juvigny. This takeover made the Germans back off the area.

The **32nd Infantry Division** men fought to capture the railroad lines at Sedan, a key German railroad hub. After three weeks of relentless fighting Pa and his fellow soldiers broke through the German Hindenburg Line. Small arms and machine gun fire blared. President Theodore Roosevelt declared, "By George, your men have hit it hard! Will you thank the Division for me?"

But to achieve this victory meant Pa crawling over the severely injured and the dead. There were 11,011 wounded and 2,250 men killed in action. His photographic memory recalled their mangled bodies. *He still could hear their voices calling for their mothers. He never forgave himself for not doing more.*

Pa used the porch room as his reading room. There his collection of WWI documentary picture books was piled in a stack on the floor. He kept looking at the pictures for places he had been and men he had known. Not that he would forget his WWI service in France. *No, the flashbacks drove him to drink often and heavily when he remembered.*

Al • 1941

Al was hopeful. Ed, an accordion player, arranged for members of the "The Al Schoen Combo," a four-man band that played small gigs, to meet Les Paul. This was a chance to be part of something big.

He was always looking for ways to better himself. Al was no slacker at trying things others might shy away from doing. A bit of nervousness was familiar to him. He did not panic. *No matter how hard it gets,* he told himself, *Keep reaching for your goal.* He was confident he would perform despite never having formal guitar lessons.

Al was a people pleaser. Along his young life, he honed this trait. Not speaking up when the teacher tied his left arm behind him in school because he knew saying something would only bring more sneers from classmates and a ruler across the arm from the teacher, Al pasted over the scars of being teased and the abruptly ended school experience with politeness and a smile. *Little did Al know that this understanding of what it was like to be different than others would give him a perspective most fathers did not have.*

He was able to find balance amidst anomalies. The experience he had being dissimilar from his classmates made him stronger to deal with his future. *Little did he know that his skills at facing adversity as a child would give him confidence his daughter with polio could do the same. Al would guide Susie through people, staring at her and frowning, and calling her "a cripple."*

Al • 1941

After commuting early morning from the farm, Al worked a shift at the chemical plant. He was tired but excited about the prospect of playing his guitar for the crowd at the Eagles Club.

Al was a bit anxious. He took deep breaths to calm himself. Family and friends thought his playing by ear was good. But he wondered if a star like Les Paul would feel the same. Les Paul was a hero for Al because he succeeded in the business although he did not read musical notes. Al dressed in his only suit and tie and stood at the stage waiting for the meeting his friend Ed had arranged.

He did not have much schooling, but Al learned by watching others. He had a talent for mimicking people. Tonight, he stood in front of the stage where Les Paul performed and took in the star's gregariousness, smile, and connection with the crowd.

A pretty woman bumped Al as she swayed to the music. He smiled at her, but again focused on the stage where his hero was performing. *This woman sure is pretty*, he thought to himself. She softly swayed to the beat, not overtaking the space, not showing off. She said she was sorry for bumping him with her hip. She offered him Wrigley's Spearmint as she apologized. Al reasoned: *This woman is kind, and pleasant.*

During a pause between songs, Al introduced himself to Margie. He told her he was waiting for the opportunity to meet Les Paul. He smiled but turned back to the stage as soon as Paul hit the first chord of the next piece. Al focused on learning what he could from an expert musician and performer.

When Ed and the others (playing trombone, and trumpet) got their turn to be on stage, Al caught a glimpse of Margie at the edge of the stage swinging to the music. He smiled in her direction. He knew he would ask her for a dance.

For Al, the evening was a success in a couple of ways. His dream to meet Les Paul and play on the same stage became reality. He also met a sweet girl he wanted to see again.

Marjorie Clare • 1941

Mary ran away with her boyfriend, Clarence, to the county courthouse and got married. Assigned to a Virginia base, he arranged for Mary to take a job with the Navy there. He departed on the *U.S.S Wisconsin* from Norfolk, Virginia, heading for the West Indies and later, joining forces at the Panama Canal.

Now Margie had six siblings to watch over. Margie was happy for the Depression decline in birth rate. However, by 1942, it shot up again. She was hopeful Pa's move to the porch room would cut down on his yelling "*MargieEmilyRichardBarbaraJimmyCarol.*" The crowded household was filled with activity and an age range from five to 58 years old.

Although Mary, the sister who usually went dancing with her had left for Virginia, Margie was not short of people asking her out on the town. Sal, a factory supervisor asked her out to the Eagles Club for dancing, but she said no. The man implied he could get her a better paying job. She still said no. The man did not know why Margie declined.

Margie knew she could not date someone named Salvatore. Pa always said "Stick to your own kind. No foreigners." Even though his own father emigrated from Mecklenburg-Schwerin Volkszahlung, Germany in steerage class on the Amaranth, Pa wanted to appear American. Margie realized people say stuff just to make them not feel part of a group deemed lower class.

Pa was like many others who quickly lose track of the "short" distance between themselves and the time their grandparents immigrated to the U.S. Why, Margie asked herself, do people who are different from us scare us so? Pa and Margie would unexpectedly find themselves dealing with the same fear of the unknown and unfamiliar a few years later.

When one evening, Emily, Margie's next youngest sister announced, "I'm heading to the ballroom on Wisconsin Avenue," Margie said, "Me too. Why not?" She knew Les Paul, a performer born on the outskirts of Milwaukee, was playing music along with his band that evening. Paul's last name really was Polfuss which Margie recognized was German in origin, so she thought there might be a crowd of German fellows she could meet. Pa would approve.

Emily and Margie strolled into the ballroom arm and arm with smiles on their faces and their dancing shoes tapping to the music. Margie, as usual, caught many guys' eyes. She looked around and wriggled through the crowd to the side of the stage to get a closer view of Les Paul playing his guitar.

Swinging to the jazz beat, Margie accidently bumped the hip of a young man who also had his eyes fixed on Les Paul. Margie caught a glimpse of Al to the side of her. She smiled. He smiled. The man, who introduced himself as Al, politely made space for Margie's "in-place" dancing. He was waiting expectantly for an introduction to Les Paul.

Al was all eyes on Paul. He did not put the rush on her like other guys. She liked that and relaxed into the beat of the music.

Les came off the stage at the break, saw Ed, and sauntered over. Margie stood motionless in awe. Les Paul started to talk to Ed and Al. Margie understood the conversation to be about tonight's show and all five of them playing together in the future. Then Les hopped back up on the stage and the show rolled on.

Margie looked at Al and he again smiled. A nice broad smile she thought. He asked her name. She asked his name. "Al Schoenbeck," he replied. Margie recognized the name Schoenbeck as the German-Jewish, Schönbeck. She knew enough German to put together German "schone" beautiful and "beke" creek. Margie knew Pa would be pleased.

After the group finished and instruments were gathered and put in cases, Al asked Margie to dance. He led her around the dance floor gracefully. She felt comfortable in his arms. After dancing, they headed to the bar. Margie looked at her watch and announced, "Ma is expecting me home. I work tomorrow."

Al told Margie he understood. He said he had family responsibilities too. They decided to meet again. Margie grabbed Emily off a guy's arm, and they rushed to the street, streetcar, and home.

When they arrived on the front porch, Emily and Margie quietly took their high heel shoes off and snuck into the youngest children's room to make sure the covers were tucked in beside their little bodies. Ma was snoring loudly. Pa was gone driving the train.

The girls breathed in a collective sigh of relief that they had not been caught. They headed up two flights of stairs to bed. It was cold on the top floor. Flimsy homemade curtains allowed the draft to stream over them through open corners in the window frames. Emily and Margie slept huddled back-to-back to keep warm. During the Depression, the only heat upstairs was that which floated up from the first and second floors.

Margie and Al met over the next months to dance and share drinks. Emily or another sister joined the couple downtown. Margie began to wonder what it would be like to not always have a sister hanging nearby her when she went out to meet Al.

Although Al was polite about Margie's sisters hovering, she wanted private time with Al. He thought the same. Al invited her for a ride in his car.

Al was worried about the war that consumed conversations. They both knew timing was everything. Relationships could be lost in a moment. They spent hours comparing notes about growing up in immigrant families. They shared their pasts, their hopes, and dreams.

Al signed up for military service when The Selective Training and Service Act required him to do so. In the first peacetime draft in United States history, it was compulsory for all men between the ages of 21 and 45 to register. Al knew that joining up would jeopardize the family farm. Already, crops lay unharvested because farmhands left for service.

Al registered and took the medical examination for the draft but did not pass because of a farm injury. Feeling ashamed not only due to his medical condition but also because anti-German sentiment was rising, he worked on the family farm and, took a second job assisting in a chemical plant. He wanted to do his part to support the war effort.

Fortunately, the United States Agricultural Department created the **United States Crop Corps** which gathered young teens and women to do farm work. One and one-half million woman and two and one-half million teens and joined the Crop Corp. Young people replaced relatives leaving for war. Some worked on Al's family farm. Al was able to be a chemist assistant full time in Milwaukee.

Since both worked downtown, it was convenient for Margie and Al to steal time together at the close of day. Their evening dates were spent not only dancing and enjoying listening to bands, but also talking to get to know each other.

It took Margie a while to become comfortable spending time with someone who cared for her. Always expected, as oldest child, to give to others at home, Margie was not at ease at first with Al's showing genuine consideration for her. She did not know how to accept Al's concern for her. Ma and Pa were certainly no examples of how to treat each other caringly.

Al sat back and listened to Margie's stories of life with lots of siblings. Margie's responsibility to supervise the brood while her mother went off like a high society lady to do charity work, made Al want to take care of Margie. He said he would gladly help Margie out when she had to supervise the younger children.

Moments of sorrow spread through Al's life early on. When Al was four, his older brother became sick with a fever. Only his mother was allowed to be with Roy so as not to spread whatever was ailing him.

Al's mother boiled a kettle of water and sprinkled in mint grown outside the front porch. She put a towel over Roy's head. He stood above the steam breathing in the vapor. Al stood back and watched. They could not afford to call a doctor. Roy died that winter.

Two years later, his mother also died. Al watched his mother develop despondency. He thought she gave up on life because she had a broken heart from losing Roy. People whispered about suicide. He had wished he could have made her smile. Al hoped his mother could have survived her sorrow. In response, he developed a mantra that would guide his life: *No matter how hard it gets, you will survive. Feel sorrow and let it go. Keep reaching for your goal.*

Margie and Al found they had similar family dynamics: discipline, hard work, and putting family above everything else. Each had been taught the German proverb: *Taten sagen mehr als Worte*: Actions speak more than words. They were each expected to contribute to their families through selfless, diligent work.

Together they planned. Margie could not abandon her household yet. Her job did not pay enough. Al was commuting from

Milwaukee back to the farm to sleep and help. They decided the best thing was to ask Pa if they could marry and move into the second-floor apartment at Margie's family house.

There was a shortage of housing in Milwaukee. Families often lived together sectioning off cramped spaces to make room for brothers and sisters, their wives and husbands, and young children. It was in these circumstances— an apartment carved out of a three-level East side home in a tightly packed German immigrant section of the city—Marjorie and Al found themselves as a newly married couple.

Al did not have the means to buy Margie an engagement ring, so he gave Margie his mother's wedding ring. With Pa's blessing, they drove to Iowa one evening, were married the next morning, and were back at work the following day.

Al still had a thick German accent which Pa corrected him on especially when Al pronounced W words such as water as "vater." But Pa liked Al because he was hard working, organized and respectful. He trusted Al to care for Margie.

Since churches did not hold what Pa called common sense religion, Pa did not mind that Margie eloped with Al in front of a judge with one witness. Pa preached to Al that a church was just a building, and the important part of religion was people helping and loving one another.

Pa and Al hunted pheasant and duck together at Horicon Marsh. Looking out over the water, they split a lunch of sausage on rolls that Margie had packed. Pa did not mind when Al reverted to his German accent when they were alone at these times. The marsh was a place where Pa felt the freedom to do so also.

What came away from the marsh was not just the ducks and pheasants. There grew a deep bond between Pa and Al. They got to know each other…all about their pasts…and their dreams for the future. *Little did they know then that later they would count on each other to help the girl that doctors said would never walk.*

Pa listened to the story of Al's grandfather Wilhelm, fleeing persecution, and surviving coming over on the steamer, Polynesian, in steerage class with his family. Pa was impressed when Al told him about the preparation Wilhelm had done to get his family ready to leave their homeland. Wilhelm led the family in daily exercise alternating with enforced rest periods. He taught them to move about the rooms of the house in darkness to find objects Wilhelm had hidden. He designated hours of silence as practice for when there could be no crying out.

Al's grandmother sewed thick lining with pockets into the children's clothes. Just before dawn on the day they walked to the harbor, Fredricka filled the hidden fabric pockets with coins and bits of hard rolls.

Pa understood the need of Al's family to immigrate because he had also seen firsthand the devastation of war. Al in turn listened to Pa's frightening war stories. He felt sad for the man who could not forget those he left behind in France. Al understood Pa. Al always did the driving to and from the marsh so Pa could have his "shot and a beer" (often more than one) on the way home from hunting.

Margie's younger sisters and brothers were all smiles when Al and Margie cleaned up the second-floor apartment to move in. Like the floor below, the apartment had a living space, along with three bedrooms. They would have to allow Margie's two brothers to continue to stay in one of the bedrooms. A small kitchen abutted the stairway down to Pa and Ma's place. Stairs led up to the drafty third floor extra sleeping area. The main way in and out of Margie and Al's apartment was through Pa and Ma's place via the back stairway and then to the outdoors through Pa and Ma's front door. The alternate route was the back stairwell to the alley.

The family now including Al always had Sunday midday meals together around a large dining table. Ma made German treats such as cheesecake (Kasekuchen), Schaum Torte, and Blitz Torte. Younger children whose attention span did not allow them to sit through lengthy conversation and eating and drinking munched on Linzer cookies as they ran about the house.

Pa's job with The Milwaukee Road gave him enough money to buy ingredients for food that Al was not accustomed to such as fancy desserts. At the family dining table where before he had to look around and make sure there was enough food for everyone before filling his plate, Al now tasted sugary, butter-laced treats new to him.

While Pa still yelled and Ma bitched back at him, Margie's name was dropped from Pa's "*MargieEmilyRichardBarbaraJimmyCarol*" rant. Now she and Al belonged together and were a part of a bigger family.

Family members moved up and down the stairs, in and out to school, and to and from jobs. Ma continued her charity work. Everyone was in touch daily. *Margie and Al would later wonder if one of the family brought home the polio virus.*

Marjorie Clare • 1945-1946

The year was 1945. It was a snowy, cold December day in the Great Lakes region of Milwaukee. Al snapped the perfect picture of Marjorie Clare holding her newborn in the holiday warmth. Margie smiles at her daughter, with a silvery tinseled Christmas tree and a radio in the background. *Margie knew not what lay ahead to muddle the future she was picturing in her mind this wintery day.*

Mama holding Susie

Marjorie Clare • 1945-1946

Margie and Al were overjoyed to welcome a second child to join with their three-year-old-son, Michael (Mike). Susie was a small baby...skimming the scales at six pounds. By seven months, she was a healthy eight pounds.

The war had ended but fear and terror came now from another source. Cases of polio had escalated throughout the country.

Polioviruses circulated widely before the 18th century. Maternal antibodies were transferred to offspring in early infancy. With the advent of improved sanitation measures, contact with the virus was reduced, and immunity waned due to less frequent exposure. This series of events lead to epidemics.

The first outbreak of polio was documented in the U.S. in 1843. England had reported cases in 1789. Egyptian carvings show pictures of people using canes to support withered legs thought to be caused by the polio virus.

In the 1940s, people believed that most babies and children either inherited immunity to polio from their mothers or experienced mild cases. **Symptoms of mild polio infections** in children included: fever, an upset stomach, sore back or neck, headache, fatigue, vomiting, malaise, muscle weakness, and pain in arms or legs. Most times, these signs of polio lasted a few days up to ten days. Such cases were referred to as "abortive poliomyelitis." There was no damage to the central nervous symptom, hence no paralysis.

Serious forms of polio involved paralysis which could affect the diaphragm leading to **difficulty breathing** and **paralysis of limbs** resulting in decreased reflexes and muscle action, severe muscle spasms and aches. Limb paralysis was usually asymmetrical, most often affecting one leg.

Parents were scared and on the outlook for any sign of polio. Some children had minor symptoms separated by a day to a week from severe symptoms. "Vigilant surveillance" were community watch words.

Muscle strength could return. Some people with polio seemed to make a complete recovery. Muscle weakness or paralysis might remain permanently.

Polio was not known to affect a person's thinking in the acute or early rehabilitation stage. Hearing, vision, and sense of smell and taste were not altered.

Not everyone who had the disease had observable symptoms. Many (72% of children and 95% of adults) were "asymptomatic spreaders" meaning these people carried the virus but did not feel sick.

Worldwide at its peak in the 1940s and 1950s, polio would paralyze or kill over half a million people every year. Disease onset at an older age was correlated with increased severity of the disease symptoms and death rate. Death rate was higher with **bulbar** polio than **paralytic** polio.

In 1946, the number of cases of polio in the United States—more than 28,000 with 1800 deaths—was greater than any year since 1916. The total number of cases in the preceding four years (70,288) exceeded the previous ten years combined (69,456).

In 1946, Wisconsin reported 483 cases of polio. Milwaukee's cases spiked to thirteen cases in a single day. Newspapers reported children's deaths. Parents were horrified.

People dreaded being found out to be a carrier. There were cases wherein people with mild forms of the infectious disease went unreported. Unrecognized cases were more common in non-epidemic years and in areas where polio was not as rampant.

People feared the unknown. No one knew then how polio was transmitted. It came in bursts. Summer and Fall had the worst outbreaks. It spread from hidden carriers...friends, relatives, neighbors, co-workers, and others. Communicability within a household was high.

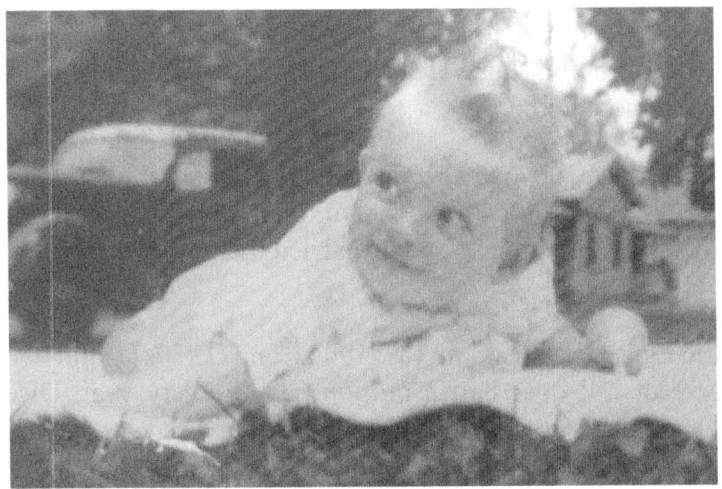

July 1946 - When Polio Struck

Polio is classified into three types each representing the neurological dysfunction caused by the virus. In **bulbar polio** (2% of total cases), the virus attacked the brainstem, and the nerve centers that control breathing, swallowing and blood pressure. **Spinal polio** (79%) led to paralysis of legs and arms and as later learned, damage to other nerve innervated systems of the body. In **bulbospinal polio** (19%) of cases, the polio virus spread both within the spinal cord and brain.

All polio survivors suffered damage to the bulb of the brain. Not all polio victims had widespread enough disturbance to cause difficulty breathing, swallowing and disturbances in control of blood pressure and heart rate. When these symptoms were observed, the patient was given a formal diagnosis of "**bulbar polio.**"

Transmission of polio is person-to-person via the fecal-oral route. Oral-oral transfer is also possible. The polio virus is passed on from one person to another when tiny amounts of feces or saliva from an infected person end up in the mouth of a healthy person. Transfer can occur via unwashed or improperly washed hands.

Infectivity of polio is highest seven to ten days before and after symptoms develop. However, polio virus is present in stool samples from three to six weeks after infection.

Case counts were not thought to be always accurate or reported in a timely manner. Parents had to notice a child's symptoms and get a doctor to come out to their house to look at a child before a guess at the diagnosis could be made.

In July, the summer of 1946, Margie was feeding Susie. She noticed her baby's head felt warmer than usual as it pressed against her breast to feed. But Margie knew everyone was a toasty uncomfortable on this hot and muggy July day. She thought Susie was a bit fussier, but so was she due to the intense Milwaukee heat and humidity.

Margie was always on the lookout for her son Mike having a stomachache, breathing difficulty, being very tired or not toddling along playing as usual. She took his temperature when she was worried.

It could just be the heat that is making Susie cranky, Margie thought. But later when changing Susie's diaper, Margie saw irrefutable evidence: one of her baby's legs lay limp. Susie wasn't doing her regular kicking when Margie pinned the cloth diaper. A sickening feeling enveloped Margie. Grasping to disbelieve what she saw before her—that her baby could be infected with polio, she picked up the phone and called the family doctor.

Making a house call was not an unusual physician practice in 1946. Upon examination, the doctor instructed Margie to call her husband to immediately take Susie to the isolation hospital.

Margie held her fears inside as she watched Al cradle Susie in his arms. Holding her, Al ran down the back staircase to the alley where he had parked the car. He laid his baby daughter on the front seat and placed a rolled-up tarp from the trunk on the seat by her side so Susie would not roll off. Al quickly steered the car away. Margie trembling and fearing the worst, could do nothing but wait at home with Mike.

Curious when they heard the commotion, Margie's brothers and sisters peeked out the back doorway of the first floor but did not come up the stairs to see what was happening because Ma bellowed at them to stay where they were. Ma yelled, "Margie, what is happening?" Elbowing the little ones back, she shrieked loudly up the stairs, "You got the polio up there? If you do, shut your door now!"

Margie said nothing as she slid the door shut. Clutching her arms around herself, she laid her back on the door and slid slowly to the floor. *Seeing your baby taken away should never have to happen to any mother.* Margie's life had just been turned upside down and altered in ways she never expected. *After this day, life would never be how she had previously imagined it.*

Mike was crying and wanting attention. He nestled his head on Margie's leg. Margie kneeled and pulled him into her arms. Shocked and frightened, Margie started to blame herself: *My fault. Everybody will talk about us. I must be in control.* Margie took a deep breath and whispered, "It's okay, Mike. Daddy is just taking Susie for a check-up. Let's find some toys and play."

Al • 1946

The doctor called "parent of Schoenbeck baby." Al walked from the waiting room into the polio ward. A nurse him led to the iron lung where Susie fitfully slept. A sleepy-eyed medical student stood beside a tray of medical equipment on a metal rolling cart.

Upon examination at the isolation hospital, doctors figured that Susie had bulbospinal polio. When Al arrived with her, Susie was immediately placed into an iron lung because she was gasping for breath. The doctor had to perform a lumbar puncture quickly not knowing how long Susie could tolerate breathing on her own outside the iron lung.

"We need you to hold your daughter while we get a sample of her spinal fluid, Mr. Schoenbeck." Al backed away. He began to sweat profusely and felt weak in the knees. Visions of seeing only Susie's head of blonde hair and face sticking out of the iron lung sabotaged his mind. She was pale. Her blue eyes were closed. It's like a coffin, Al thought.

He remembered when last he held Susie and she squiggled and screamed in a way he never had heard a baby cry before. Al talked to himself: *No matter how hard it gets, you will survive. Feel sorrow and let it go. Keep reaching for your goal.*

Squeezing Al's arm gently to convey empathy, the doctor took Susie out of the iron lung and gently transferred her to Al's arms. The doctor explained again what would be happening. Al needed to hold Susie tightly. The doctor said that Susie's body must be arched on his chest so the doctor could place a large needle into her back in an area around the spinal cord. The doctor would withdraw fluid.

Al gripped Susie tightly across his chest. The medical student cleansed the lumbar area of Susie's back. The older doctor inserted the needle into the space between two vertebrae. Susie wailed and squirmed. Al was holding her as securely as he could. His tears were falling. His sobbing caused him to shake.

The younger doctor began crying too and grasped a table to balance himself. The older doctor put the fluid sample in a vial for the laboratory analysis and sent the younger man away with it.

Al kissed Susie's forehead again, and again. Then he gingerly handed her back to the older doctor. Al knew he must sit, or he would pass out on the floor. The doctor sensed this and pulled over a chair. Al again told himself: *No matter how hard it gets, you will survive. Feel the sorrow and let it go. Keep reaching for your goal.*

Al knew he had to let Margie know the doctors evaluated Susie's spinal fluid for polio virus. But he would not tell how both he and Susie cried. Best not to upset Margie, he thought. His time was up in the isolation unit. He headed for home.

When Al left the polio unit, a nurse called another parent's name. The man looked back at Al as he walked through the door. He nodded. His eyes reflected their shared unspeakable grief.

Susie • 1946

Things are not always as they seem, or as we wish them to be. You would think a hospital ward would be a quiet place for rest and recovery. It was not. Descriptions of hospitalization for polio patients at South View Hospital and other hospitals with isolation units provide another picture. A polio ward could be a chaotic, noisy and a frightening place to be.

Nurses grabbed me out of my father's arms and placed me in an iron lung because I had trouble breathing. Alone and lying on my back, the rhythmic whoosh of the bellows of the iron lung was a constant drumbeat.

Every polio patient had some damage to neurons in the brain stem (called the bulb of the brain) but not all polio survivors had widespread damage. When damage was severe and neurons ceased working, the patient was diagnosed with **bulbar** polio and assigned to an iron lung. How long a patient remained in an iron lung depended on the severity of **bulbar** destruction the polio virus wielded.

An iron lung is a respirator, a breathing machine. It does the job of inflating and deflating the lungs when a person cannot move the muscles of respiration on their own. Iron lungs preceded ventilators as assistive breathing devices.

An iron lung was a box sealed to outside air. It worked using a two-step system of alternating pressure. Air was drawn out of the lungs alternately with air being pushed back into the lungs.

This alternating pressure system caused the patient's lungs to expand allowing inflation of the lungs when pressure in the iron lung was decreased and to deflate the lungs pushing air out of the mouth when pressure in the iron lung was increased.

Nurses describe working through port holes to deliver care including giving baths, combing hair, feeding, administering injections, and providing diapering, urinals, and bedpans. At times, the iron lungs were opened for physical therapy. Such treatment had to be completed within the amount of time children were able to muster enough strength to breathe on their own.

The children and young people in iron lungs could see the face of a caregiver who stood close by. The child might catch more glimpses of their surroundings, through a mirror hinged on the outside of the iron lung.

The sound of bellows sucking air out of iron lungs could be heard throughout the polio ward. Polio survivors talk about later on in life sleeping with a fan on to replicate "whoosh" of the iron lung inflation and deflation. Familiar noise is soothing.

The bellowing of the iron lung machines reminded nurses of the hypervigilance required of them. A nurse described how she was assigned care in a room with two iron lungs when she was four months post-graduation from nursing school. The nurse, then in her early twenties, was working as an operating room nurse but when surgical procedures stopped so staff could care for a blitz of polio patients, she was re-assigned to the polio isolation ward.

The mechanical ventilation moving air in and out of the child's poorly functioning lungs required electricity to power it or a nurse to manually pump the bellows. Each nurse on the polio unit was trained and evaluated regarding her ability to hand pump the bellows of the iron lung incase electricity was disrupted. The nurse's hands at times might become the child's resource for breathing.

One nurse was expected to effectively pump two units if the power went out. The nurse had to stand and push on the bellows for however long there was no power. When there were electrical failures, nurses recall the supervisor calling the electric company to come and hook up the hospital to a generator. Hospitals did not have their own backup generators at the time.

Nurses sometimes manually ventilated a polio patient with a mask attached to oxygen on one end and a tube inserted into the patient's trachea on the other. Things went wrong and tubes kinked. Oxygen bags became worn and broken. Nurses had to move heavy oxygen tanks and open them using wrenches.

Patients at times required suctioning. Nurses placed long catheters into a patients' tracheas. Using a procedure that would not damage the inside of the trachea, nurses removed fluid that otherwise might have clogged airways.

The words of nurses now in their nineties who recall their experiences taking care of children with polio:

> "The saddest time of my nursing."
>
> "Memories I cannot erase."
>
> "A time when everyone was worried about spreading the infection."
>
> "The most frightening experience of my 45-year career."
>
> "When I cried seeing parents sleeping in the lobby hoping to be let in to see their child."

Upon arriving for shift duty on the polio unit, nurses employed a variety of methods to reduce their exposure to the virus and to prevent passing on other germs to the patients.

- Scrub gowns: Nurses entered an outer section of the isolation ward where they changed out of their regular uniform. Each nurse put on an operating room scrub gown. A nurse was not allowed to walk outside the unit in this outfit. The scrub gown was left onsite to be washed by hospital personnel.

- Handwashing: The nurses washed and brushed their fingers forcefully with nail brushes. Nurses remarked that their knuckles became reddened and sore during their polio unit days.

- Gloving: Rubber surgical gloves were worn on the polio unit. Gloves were changed between caring for different patients. (Latex was not used to make gloves until 1964. Some wearers reported allergies to latex. Nonlatex gloves came into use in the 1990s.)

    o In the time of polio, gloves were not disposable. At the end of each shift, the nurse had responsibility to put the gloves in a 14-minute glove washer before she left the polio unit.

    o Hospital shift workers turned the gloves outside in. Then they put them back into the washer for another 14-minute wash.

    o After washing, gloves were set on a drying rack. Staff had to turn the gloves once a side was dry.

    o When gloves were dry, they were wrapped in cloth squares hemmed by volunteers and placed in an autoclave for disinfection. Autoclave sterilization uses heat to kill microorganisms. The autoclave provided pressurized steam required for sterilization.

    o After autoclaving, gloves were placed in a machine that lightly powdered the gloves so they could easily be slipped over fingers.

- Masks: Each nurse was given a bag of masks just before entering the unit proper. If at any time, a nursing supervisor observed the nurse touch her mask, the nurse was instructed to remove the mask and get rid of it as it was considered contaminated by the nurse's fingers.

Hospital staff wanting to contribute to the fight against polio —often volunteered to make masks after their shifts ended. Sitting at long tables into the night, they cut gauze and wove string through the mesh for ties. Each nurse carried a muslin bag on her waistband that contained five masks made from gauze and simple string. These masks, they hoped (later disproved), would help save them from contracting polio.

All the pressure of working on the polio unit was not only a challenge, but often a *calling* answered by brave and dedicated nurses. The families of these nurses often pleaded with them to not work with polio patients.

Then a young nurse, Rosemary, now ninety-one years old described being "very scared" that she might contract polio. But schooled by the nuns who ran the diploma nursing school from which she graduated, she and others were armed with a sense of purpose, in those uncertain times, to care for children with polio. Getting close was the only way to do so.

The nurse recalls washing her hands "a hundred times a day." As time with the virus brought new knowledge, scientists found that polio was caused by an enterococcus virus and spread via fecal matter spread through contact with unclean hands and surfaces. She remembers being cautioned to meticulously wash fresh fruits and vegetables for fear of them being contaminated by polio virus and the virus being transferred into the mouth.

Once a decision was made that I could maintain breathing on my own, I was taken out of the iron lung and placed in the general ward on my back in a mint green crib. The cacophony was exacerbated by the grating of dozens of metal crib bars being lowered and raised to attend to moaning and wailing children.

Outside a polio unit door affixed with a glass window for observation, mothers and fathers held wet, bunched handkerchiefs catching their tears and muting howls of grief that only a parent of an ill child fully understands. Parents took turns at the window to catch a glimpse of their loved one inside the ward.

Unable to breach the door unless invited to come in occasionally, the waiting mothers and fathers were a body of grief that moved like a heavy fog around the waiting area. There was no socialization. Polio was all too horrific to discuss. Parents talked with hushed voices wife to husband and husband to wife.

The sturdiness of the door muffled the babies' and younger children's crying out in pain and the older kids begging to be allowed out of their braces. Parents witnessed children repeatedly calling out for their mothers—*a plea people universally demonstrate when they are afraid*. Nurses recalled that many children gave up asking for their parents, instead withholding their feelings within the confines of their own heart and mind.

On the edges of the unit, there were smaller rooms each occupied by two patients in iron lungs. The symphony made by the baffles of iron lungs "breathing in and out" became my reality, my lullaby even when I was placed in a crib in the larger central room.

The noise was never-ending, and the glare of bulbs was ever bright. Lights in the wards were on day and night so we polio kids could always be keenly observed. For us, time had no meaning. We patients were all on our backs either in iron lungs or cribs out of which we could not crawl. On warm, sunny days, we would be strapped in a row on a long rolling cart positioned outside so we were exposed to sun and fresh air.

I remember laying alone at the hospital in a mint-green steel crib when doctors would come by with their white coats and mesh masks. Crib rails clanked as they were lowered for doctors to inspect and probe me. Nurses' faces were masked while they fed me.

I recognized the familiar scent of some nurses even though they were not allowed to wear cologne. Tension can cause sweating. Nurses were scared. Their unease could not be hidden and was conveyed adding to how frightened I felt in the space.

Stories of polio survivors confirm they submitted to whatever procedures done to them because they were afraid to not do so. Common experimental surgeries were muscle transfers, tendon lengthening and procedures involving drilling into bones.

When the men in the white lab coats (doctors) visited, I smelled them and watched them as they touched me. Usually the "White Coats" came with tools that caused pain. Pins to poke and prod. Gloved hands to lift and drop a limb to see what might happen in response. Their gloved fingers that they put into me to see if they could elicit a response.

Each day, one doctor in the group took a small hammer and hit my knee to see if my leg would move. It did not. The "White Coats" checked each kid's polio limb to see if a leg was getting better or permanently paralyzed. Same hammer from bed to bed.

One of the "White Coats" took notes about what the others said. He stood back a little. He was more cautious not actually touching me.

Sometimes my father would join the "White Coats." Dad would be wearing a nurse's scrub apron over his clothes. The "White Coat" who did the writing would give my father instructions to hold me tightly to his chest. The chief "White Coat" stuck a big needle attached to a tube into my lumbar spine to draw out cerebrospinal fluid, a procedure called lumbar puncture, (LP). The fluid would be checked in the lab for confirmation of the presence of polio virus and lymphocytes (white blood cells that are part of the immune system).

Lumbar puncture was a controversial diagnostic procedure in the 1950s. It was believed to relieve pressure on the spinal cord. However, studies conjectured that paralysis increased in some patients after lumbar puncture.

While I keened, my Dad held me snugly. My body curled into his when I smelled his familiar pheromones...the scents I associated with his rocking me while singing. His tears fell onto me and blended into mine. Dad's presence comforted me and taught me how love felt.

What happened next materialized without any conscious thought or direction from me. When the needle pierced my skin, *I sensed I was suddenly above my body* and all the "White Coats" surrounding my father holding me. I could see my body below and hear all that happened during each lumbar puncture from a place where I hovered above the group. While I was there in this place outside my body, I felt no pain. But I saw and heard myself as I squirmed and screamed.

Awareness that you are out of your body, looking down at it is an **out-of-body experience (OBE)**. This dissociative state—feeling separated—occurs commonly when people are in physical or psychological harm. OBEs happen spontaneously which means you cannot just call one up to happen.

People who report OBEs describe them as floating above and being in a state disconnected from their body. A person can see and hear what is going on around them but for unknown reasons cannot feel agonizing discomfort going on in their body. Military personnel and victims of car accidents report lack of pain sensation while they are having an OBE despite extensive injuries.

When the "White Coats" took me from my father, I popped back into my body. The feeling of my pain returned. I longed for the scent of my father.

After the "White Coats" were done examining me, my father sat on a chair and sobbed. His tears pooled into big spots on the apron he wore. The "White Coat" who was taking notes told my father to get out.

My father later told me he noticed that every time I saw a doctor in a white lab coat, I would cry in anticipation of the things they would do to me. I feared the doctors because what they did hurt me.

But I did not reveal my feelings. I "cocooned" my feelings and emotions. I stopped crying. Tears and screaming got me nowhere. *You can hurt me. I will not tell. I won't cry.* This mantra would become a life theme.

My leg would become permanently deformed and my posture and gait wobbly due to gravity and muscle imbalance. But I was one of the lucky ones, I eventually got to go home.

Iron lung

Who, What, When, Where, & How

Who was placed in an iron lung? Polio patients with **bulbar** or **bulbar spinal polio** who struggled to breathe were placed in iron lungs. Their muscles paralyzed by the polio virus could not move air in and out of their lungs normally.

Once settled in the iron lung, polio patients made statements that they were no longer *"frightened," "fighting for air,"* or *"gasping for breath."* On average a patient would spend two weeks inside an iron lung.

However, for some polio victims, the iron lung became a long-term remedy for the damage the polio virus inflicted on their breathing muscles. Polio survivors who could not be weaned— which means gradually withdrawn from the assisted breathing the iron lung provided— remained on the machine through adulthood and some until death.

What is an iron lung? An iron lung is respiratory assistive device which by increasing and decreasing pressure inside an airtight box mechanically moves air in and out of the lungs. This machine copies the way the body's chest muscles and diaphragm move air into and out of the lungs.

Patients laid on their backs often on beds that slid in and out of the iron lung. The patient's head rested on a platform outside the machine. A rubber collar provided a seal to maintain the closed environment.

Caregivers accessed the patient through openings called "portals." A mirror placed at a 45-degree angle over the patient's head allowed the polio survivor inside to view life outside the iron lung in a *mirror image* meaning the left and right sides were reversed in the patient's view.

Invention of the iron lung came about by chance. **Philip Drinker** (1894-1972), a Harvard industrial engineer who was at Boston's Children Hospital consulting on a climate-control issue, passed by children dying of respiratory failure due to polio. Moved by the sight of children gasping for air, he remodeled a machine he had invented for resuscitation of victims of electric shock or gas poisoning into the first iron lung. His device was expensive ($2000 in 1930) and clunky.

In 1931, the less cumbersome and lower-cost machine known as the Emerson Respirator after its designer, **John Haven Emerson** (1906-1997), came on the market.

When were iron lungs used? In the acute phase of polio during the 1930s, 1940s and 1950s before the development of the polio vaccine and thereafter, by those who polio survivors who could not be weaned from the device.

During the height of the polio pandemic, one out of every two hundred polio patients was placed in an iron lung. In 1939, 1000 iron lungs were in use in the United States. In 1959, 1,200 people were treated in iron lungs. By 2017, the count of people in iron lungs was down to three.

Where: There was a mass distribution of iron lungs throughout the United States in 1939. In 1941, the **National Foundation for Infantile Paralysis (NFIP)** donated iron lungs..

How it was: Stories from inside the iron lung

In 1958, a mother who had been confined in an iron lung at New York City's Bellevue Hospital for three months gave birth to a healthy daughter.

In 1963, a Texas polio survivor became the first person to graduate from a Dallas high school without physically attending a class. Gradually, he spent time outside the iron lung and graduated from Southern Methodist University in Dallas and law school at the University of Texas at Austin, while sleeping in the iron lung at night. He became a lawyer appearing in court in a modified wheelchair that held his paralyzed body upright.

In 1990, a retired Texas oilman opened his daughter's iron lung, and shot and killed her. He then took his own life. Paralyzed by polio, the woman had been living in an iron lung for thirty-nine years.

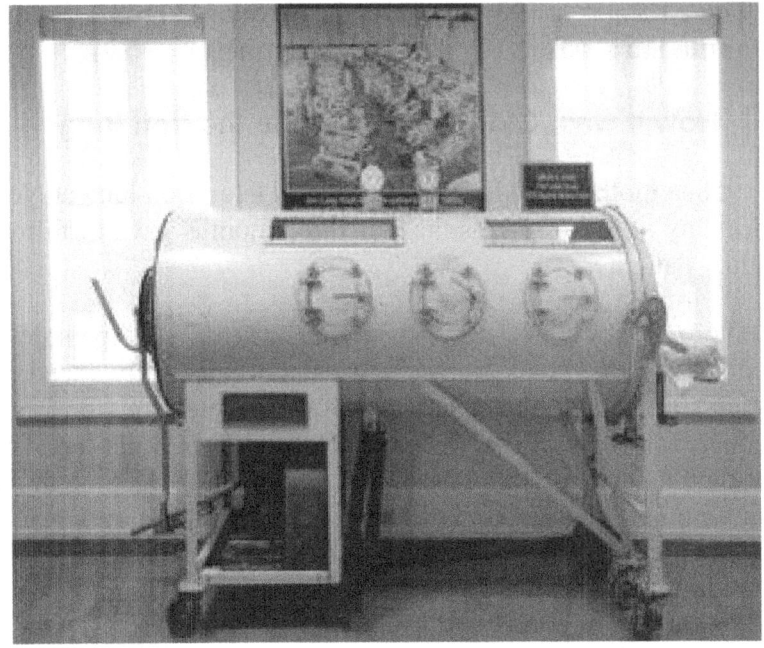

Iron Lung (c.1933)

*Mobile Medical Museum, Mobile, Alabama digital file
https://www.loc.gov/resource/highsm.05216/*

Marjorie Clare • 1946

When Margie saw Al return from the hospital without Susie, she collapsed in his arms. The little girl whose birth she had joyously welcomed just seven months earlier was gone. It would be weeks before Margie saw her baby daughter again and then, it would be from afar through a glass window.

After Al repeated instructions from the chief doctor at the isolation hospital to scrub the apartment clean, Margie could not sleep. Using lye soap, she filled her bucket over and over with hot water. The doctor instructed parents to wash all the surfaces in their homes. He said that soap and the friction of scrubbing of walls, countertops, furniture, appliances, and bathroom fixtures could remove the polio virus. Margie stayed up all night cleaning the apartment. She worried what people would say. In her mind, Margie repeated: *My fault. Everybody will talk about us. I must be in control.*

Al awoke to a nasty smell of ammonia. Lye soap, first used by Romans in Ancient Egypt to treat wounds, releases a pungent scent due to its high alkalinity.

Before the war, manufacturers mixed lye with fats to provide an emollient factor which reduced the harshness of the lye on skin. But WWII brought a shortage of vegetable fats and oils for use in household goods.

Al found Margie's hands red and inflamed. The bar of lye Margie used for scrubbing irritated her skin. She hadn't noticed the irritation because she was so intent on her cleaning.

How polio was transmitted was not yet widely known. Word on the street was that it spread through water contaminated with feces. Margie cleaned in part to remove debris and also to calm her nerves.

When polio changed her daughter's life in inalterable ways, it transformed hers too. Margie, who before had responsibility to care for her seven younger brothers and sisters, (Twins were born to Ma and Pa in 1944.) could no longer be with her parents and siblings.

The family became fractured by polio. Ma made sure of that. She hung up a sign on the back door to the first floor of the family home that read: ***No Polios***. Margie's brothers moved from the second-floor apartment where they had lived with Al, Margie, and Mike, to the attic sleeping area.

Ma told Margie and Al only to use the back stairway leading to the alley to come in and go out of the house. She yelled that they could no longer walk through the first-floor space where Ma and Pa lived. She said the attic area where the boys slept, and the basement were off-limits too. Having a polio child pivoted Margie into becoming an ashamed recluse on the second floor of the big family house.

This meant Margie could not use the wringer-washer in the basement. Pa snuck up a box of Tide detergent (first made in 1946), a long piece of rope, nails, hammer, and clothes pins. Margie sprinkled Tide into bathtub water where she soaked the family wash. She did not complain about the arduous task of wringing out clothing, and linens. She hung up pieces of laundry on a rope line strung across the living room. Margie opened wide the living room windows in pleasant weather hoping to catch a breeze to help dry everything.

The physicality of the housework made Margie tired. She sometimes got short with Mike. By the time Al came home in the evening, she was ready for the drink he would pour her from a bottle he retrieved from a high cupboard. Although World War II changed the gender roles of people, Al kept charge of the alcohol in the household. Margie drank to relieve stress and disillusionment too.

With only Pa climbing up the stairs to try to cheer up his eldest and favorite daughter, Margie was depressed. No one offered to watch Mike so she could make a trip to the hospital. (Margie had yet to learn to drive a car.) Spread of the virus terrified people so much it was not unheard of to cut off ties with their family members who had children with polio.

Margie heard a quiet knock on the back door. Her sister, Susie's godmother, Emily came up the back stairway when Ma was out of the house. "I want to help," she said. "I have seen Pa sneak up here. When Ma goes to the charity next time, I can come up and watch Mike so you can go with Al to see Susie in the hospital." Only Pa, and Emily watched Mike so Margie could go to the hospital with Al.

The children's ward in the isolation hospital was not a friendly place. Margie found parents of polio children did not introduce themselves, due in part to the stigma of having a polio child. In addition, parents walked a tenuous tightrope. Doctors could not tell them how long their child's symptoms would last or if their child, at worst, would die. The uncertainty paralyzed parents' lives. They waited. Many parents prayed aloud.

The unpredictability and confusion were heartbreaking and made it hard for Margie to hope too much. There was no template for how to be the mother of a polio child. Margie felt she couldn't love her baby too much because her baby might die. The image of a daughter who would be normal was already gone. Margie did not know what to put in its place.

Margie's visits to the hospital declined. She felt more comfortable staying at home with Mike. Margie anticipated that everyone would look at her as the mother of a child who contracted polio and say she was not a good mother. Over and over, she ruminated: *My fault. Everybody will talk about us. I must be in control.*

Al visited Susie every chance he got. He would look through the window of the isolation wing door with hope. He was already figuring out the physical therapy routines he observed done with Susie. Al's thoughts were: *No matter how hard it gets, you will survive. Feel sorrow and let it go. Keep reaching for your goal.*

Al • 1947

For an hour, Al paced back and forth in the small anteroom off the polio unit. With other distraught parents of polio kids, he nervously waited his turn for his five allotted minutes to catch a glimpse of Susie.

When Al gets to look through the small window of the locked door of the infant section in the polio unit, he watches and wonders. Susie is whimpering softly. There is nothing he can do about her distress. He sees a nurse take squares of cloth from out of a steamy bowl of water and place them around the lower part of Susie's polio leg. His minutes at the window are up. He feels the nudge of an elbow of another parent.

Al waits again in the anteroom. Time is all he has to give Susie now. He gets another turn at the window. Susie is now sleeping. A nurse removes the cloths. She stretches out Susie's right leg, the one that does not move. The nurse moves the floppy leg back and forth again and again. Susie writhes her head side-to-side.

When allowed in to visit Susie, Al listens to the nurses. They teach him the reasons for moving Susie's polio leg up and down again, and again. Nurses explain how volunteers sewed the warm packs. They demonstrate where to position them on Susie's leg.

Al can see that warm cloth placement soothes Susie's pain. After the cloths are on a half hour, Susie's arms flop down by her sides. She stops thrashing her head about and falls asleep.

And at the end of the visit, Al gazes at the rows of bedridden children crying and unable to move around with heavy steel braces on their legs, He says to himself, "I can do this at home."

Al goes back to the anteroom to await his next turn to see Susie. The chief doctor comes to the waiting area and says, "Parents of the Schoenbeck baby." Al steps up to the door. The doctor puts his arm around Al and leads him to a small room.

He explains that Susie is fortunate that she no longer needs the iron lung. But, the doctor says, she will never walk. Her right leg remains paralyzed. The doctor tells Al about a new surgical procedure. Al puts his hand to his forehead and takes in a deep breath and sighs. Susie has gone through so much already.

The doctor explains the surgery is experimental. A surgeon would cut a functioning tendon out of Susie's "good leg" and put it in the paralyzed one. The hope would be that the transplanted tendon would spur on movement of the leg affected by polio.

"There's time, Mr. Schoenbeck. The surgeon who has done this elsewhere with success will not be in Milwaukee until the week after next. It's an opportunity to make Susie's leg move." He encouraged Al saying, "Your daughter doesn't have a chance to walk without surgery."

Al waited a bit before asking if the doctor could speculate that Susie would recover with the surgery. The doctor said, "There are no guarantees, but I'd like to do it with this surgeon. Mr. Schoenbeck, Susie will never walk without it. Never."

Al could not imagine surgeons cutting into his baby. "God what do I do? I do not know." Exhausted, he returned home to Margie and Mike.

After dinner, Al lulled Mike into sleep by singing old farm songs. Margie asked how Al's visit went. "How was Susie?" Al told her about the therapies he saw done at the hospital. He told Margie that the nurses said Susie didn't cry much anymore. They said

Susie had become noticeably quieter. She spent most of the time looking up at the ceiling. Al knew Susie wasn't happy.

Al continued on, "The chief doctor told me Susie might be able to walk if we consent to surgery on both of her legs. The procedure could be done in two weeks. A surgeon who has performed the procedure a half dozen times before is coming to Milwaukee. This doctor would lead the surgeon at South View Isolation Hospital to do the operation. The doctor said he cannot say surgery will work for sure."

Al and Margie stood together holding each other, their heads resting on each other's shoulders. Disbelief and despair furtively seeped into every pore of their bodies. "The doctor's words: "Maybe…only maybe the surgery will help. Not sure. Done a few times before." lingered in Al and Margie's thoughts.

Al told Margie that the nurses at the hospital taught him what to do for Susie's polio leg. He said he would do the same at home. "We can organize treatments to be done morning and night on workdays and weekends. So many things are important to do regularly. Having a set schedule at home is no different than working on the farm. Doing Susie's therapy would be like doing chores. We could build the polio therapy Susie needs into our life," Al reassured Margie.

He said exercising Susie's leg would not be a burden. "I feel lucky I have strong arms from farm work. Moving her polio leg is easy for me." Al went on to describe what the nurses taught him: "I do fifty repetitions up and down of each leg. The nurses cautioned me to not do more. Tiring out the weaker leg is not good, they said. The nurses demonstrated the therapy movements. I showed them I could do them."

Al understood that the Susie's polio leg could not be in the steel brace all the time. He knew that if someone did not exercise the leg, it would become even more withered.

"When I was talking to the nurses," Al told Margie, "They knew, we are thinking of bringing Susie home. One of us would need to read and sign a paper that we were taking Susie out of the hospital *Against Medical Advice (AMA).*"

Al pressed on saying, "The nurses have taught me and watched me place Susie's little leg brace on in a jiffy. I looked for redness on her polio leg. We would need to check her skin every day in case the brace becomes too tight. One nurse gave me a tiny can of oil for the brace latches. Another nurse made a schedule on paper we would need to follow. They said I could phone them if I had questions. They gave me more than instruction. The nurses gave me confidence we can care for her at home."

Al realized, after losing his brother and mother early on in life that being deprived of a mother is unbelievably painful. *You never really get over death of a loved one,* he thought. Al knew Margie needed to bond with her baby.

Al looked at Margie as tears flooded both their eyes. "Susie needs to be with us," he said. "Even though our days doing therapy would be full, Susie would be in our arms. No matter how hard it gets, we will survive. I know you feel sad. Let the sadness go," Al spoke trying to reassure Margie as he enclosed her in the grip of his strong arms.

Margie asked Al to pour her a drink. She lifted the glass up, lit a cigarette and stared blankly out the kitchen window. Then Margie suddenly moved to her sewing machine and busied herself. Being active doing something always helped relieve her anxiety. She made a new outfit for Susie to wear home from the hospital. Margie cut it out of an old dress of hers. The material had sunny yellow flowers all over it.

Al was not able to fall asleep wondering if they were doing the right thing. Margie's constant looks of sorrow flash through his dreams. Al could not stop worrying about Margie. "She keeps blaming herself," he thought. Al had heard Margie repeatedly say, "It just takes one. It could have been me." He was not able to reason with her that it could have been anyone carrying the virus. People did not necessarily show symptoms.

Al's heart ached feeling Margie's despondency. Mike distracted her sometimes with his cheerfulness and wanting to cuddle and play. Al was grateful Mike was healthy and happy.

But the heaviness of Margie's sorrow shadowed Al's dreamtime. Scenes of the rows of bedridden children crying and unable to move around with heavy steel braces on their legs startled him awake.

In the morning Al said, "I am ready to bring Susie home. Living like this with her so far away and us so broken apart isn't right. I do not want to put her through more than she has been through. Surgery is not guaranteed to work to make her leg move. It could make things worse. We can care for her here. I will do what I see the nurses doing. I will carry her…if I have to…for her whole life."

Margie nodded in agreement. With the decision made, Al said he would arrange to bring Susie home that evening. Margie wanted to go with Al to the hospital, but there was no one to watch Mike.

Al could not really read the *AMA* document, but he would sign it. Margie had taught him to sign his name in cursive just before they got married so he could formally sign their wedding certificate. This would be the second form he ever signed with handwriting instead of using block print to write.

Al picked up Susie to begin the journey home where they would deal with having a polio child. Life has its happy moments. Carrying Susie out of the isolation hospital was one of his happiest.

He rushed to get the tarp out of the trunk to hold Susie on the front seat of the car. Then, he realized the steel brace would keep her in place. His daughter could not move. Polio virus paralyzed her.

Because Susie wore the small but heavy steel and leather brace for her polio leg, everyone he passed knew she was crippled. Al saw people stare and step back from him when he put her in the car in the hospital parking lot.

When Al reached home, the homemade *"No Polios"* sign was still on the house's first floor back door. Ma peeked out but said nothing as Al walked by clutching Susie.

Al seemed to instinctively know when to massage Susie's polio leg. Margie stood by hushed, watching but not touching. Her grief impaled her to the floor and standing still she wept inside. Margie was drinking more. "I'd just like another little nip," she'd say.

Al was more the direct caregiver than Margie. Margie used her excess energy to cut up old fabric scraps. She hemmed a stack of cloths each about a foot and a quarter by a foot. She set aside a big bowl in which to set the cloths to soak in warm water. Margie scrubbed the bowl before and after use. It was, stored it in the closet, so it did not get dusty. They were trying to keep everything as clean as possible.

Margie boiled the water and poured it over the cloths to let them sit for a bit. Al tested the temperature of the cloths with his elbow to make sure they were not too hot. Al squeezed each cloth, so water did not drip all over Susie's leg. Margie sewed pads out of old blankets to put below Susie's legs to catch stray drops of water.

While the cloths were soaking, Al took off the brace and checked for red marks. He knew none should be there. The nurse said if any appear, Al should leave the brace off, rub on Vaseline and watch the area until it looked like regular skin again.

Then Al exercised Susie's legs. Al figured he should exercise both legs since Susie wasn't moving the good one to walk like a child her age would normally do. He moved each leg up and down fifty times.

Al developed a routine he described as this:

I begin to massage Susie's polio leg. I thought it would be hard to figure out where to rub, but it isn't. When the muscle is spasming, it gets tight. I put my big hand around her leg and feel the muscle in her calf.

My Uncle Babe had me rub with long strokes up and down a newborn calf's leg when it wouldn't stand right after birthing on the farm. Susie's little polio leg feels ropey when spasming like the calf's muscle did.

I press my hand up and down, up, and down, working the muscle until the ropey part softens. This I think means the muscle has given up tightening and relaxes. Susie looks at me and whimpers. I don't know what else to do but keep rubbing. If I do nothing, the muscle will stay tight and keep hurting her.

It usually takes ten or fifteen minutes of rubbing but sometimes a half hour to loosen the muscle. I watch Susie's face and arms relax when the pain goes away. Once the muscle softens, I place the warmed cloths around Susie's polio leg. I hold them on. I put my face by Susie's so she can see my smile. I love this child.

Margie stands back, and then she leaves to have a cigarette in the kitchen. I rub Susie's forehead and gently kiss her hair, brushing the wispy blonde strands from her eyes with my fingertips. Susie smiles and reaches for me. I hold her to my chest softly singing, *"You are My Sunshine."*

Nurse Elizabeth Kenny

In 1940, **Elizabeth Kenny** (1880-1952), arrived from Australia with what was described as a "controversial" approach to polio patient care. Whereas treatment in the United States focused on immobilization, splinting, and bracing of affected limbs, nurse Kenny targeted reducing muscle spasms and increasing muscle strength.

Sister Kenny demonstrated that the application of warm, wet, wool cloths eased painful muscle spasms. In addition, she advised passive movement of polio affected limbs to regain muscle strength.

Kenny was not a trained nurse. She served as a "Sister," a title given to a chief nurse, in the Australian military for her service nursing soldiers during World War I. She developed her treatment for polio survivors from her experience treating soldiers with meningitis.

When she came to the United States, doctors in New York and Chicago refused to accept her methods. They questioned her theories and lack of formal medical training.

However, in Minnesota, Kenny found that The Mayo Clinic, the University of Minnesota, and Minnesota General Hospital were interested in her work. Parents requested her therapies be used for their children.

In 1942, The Elizabeth Kenny Clinic in Minneapolis began providing treatments that Sister Kenny advocated for polio patients. These therapies helped begin a new field of medicine called rehabilitation medicine.

During the early 1940s, many physicians and parents adopted The Kenny Method or variations of it. Most physicians did not agree with Kenny's theory that polio was a muscle not a nerve disease, but doctors used her treatment methods because they recognized they brought about improvements in patients. Sister Kenny treatment centers were opened throughout the United States.

Patients using her treatments often cried out in pain as paralyzed muscles were moved and stretched. But they continued using The Kenny Method because they felt it helped recover functioning.

Marjorie Clare • 1947

Margie and Al moved out of the big Eastside multi-family residence to a small house in the Westside suburbs of Milwaukee where they could enjoy Susie's childhood however that would be. They settled into a neighborhood of new tract houses.

Margie took a job working the night shift at a bank to help pay the house mortgage. Each evening Al bundled Mike and Susie into the car to drive Margie to work. He did the reverse to pick her up again in the morning.

Al took care of Mike and Susie during the night and worked his job during the day. In the late evenings, after his shift of work, Al cared for Mike and Susie while Margie caught a nap.

Unlike most women in the neighborhood Margie not only worked, but also drank cocktails and smoked. Alcohol and nicotine became part of her daily routine. Cigarette companies gave out packs of three free cigarettes on the streets of downtown Milwaukee to office workers like Margie leaving work in early in the morning. The tobacco company goal was to get people hooked. Margie got new packs when she stepped onto the Wisconsin Avenue sidewalk while waiting at the curb for Al to pick her up from work in the mornings.

Margie's life was full. Working at night and staying awake during the day to care for a toddler and five-year-old, along with keeping a household running in the days when meals were all homemade, was physically fatiguing.

Worn out from the overnight shift work and fearful of dropping Susie because the polio leg brace was awkward and heavy, Margie left her child mostly in the crib. She fed Susie using bottles because her milk had dried up long ago. Sometimes, she propped one up on towels and walked away. Mike would look at his sister and try to grab her hand as it waved in the air. He sang her songs Al had taught him.

Both Margie and Susie were perpetually tired. The never-ending pain of polio exhausted Susie. Early pictures of mother and child show them staring out into space, too sleepy to smile for the camera.

Mama and Susie looking tired

Life drained Margie emotionally also. She did not know how life would turn out. Unpredictable circumstances accompanying mothering a polio child had changed her outlook. Her life did not have the predictability that makes a person feel safe.

Plenty of times when he returned from work, Al would find Margie sitting in a dark room crying. Mike would be pulling on her apron strings to try to get her attention. He wondered, "Did I do right by bringing Susie home?"

When he returned from work, Al stepped up to help. He would find Susie in her crib fussing and crying, persistently trying to move around with one unmovable leg. Susie was stuck lying on her back looking upward at the ceiling. She could not roll to the side or roll over. But he smiled seeing that Susie had a little *stubborn* in her trying to drag the polio leg. He did not consider her stubbornness a bad trait. Al thought her persistence a sign of Susie's determination and spunk.

Pa talked about Susie with his Milwaukee Road railroad friends. Fred, the brakeman said his two-year-old grandson grew out of a walker. It was retired to the backyard. He offered the old metal contraption missing its handle at the front to Pa who, in his basement woodworking area, fashioned a new bar for Susie to grasp. Left outside for months, the metal frame had rusted. Pa coated it with a powder blue paint. Pa was a hardworking, hard drinking railroad man but also a soft-hearted soul.

Walker

Al had the idea to hold Susie upright in the walker so her brain would register what standing was like. He reasoned that if her body understood what upright and walking felt like, she would start to move the walker Pa fixed up. He engaged Mike to push Susie in the walker while he gripped her body so she would not flop over. *No matter how hard it gets, you will survive. Feel sorrow and let it go. Keep reaching for your goal.*

Susie would have toppled out of the walker without Al's hands around her. For father-daughter pictures, Al held Susie up just like he did in the walker.

Faking standing

During outbreaks of polio in Milwaukee, the county department of health would slap a quarantine sign on the front door of houses of polio survivors. This sign came with the restriction that Susie could not go outside the limit of their home's backyard.

Quarantines were a way of keeping the spread of polio down. When city workers tacked up a new quarantine sign on the front door, Margie's heart broke more. She would quickly close the front window drapes and sit in the darkened living room. She refused to answer the doorbell knowing a case worker would want to review once more the quarantine procedure with her. Margie knew the neighbors would be watching. She felt ashamed.

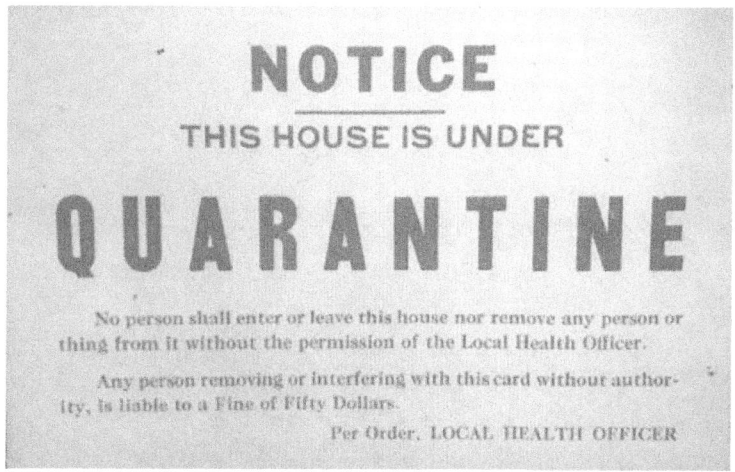

Margie's pooling tears spilled over onto Mike as he sat on her lap. She couldn't see a way out. Polio was spreading. There was no cure and, therefore, no light at the end of the tunnel.

Milwaukee County police patrolled neighborhoods making sure families cooperated with quarantine orders. Margie sat alone with her little shut-in polio kid and Mike.

With every new quarantine, neighbors would further distance themselves. Heightened numbers of polio cases were a reality, and the increasing numbers spawned more fear. Margie knew she could have been the one to bring polio to Susie. *My fault. Everybody will talk about us. I must be in control.*

Susie • 1947

I began my journey outside the hospital. Before he left for work in the morning, I recall being hardly awake when Dad would get out a bottle of rubbing alcohol and grip my polio leg in his hands. Every morning he massaged the daily spasms until the calf muscle gave up its tightness and finally relaxed.

My mother stood by watching but not touching. Heartache impaled her to the floor and standing still she wept inside, then looked away. Silence masked her feelings. Watching me squirm and hearing me cry was too painful for her. *Grief is heavy.*

Mamas suffer alongside a child who is hurting. Mama blamed herself for what she was witnessing. *My fault. Everybody will talk about us. I must be in control.* Mama wanted more for her child than herself. She went to find a cigarette to calm her nerves. Mamas cope the best they can.

After the spasms were quelled through his massage, my Dad exercised my legs moving them up and down repeatedly. He memorized how the nurses in the polio ward exercised the leg that wouldn't move itself. Then, he reapplied the brace fit with a little shoe on the end to hold my foot in proper positioning.

A distant relative urged my parents to take me to **Max Hintz** (1930-1996), a chiropractor in the small town of Burlington an hour or so away through winding roads. Dad called Dr. Hintz and explained ahead of my first visit that I was afraid of men in "White Coats." Max responded to my isolation hospital experience by wearing a powder-blue lab coat when he took care of me. Dad later told me he was relieved that I did not scream when Max came into the room like I did for the "White Coats."

Chiropractic care centers on an *"adjustment"* to the spine. Max's practice was a "hands-on" therapy wherein energy was transferred from the chiropractor to me following in the Palmer system of chiropractic. My Dad would set me down on a table and Max would touch and manipulate my vertebrae in what seemed to me as a child like a deep massage.

Chiropractic treatment was not painful. Afterward, while my father drove us back home, my mother would hold me in her arms or I would lay spread eagle out over the backseat, my brother allowing me to rest my legs—one heavy with the steel brace—on his lap all the way home. I slept for hours after each treatment.

Scholars have written that the success of chiropractic treatment has much to do with the empathic relationship established between the provider and the patient. This is true for traditional medicine also. Max Hintz focused his kind, healing intention on me. My body relaxed in his arms. I was not frightened. Empathy makes for good medicine.

My parents combined the trip to the chiropractor with an oleo run which took them about twenty miles to the Illinois border where they would bootleg the butter substitute bringing cases back for family consumption. It was illegal to sell oleo also known as margarine, in Wisconsin due to it being "the dairy state." However, my parents could not afford butter.

Their bringing back enough oleo for the rest of Mama's family in the big house on the Eastside of Milwaukee paved a road back into communication with the family. Mama and Dad did not like the way Ma treated them when I first got polio, but they understood Ma's way of isolating was what she thought best. Mama and Dad forgave Ma because they knew people act many times out of fear and you cannot blame them for that.

From Max, my Dad learned the *"use it or lose it"* theory. Max instructed my parents to put me on the floor and let me wiggle around. Eventually, this led to me crawling albeit with my strong leg pulling my braced polio leg.

Max told Dad that keeping the brace on my polio leg all the time would cause my leg to wither further. So sometimes I squirmed free of the brace on the floor. The chiropractor gave my Dad encouragement to hold me in a standing position, thus putting weight on my legs. Max wanted my body to gain the muscle memory for being upright.

My father believed in science. His belief set my body free. When he exercised my polio leg, my Dad would say to me, "Someday you will be able to move your leg without me." I grew up believing I could accomplish what he expected even though movement was painful.

My Dad learned little healthcare tips from watching the nurses. He noticed the hospital staff practice of opening windows to get crossflow ventilation of fresh air in the polio ward. This was a Florence Nightingale custom in The Crimean War. Dad drilled soup-can-sized holes in the wood of my bedroom windows. He made metal panels that could slide up and down over the holes. The window openings could be adjusted to be narrowed or widened to allow fresh air flow during the night.

Every evening Dad ensured that after exercises, he wrapped warm cloths around my polio leg. Afterward the heavy steel brace with a shoe affixed to the end (to minimize foot drop) was latched back on for the night.

A month before she died, my mother gave me a box containing her personal letters. Within it were handwritten notes from Max Hintz. She had repeatedly requested bills from him for the services he gave me. Max wrote back in response that there were no charges. There would never be charges. Sometimes people come into your life and change everything without asking for anything. I learned through Max this kindness is the way to be.

Susie • 1948

In Winter, when Dad drove Mama to work for her night shift at the bank, Mike and I shivered against the cold. Mama took one last drag on a cigarette while Dad put our jackets on over our pajamas. Dad wrapped old blankets around Mike and me. We huddled together in the back seat.

Sheltering us in his arms, Dad carried both of us at once into the house when we got home. He put Mike in his bed, then removed his outer clothing. I laid on my back, the steel brace holding me in place on Mike's mattress until Dad picked me up and pulled the blankets over my brother, kissed his forehead, and put me on the other bed.

Then Dad took my brace off and rubbed my leg with Ben-Gay, an ointment used for muscle pain. Dad rubbed the medication on my leg every night using it more than the recommended number of times each day.

People with sick kids crying from unending pain understand. Parents do what they believe helps their child and just don't tell. People use drugs if they can afford them and they work to relieve pain, no matter the risk. Exasperated by my obvious distress, sometimes my parents would rub brandy on my gums to stop my whimpering and thrashing around.

When he wasn't in too much of a rush, after the drive to and from my mother's downtown Milwaukee workplace, Dad would take time to apply moist warm cloths to my legs before the Ben-Gay. The combination produced a soothing vapor.

Ben-Gay contained menthol and methyl salicylate which is in the family of compounds that include aspirin. Aspirin reduces mild pain by blocking the production of prostaglandins which regulate pain and inflammation. Aspirin, gathered from the bark of willow trees, is an ancient remedy first noted as used in Egypt.

Ben-Gay being a simple non-prescription medication appealed to my Dad who, as a chemist assistant, wanted to know what was in compound medications. Plus, it did not cost much. Mama could stretch the budget to include Ben-Gay. My parents rarely gave me aspirin due to the 1940s "high price" of fifty-nine cents a bottle.

I usually fell asleep before Dad got my brace latches fixed. I just hated that brace. Wearing it increased my pain. Turning over or removing it was impossible. During these times, when I was very young, I began to, without intention, find myself in a state removed from my body and floating above it in a place where I could see myself lying in bed with the brace on.

I had no idea how I escaped my body. It did not occur to me until much later in life that this did not happen on occasion to everyone. I told no one about this realm of being outside my body where I could see from a place above, hear what was going on and be free of pain.

When I was young, I had no words to describe my polio experiences. My parents taught me to not gripe about soreness. We all pretended to the outside world it did not exist. Pain was a reminder of the polio that people wanted hidden from view. My parents wanted no pity. I followed their lead and kept my out-of-body (OBE) experiences secret even from my parents.

These times as a child enabled me to understand that beliefs are like guests that come up and knock on your door. You accept as real those experiences you invite in. As a child, I had no barrier to letting OBEs in and floating out of my body. OBEs were the only mechanism that fully removed my extreme pain.

There were certain times my parents released my leg from the brace. One was for warm baths which were soothing. Another was for snapping photographs. My Dad would grip me tightly around my waist making it appear in the picture I could stand on my own. My brother sat behind me with his arms holding me upright to steady me. Pa liked to be photographed holding me on his knee my polio leg flopping to the side nearest his body, so it was not so noticeable.

Pa and Susie on knee

Whenever possible my family presented me as non-disabled. That's how it was for polio kids. Our deficits were hidden whenever possible. Parents presented us as normal to block any discussion of the polio experience still horrifying the general public.

Braces, Crutches, and Wheelchairs

The priority for polio patients arriving at the hospital was an assessment for the urgency for an iron lung. This was always an emergency in the eyes of medical staff. Evaluation of the need to use crutches and braces came after the patient moved through the acute stage of polio.

In contrast, the first image a patient often had when being told they had polio was of being seen as a cripple. This viewpoint was thought to be an outgrowth of promotional materials of the **National Foundation for Infantile Paralysis** and **March of Dimes** which depicted the polio survivors using crutches, braces and/or wheelchairs. This picture was purposely placed in the public's mind as a sign of weakness to evoke compassion in the eyes of potential donors.

Polio survivors recounted their fear of using assistive devices because of the stigma attached. Patients felt people would look at them differently when they used crutches or wore a brace. Mechanical support meant they were no longer whole.

They voiced worry that people would both literally and figuratively look down at them in a wheelchair. Some polio survivors refused to be seen by anyone but hospital staff and family in a wheelchair. They talked about feelings of shame and resignation that they might never walk that accompanied wheelchair use.

There were survivors who grasped onto the prospect that using crutches, braces, or a wheelchair might lead to eventually being able to walk independently. They hoped the devices were helping their muscles get stronger. While some progressed to walking freely without crutches or braces, this was not always true, and many polio survivors had to come to terms with wearing assistive devices their entire lives.

There were reports of children rambunctiously racing through hospital halls in wheelchairs. Many children realized that wheelchairs meant they could be out of bed and on their own. This freedom led them to devise wheelchair stunts and wheelchair race competitions.

Going home into the community with crutches, braces or a wheelchair was viewed differently than being part of a hospitalized group using assistive devices. It wasn't the actual type of device that mattered. It was how other folks pictured the polio survivor using the device that counted. "The look of pity," being marked as "different," and the added pressure of parents and friends for the child to walk to overcome use of the devices all bled onto the happy picture of returning to live with family.

Many survivors shed their braces at discharge. Often it was a family decision without consultation with a physician. The muscles of most polio survivors recovered sufficiently to give up crutches, braces, and wheelchairs at least until their muscles aged when many resumed using devices. Post-polio symptoms forced some survivors to return to what they had worked so hard to put aside.

Al • 1948

Polio disturbed everyone in the family. Susie slept in a bed beside Mike's bed. She was a fussy child, moaning when she was in dreamland. Hearing her sighs of aching, Al would get up and walk with Susie in his arms until she fell back asleep. He wasn't getting much sleep himself.

Susie's crying out at night in pain would awaken Mike and he unlatched the levers on her brace. The brace fell to the side and off Susie's polio leg. She then might roll over and quiet back down into sleep. But if Al heard the drop of the brace to the floor, he would get out of bed and place the brace back on.

No one was getting a full night's sleep. On weekends, Margie would awaken to the noises, but not get up. Al told her to stay in bed because she was up all night five times a week working her bank job. Margie did not fall back to sleep readily. She worried about the future. The epidemic of polio was not going away. No one could give parents an idea of how life would be for their polio kids. She looked back with regret and forward with uncertainty.

During the day, Mike was curious about his sister. He sang her songs his father taught him like *The Happy Wanderer*. He mimicked his father's actions by rubbing Susie's leg albeit the one without the brace. He would make up games crawling on the floor to show Susie how to move.

When Margie would put Susie in the walker Pa fixed up, Mike would hold Susie up with his hands around her to keep her secure as he pushed it. Since parents of his neighborhood friends prohibited their children from coming into a house where there was a polio kid, Mike had more time when he was alone to entertain his sister. Al brought Mike penny candy to reward him for being a good big brother. Margie read to Mike to reward him for playing with his sister.

Mike guarding Susie

On rare evenings, Al drove the family to Pewaukee Lake. Mama and Mike swam alongside other families in weed-laden water warmed by hot, humid days. Holding Susie gently in his arms, Al would go away from the crowd and let Susie float in his arms buoyed by the water. He would move her legs up and down pretending she was swimming. Susie could see Mommy and Mike swim by. Loving the water, she spontaneously kicked her good leg and paddled with her arms.

One day, Al thought he saw the water around Susie's polio leg moving. He watched expectantly. He was not sure. So many days, so many times, hope had carried his mind to picturing Susie walking. But she could not. And, then Al once more would face disappointment. He could not shake off the words of the chief doctor at the isolation hospital: "Your daughter will never walk."

He could not rid himself of hope either. Life without hope would not be living for Al. As a young child he met sickness and death. He experienced firsthand people judging others wrongly. Life's hard lessons may give birth to the courage to go on and hope. *No matter how hard it gets, you will survive. Feel sorrow and let it go. Keep reaching for your goal.*

Not trusting that he saw Susie's leg move in the water, he called Margie over. "Margie," he yelled, "Come here." The weeds were thick. Margie tore piles of them away so they all could see into the water better. Margie, Mike, and Al watched the little polio leg move just a tiny bit on its own.

Moving to the suburbs placed the family closer to the lake. Al and Margie spent every evening possible the rest of the summer taking Mike and Susie there. Eventually, supported by Al's hand under her belly, Susie, using her arms and one good leg, pulled herself forward dragging the polio leg along with her.

Mike yelled, "My sister can swim!" Al and Margie teared up. Other swimmers kept their distance but looked over and smiled. Al continued his daily exercising of Susie's polio leg. Susie continued to creep across the floor holding herself up on one elbow and dragging her polio leg behind her. Hope can give vision to our dreams in anticipation of reality setting in. Al never set aside hope for Susie to be able to move forward.

Marjorie Clare • 1949

Margie's daily life on the Westside of Milwaukee was not easy like the one depicted in the *Father Knows Best* TV show. She wasn't just baking cookies in the suburbs and greeting her husband with a smile when he came home from a day at the office.

The move was a big adjustment. She had never lived apart from Ma and Pa. While still living with the family in the big house on the Eastside, Al and Margie passed by Ma's "**No Polios**" sign on the first-floor door each time on their way out to the car parked in the alley. Living isolated in the same house not speaking to each other was deep heartbreak for her.

Moving brought unknowns. Margie feared how accepting new neighbors would be of a family with a polio child.

Former family relationships fractured by fear of polio snowballed into Margie's personal insecurities that heightened into walls she built up to separate her from feeling potential rejection. Nurses taught Al that being outside in the sun promoted health, so she played with the kids in the yard every sunny day. She kept to herself mostly not taking the kids outside the yard except to walk to the nearby grocery store to get milk or bread or to visit the library.

Margie was always worried about keeping the house meticulously clean. Scrubbing away the polio virus when Susie was in the isolation hospital stuck with her as a way of coping. Cleaning up relieved her stress. Having an orderly house made her feel more in control when she and Al did not know what the future held.

She kept a mop and wringer bucket handy in the kitchen closet. Al put them outside in the sun on the back porch once a week. Margie sponged down every countertop, cupboard, and appliance with an ammonia solution daily. Al told her they could have eaten off the floor. Clutter made her feel guilty, like she should be doing something. So, everything in the home had its place.

Margie hung laundry outside on a rope line in the fresh air to dry. Margie wanted the sun to kill any lurking germs. Housekeeping and laundry kept Margie's mind busy and off Susie's condition.

One sunny day, a neighbor waved. Margie, afraid to be too forward, gave a slight hand movement back and forth. She wondered if the woman knew about Susie having polio. Margie saw two children playing in the woman's yard. Rather than feel rejected, she grabbed Susie from the stroller and called Mike into the house. *My fault. Everybody will talk about us. I must be in control.*

Later that morning, Margie heard a knock on the door and kids talking on the other side of it. She quickly put Susie in bed. Cautiously, she opened the door. The woman who waved stood with an outstretched arm holding a plate of cookies. Margie backed up a little. The woman tilted her head to the side as if to say, "What's up?"

Marie was Margie's first and as it turned out only visitor. Waiting to be asked in, she smiled and told her children to calm down. The boy looked younger than Mike. A girl appeared his age.

Margie opened the door and took the plate saying, "Thank you," while thinking, "I can't believe someone wants to come in." Catching the woman's eye, Margie said, "My daughter is sleeping now."

Mike came to the door and looked out at the boy and girl. "That's okay," the woman said, "We wanted to invite your boy to play in our yard. I am going to turn on the sprinkler so the kids can run through the water and cool down. I can watch him with my kids. He will be fine."

So, Mike was the first one to make a friend in the new neighborhood. Margie got him in swim trunks and took his hand leading him over to the neighbor's backyard which was a small patchy bit of grass abutting a large dug out space where a garage should be. The sprinkler sat where the thickest, tallest grass poked up.

While Susie slept, Margie sat on her own back stoop two yards away watching Mike play with the girl and boy. She wondered what the future might hold. She was hesitant to hope that friendship could be possible, yet she knew Mike needed kids to play with. Margie was cautious to not be too hopeful.

When Al came home from work, Margie told him of Marie's visit. They ate the cookies for dessert after supper. Al offered to take the plate back. "No," Margie said, "I will. I must take the chance she might be a friend. Maybe she has never noticed when the quarantine signs have gone up."

Margie combed her hair, put on her best shirt and slacks, and walked down the block. Al noticed there was something different about Margie when she walked back through the front door. Her face wasn't staring down as usual at the pavement. Margie was looking up and smiling. She passed by the cigarette pack laying on the kitchen table.

"Al," Margie exclaimed, "Marie, the neighbor, is a nurse! She works nights, like me! Her husband delivers Omar Bread. That's why we have seen the Omar Bread truck at their house in the dugout place where a garage should be."

Margie felt a glimmer of hope. Marie was someone who didn't back off from her because her child had polio. It was a good feeling to not be perceived as a mother who was dirty but as a person whose life circumstances were unpreventable. Like everyone, Margie wanted her family to be accepted even if their circumstances were different than others.

Marjorie Clare • 1950s

Against the chilly wind, Margie pushed Susie's stroller to the corner to catch a bus to the Burleigh branch of the Milwaukee Public Library. Since Al took the car downtown to work during the day, walking and the city bus were the transportation options for Margie and the children.

As a youngster, Margie discovered that reading could bring relief from the doldrums of daily life. Grabbing a book, she could hide away from her younger siblings in the big house on the East side. Pa encouraged her reading because he realized Margie was smarter than average. He winced overhearing the other kids tease her about being "Miss Smarty-Pants." He understood books can draw a reader away from what was bothering them. That's how reading worked for him.

During her childhood, reading together drew Margie close to Pa. They carved out quiet, thoughtful times amidst chaotic household life. He read to her from his treasured National Geographic magazines with their pull-out maps. His favorite edition contained a 1918 map of the WWI war theater. Pa posted it on a wall inside a walk-in closet off the dining room. Margie watched Pa rub his fingers over landmarks of towns while he remembered war buddies of the past—*haunting memories.*

They shared in depth philosophical discussions. Pa told Margie he believed in the reasons he went to war, but he wished there were ways to present opinions without bloodshed. Pa told Margie that a person needed to read to understand what was happening in the world. He said reading taught a person about their own feelings.

Pa kept his National Geographics lined up by date on a long shelf in the closet. When the household got too noisy for his liking, he would go there and sit on a ledge he built just for doing so, shut the door, and read. The magazine's photos took Pa to places he had been and countries he would never visit in person.

When Margie was young, everyone knew that she was Pa's favorite child. If someone was looking for the two of them, they first checked the closet to see if they were snuggled up reading. Pa and Margie loved their quiet times together. When separated from family bickering, a calmness settled over both of them.

So, seeking the comfort of books despite it being a blustery day, Margie headed to the library. It not only housed an extensive collection of books, but also had a carpeted area where children could play with books and toys. Margie stuffed a bulky blanket around Susie's waist and legs in the stroller to hide her brace and steered against the wind.

People who looked down on polio kids and their parents sometimes asked the librarian to bar Susie from the library. Overhearing a request by a library guest asking for Susie to be taken out brought back frightening and embarrassing memories to Margie. At these times, the pain of polio spilt over from child to mother and Margie became noticeably anxious and afraid.

Margie understood that people were worried about contracting polio. The public got uncertain messages about whether or not children who had polio could spread it. Milwaukee public pools were not letting kids who had polio come in the water to swim. There were signs at pool entrances indicating polio survivors were not welcome. So naturally, people were scared to be with polio kids in other places also. It was not common knowledge that a polio survivor developed antibodies against the virus when they were ill.

When faced with a library guest demanding the *polio child* be removed, Margie would cast her eyes downward toward the floor and scramble to hoist Susie into the stroller without engaging the person asking about Susie or checking out the books she had set aside. Margie pushed the stroller quickly to head for the library exit. *My fault. Everybody will talk about us. I must be in control.*

The librarian showed understanding of the predicament. She did not stand back and do nothing like we all have seen people do when witnessing potential confrontation. She acted when she saw Margie's trembling hands, downtrodden look, and hurried pace to exit.

Stepping down from a wooden ladder, the librarian wound her arm around Margie's shoulder and said, "You and Susie are welcome to stay. I love reading to your sweet little *polio girl.* Margie would remember how softly the librarian strung the two words *polio* and *girl*. It was the only time she had heard the words said together not harshly, but in a calm and kind way.

As mother of a child who had polio as an infant, Margie listened to random strangers unsolicited views such as:

"Your poor child, it must be awful."

"It must be miserable for you."

"No one in our family has gotten it."

"What will become of her?"

"I am so relieved no one has gotten polio in my family."

The quickness of people to judge and distance themselves from the disease made Margie's body tense up. The librarian's reassuring words in contrast soothed Margie.

When she had extra time, the librarian would come to the children's room and offer to read to Susie so that Margie could stand by the card catalogue and flip through it to find books she would like to take home and read. Without the kindness of the librarian, Margie may not have returned to the library each week. But, because the librarian made the atmosphere feel comforting like reading at home with Pa in the big house on the East side, she did.

The librarian chose to overlook the eight-book check-out limit for children allowing Susie take home all the books she and Margie could carry. Susie, stubborn to take as many books as possible, would get out of the carriage and fill it with books. She would place one of her hands in Margie's and grasp hold onto the stroller with the other while dragging her polio leg in the brace behind her. Susie walked out of the library with her cache of books.

Who are the people we remember with fondness as we review our lives? Margie spoke to Susie decades later about the librarian who made a difference in their lives. It was she who made Margie feel comfortable and accepted at a time when others' comments caused her to feel alone and afraid. It doesn't take a degree in rocket science to change someone's world. Someone stepping up to be kind will do.

Margie would read books to Susie before she put her to bed for a nap. Then she was able to steal away an hour to rest which was much welcome since she was facing an overnight shift at the bank.

Later in the day, Margie and Susie would walk to pick up Mike from school. In the Spring of 1950, Mothers lined up in front of the six steps up and twenty-foot-wide set of stairs leading into public school (P.S.) 68. Margie stood back from the crowd. As each child ran out, a mother grabbed a hand and the crowd thinned. Margie always hoped Mike would be one of the first ones down the stairs so she could leave quickly for home.

Other mothers already knew Margie was the one with a *polio kid*. Even with the blanket covering her legs, people looked over at Susie. Margie wondered what gossip was going around. People were curious. They stood on tiptoes wanting to catch a glimpse of Susie from afar. *Smile, so they will not feel so badly*, Margie coached Susie. Margie brought up Susie to think of other people's feelings and fears. She said understanding others helps you forget about your own pain.

Margie registered Susie for P.S. 68 kindergarten. Dropping both children off would give her time to sleep after being up all night at the bank. Margie was tired and looked forward to Mike and Susie being at school.

Toward the end of Susie's first year of school, the principal, **Ms. Demand**, distributed a notice to students that the faculty would hold the annual May Pole Dance at 10 am on May Day. Mike brought a note home. Susie did too and handed it to Margie. Susie's announcement of the event had an extra handwritten paragraph on the bottom which stated, "Susie can sit on a bench on the playground during the May Pole dance. She can watch from there."

Margie did not welcome the principal's idea. Barring Susie from dancing around the pole with the other kids was not acceptable. Al, Marge, and Mike had worked hard together to help Susie learn to walk albeit with a limp. She phoned to get an appointment with Ms. Demand.

Margie listened to Ms. Demand who told her the May Pole dance was an honored tradition at P.S. 68. She said parents would be coming to see their children perform the dance. Parents would take photographs. Ms. Demand said that Susie's limping would make the dance not look uniform and parents would be upset and complain. She said two family members had already asked her if the *polio girl* would be sitting out.

Margie thought, "The principal is worried about how everyone will talk about her not putting on a good May Pole dance. I get it. I am always worried what people will think of me. Margie told herself: *My fault. Everybody will talk about us. I must be in control.*

Margie began what she called her "protest talk" by telling the principal that exclusion for having a limp was not a humane reason for not letting her daughter participate. She explained that Susie could get up quickly if she fell, and she didn't cry when scrapped up from falling on pavement. In fact, Susie did not cry when hurt so Margie told the principal that she need not worry that the May Pole Dance could be disrupted by tears.

Margie asked when May Pole dance practice would be the next day. She told Ms. Demand she would be there to watch Susie practice with the other children in her grade.

On May Day, 1951, Susie joined her classmates and walked ribbon in hand around the May Pole. Margie was happy that Susie did not fall. Susie did not cry either although Margie could see her daughter rubbing the calf of her polio leg which meant it was spasming and hurting from walking many loops around the pole.

The May Pole Dance went well. This success spurred Margie on to speak up again.

When Susie became a Brownie Scout in the troop at the grade school, Margie met resistance in letting Susie fully participate due to her polio. "Yes, she can," Margie said to the Brownie troop leader when told the group was taking a quarter mile walk to get a badge and Susie did not need to come along since she had polio.

"I'll make sure she is alright during the walk. I'll be there," Margie told the troop leader. Margie realized that she might have to speak up again to make the people understand her daughter's capabilities. She would also have to learn to drive.

Most women did not drive in the 1950s. Marie, Margie's friend two doors down, took the bus to her nursing job. Margie did not know any woman who drove a car. Practicing with two squiggly, giggly, impatient children in the backseat would have deterred most women. But Margie had a goal and a husband who supported her in reaching it. Al told her: *No matter how hard it gets, you will survive. Feel sorrow and let it go. Keep reaching for your goal.*

Driving a car set her apart from other women in the neighborhood. Now she was the mother on the block who smoke, drank, and drove a car.

To have a car during the day, Margie had to drive Al downtown to work. Following the Brownie Scouts who were walking on the sidewalk, Margie clutched a slow pace moving the car along the curb. She kept an eye on Susie walking with the other Brownie scouts on the predetermined route. The horns of vehicles beeped as Margie drove with the car hugging the side of the road. Some drivers passed around her car. Margie told herself: *My fault. Everybody will talk about us. I must be in control.*

Margie took control. Once every ten minutes, Margie called Susie over to the curb to rest. The scout leader agreed with letting Susie up catch up by Margie giving her short rides in the car. She also said Susie could walk the yards she missed around the schoolyard after the next Brownie scout meeting.

Margie was grateful for the scout leader's compassion. Later, as repayment for the woman's kindness and despite her being the only woman who worked outside the home in the group of Brownie scout families in Susie's troop, Margie ran the annual cookie drive. Brownie scout cookie boxes were heaped floor to ceiling for months in the tiny living room space of the family's small tract house. People so infrequently were nice that Margie made a big deal to pay back someone who showed kindness.

Margie realized that she needed to speak up so others might understand her daughter. Each time she protested for people to accept her *polio girl*, Susie had more opportunity to become the best she could be.

But Susie's early growing up was a lonely time. Having a child with an illness took all Margie's inner strength and permeated her life. The once dancing girl that people called the "pretty one," was replaced by the mother of the *polio girl*. Margie's eyes drifted to the sky outside the kitchen window while she lit one cigarette after another and sipped on the drink Al made her.

Susie • 1950s

"Stand up straight!" Mama yelled at me on school day mornings. My mother wanted me to have good posture so I would not look any more crippled than I was.

"Get over here!" she demanded. I would march into the hallway and lean on the wall for balance. She had a firm grip on my arm to let me know she was in charge. I kept my eyes cast downward and complied. *You can hurt me. I will not tell. I won't cry.*

I stood very still and erect in the hallway while she reached into the closet to grab the small circular metal container that contained rouge. I wished I could hold the fancy rouge, but Mama never let me because this was costly beauty stuff which I might drop and break.

Rouge came with a powder puff that Mama used as a brush to pinken up my cheeks just below my eyes. I do not know how much it cost but I do know that rouge was one of those supplies I was not to touch. Thus, its placement was on a high shelf in the hall closet.

Mama dusted my cheeks with rouge every school day so I would not look sickly. If I looked ill, the teacher could send me home interrupting Mama's needed sleep before she again worked a night shift. This routine taught me that people may believe how you look on the outside is how you feel on the inside. It took a while for me to realize this is a game people play with each other.

My grade school principal, Ms. Demand, was surprised that I could read when I began school. She set aside time every week to hold special classes with three children she found interesting. When she told us that we were in her office because we had "sharp minds" we shrugged our shoulders and looked at each other. I was not sure if sharp meant good or bad.

Ms. Demand refused to give up teaching when she became an administrator. She marked the three of us children as her special project and taught us throughout our elementary school time. We sat in a semi-circle in her office while she read aloud to us. I am sure my jaw hung slack open at times when her voice mimicked the speech of the book characters. She knew their world and transported us there. Ms. Demand showed me that a reader could find long lasting friends in books.

Ms. Demand's love of teaching enlarged my world. She introduced us to her favorite subjects which were archeology and anthropology. Because of her support, I read everything I could get my hands on. I lugged heavy library books home. I was fascinated by the pictures of faraway places. I opened the books and dreamt I might someday see these places in person.

Ms. Demand would say, "This book is homework," giving me justification for taking time to lay down, read and relax my body, distracting me from pain. I wonder if she knew her gift would last a lifetime.

Her belief in my intelligence was a self-fulfilling prophecy that spun me to the top of my class. Sometimes you take upon yourself qualities secondary to how people make you feel.

The principal's backing got me moved me up early to the first grade. I suddenly faced not only new classmates but an unmovable object, the cloakroom—a dark, long, windowless room with hooks for outer garments and bins for boots. Kids had to take off their outer garments (which in Wisconsin winters were many) place them on the hooks and get into the classroom before the bell rang.

This scenario was problematic for me. Girls wore dresses to school in the 1950s. I wore slacks under my dresses to school to keep my polio leg warm. Cold temperatures heighten polio leg pain.

In the kindergarten setting, girls could sit on little chairs and take the slacks they might wear under dresses off. But first graders had to independently take off their outer clothes and slacks and meet in the classroom. I could not do it. No way could I stand on one leg and pull off my slacks.

I tried sitting on the floor but then worried my dress would bunch up displaying my underwear. So, defiant of the rule of the time that girls wore dresses and boys wore the slacks in the classroom, I wore my slacks into the classroom under my dress. The teacher told me I could not. I had already learned from my parents to never believe you cannot do something.

P.S. 68

Al • 1950s

Rituals restore equilibrium. Once Susie was able to manage walking, Al made a habit of taking Susie for evening strolls in the neighborhood. During this time, Mike could play ball outside in the alley with other boys. This routine gave Margie a block of time when she did not have to worry about kids.

Al always washed up the dinner dishes before the after-dinner walks. Mike and Susie dried them. Growing up on the farm, Al believed it important to teach children to do chores when they were young even if Susie was sitting on the floor only drying unbreakable pots, and pans.

The family house was on a boulevard that came to a triangular point where it intersected with a busier street. The intersection did not have a stoplight. Walking to the corner and across the street was a challenge for the father and daughter. Al held Susie's hand and sometimes had to pick her up and carry her to be fast enough to stay out of the way of traffic.

Al and Susie were always excited to go into the general store. The place had a silver-edged soda fountain set up to serve ice-cream floats, a magazine rack, toys, tools, and pharmaceuticals.

On these trips Al would heave Susie with her heavy brace onto a stool at the counter. The store owner rewarded Susie with an ice cream cone for making the trek.

Al browsed the monthly *Hit Parader, a* magazine that presented lyrics and chords to popular songs. *Hit Parader* began publication in 1942. For Al, a look through the pages was sweet as candy. Since he played instruments without needing to read notes, all he had to do was buy this magazine each month and he could perform the songs with his group of friends.

Sometimes as Al read lyrics, the shop owner, Joe, picked Susie up and sat her on the red tricycle in the window display. Susie would wave and people walking by would smile and wave back.

As they walked along together, Al would tell Susie short stories he made up. Each story contained a lesson. He told Susie that all stories have a beginning, middle and an end. Al explained that not all stories have happy endings and that is the way life works. He told her that if a person gets stuck in the beginning or middle of a story, they may have to work hard to fix the things as best they can. Al coached Susie saying, "No matter how hard it gets, you must keep trying."

The Worm was one of the stories Al told. Al said, "Worms live inside long tunnels in the earth. On special days when it rains, the worms come up and say 'hello.' You can find them on the grass and the sidewalks. Worms help make the earth better. Be sure to smile at them and say 'hello' back."

Al was trying to teach Susie that everybody has a choice whether or not to smile and be friendly. He said smiling is part of good health. Susie liked walks after it rained and always looked down to find worms at which to smile. Fellow walkers had often squished worms on the pavement. Susie learned *The Worm* story was one that did not always have a happy conclusion.

"I have a story with a happy ending," Al said as they walked. "This story is called *The Germ*. One day long ago in Milwaukee, there was a germ running around the city. It got inside people and made them sick. No one knew why. One warm day, Mommy found Susie very sick. Daddy took her to the hospital where the doctors told him that the germ was inside her."

With the biggest voice he could muster, Al said, "Go away. I do not like you inside of Susie making her feel sick. *The Germ* story has a happy ending. The germ is gone from you. You can walk!" exclaimed Daddy.

After a long workday, Al looked forward to dinner and then strolls with Susie. This ritual gave him purpose and joy.

Viktor Frankl, an Austrian philosopher observed that when the lives of people have meaning, they can make their way through troublesome situations. People may build resilience going through challenging times such as the illness or death of loved ones. This was true for Al.

Later when Susie's polio leg strengthened, Al and Susie began to take their evening walks without wearing the cumbersome brace. They traveled further. By bracing her hip against Al's, and putting her arm through his, they ventured for miles stopping for ice-cream or custard along the way.

Susie would play outside with Mike, and other kids on the block. With neighbor children, she went into the cemetery across the street where older boys on the block told stories about ghosts to frighten the younger kids. Susie was not afraid because Mike was always close by.

Sometimes Susie fell, but Al taught her to get right back up. Al did not view falls as a barrier to getting out and walking. Susie never received serious injuries by falling. She never broke a bone. Al cleaned and bandaged her scrapes. Replaying in his mind the prediction of the chief doctor's statement at the isolation hospital that his daughter would never walk, Al was grateful for the progress Susie made. In Al's mind, falling and getting up counted as exercise. Al believed movement was essential medicine.

Little did Al know at this time that he would later count on Susie when he was in his nineties to speak up at a meeting about his wish to be discharged from a healthcare facility back to his home. Al wanted to exercise his right to choose the risk of falling in his own home even if he might get injured. He preferred walking around his home which was familiar and comfortable rather than living in a nursing facility.

Susie told the nursing home staff about her father's beliefs about walking. Sixty-five years before, Al took the risk of taking Susie home from the isolation hospital. Al moved Susie's polio leg until she could move it herself. He knew Susie would lose the gains in strength she had made if she stopped walking. He understood the same was true for him. Mike drove him home and monitored his safety. Al exercised daily. He never fell.

Susie • 1952

It was a hot July Saturday. In the early morning, my friend and I picked ripe red berries off bushes in our backyard garden. Mama was getting ready to cook up current jam.

We became bored and decided to build a tent by pinning old blankets on the clothesline. Mike and his friends swooped in and grabbed the clothespins off the line causing all the blankets to fall on top of us. The boys ran away as we struggled to make our way out of the mess.

We looked for the culprits in the garage. Sometimes the boys hid there. A neighbor rented a space for his car from dad so there were two cars parked side by side. Crawling on all fours on the concrete we peeked below each vehicle. We did not find the boys.

Now bored, we decided to take turns swinging between two parked cars as if we were acrobats in a circus. Grasping the hoods on each side of us, we swayed between the cars all the while yelping as we moved back and forth. Suddenly my arms grew tired, and I fell onto the concrete floor.

"Mrs. S., Mrs. S. come quick!" screamed my friend as she ran toward the house. I could see her running although I was unconscious on the garage floor.

My thoughts moved quickly to Mama being mad at me for using the cars like gym parallel bars. It wasn't on the forbidden-to-do-list only because she had not caught me doing it yet.

I am floating above my body looking down. I see the kid who lives across the alley touching my hair. "Stop!" I want to yell. But he cannot hear me shouting from above. I do not want him poking at me. He says, "Susie, wake up!"

My mind keeps looking down at my body. Like in the hospital, I have flipped out to a place where I can see and hear what is going on around my body. I am hoping I do not go back into my body until Mama gets to me. "When Mama comes," I say to myself, "I'll go back in. Not until then."

My childhood **out-of-body experiences (OBE)s** occurred in two types of circumstances which were when I got injured or when I experienced unfathomable pain. The span of time I was outside my body gave me relief from fear and agony.

The worst times of pain and most frequent occurrences of OBEs happened when I was strapped in the steel brace unable to move side to side, or when I experienced long-lasting muscles spasms. Most everyone has had a *"Charlie Horse,"* cramp in their calf muscle. Picture a cramp unrelenting and going on for hours, days, a week and you have described what polio pain can be like.

OBEs are a blessing for which I am thankful. Not everyone believes they are real. I understand people ignoring stories about phenomenon that are not within the realm of their experience.

Out of Body Experiences During CPR

Patients in critical care after open heart surgery told stories of going out of their bodies when nurses and doctors took turns performing compressions on their chests and shocking them. When others walked away shaking their heads, I stayed by the bedside and listened to their stories. My living through such events from the beginning of my life with polio gave me an understanding mind.

One of my areas of research is near-death experiences of patients undergoing CPR. The recounts I have heard reveal common

> characteristics within patient stories. The voices of patients are reported in articles I have authored in *The Journal of Near-Death Studies* and numerous other professional journals, lay articles, and books.
>
> I continue to give talks about what I know to be true, i.e., there is a place human beings can exist outside their bodies. We never know how our own lives will thread with others throughout time. That we are not fully in charge of our lives is quite apparent to me.
>
> Looking back, I wonder if my early childhood OBEs happened in part so I could help patients come to understand their own.

Back to the story at hand in the garage: I watch. I wait. I am comfortable although my arms are sprawled out at odd angles and my scrawny legs splayed crookedly to the side with my head on the cold, hard floor.

I see Mama rush to kneel beside me. She gently touches my face and brushes my hair across my forehead. I find myself popping back into my body. Only then do I feel the pain and reach up to touch the side of my head. "Ouch, it hurts, Mama," I cry.

Mama lifts me in her arms and carries me into the house. She puts me in her soft bed and plumps both pillows under my head. She sends Mike, who has reappeared from his hiding place to fetch Marie, the nurse, Mama's one friend on our block.

Marie moves my arms and legs while asking mama to bring her a flashlight. She checks my pupils. I fidget and squirm. I do not like to be poked. Marie declares I need to be watched and kept awake. She says that I may have a concussion.

Mama knows the routine Marie has taught her. Mama checks my pupils every fifteen minutes and makes sure I do not fall asleep. She puts the flashlight on the floor by the bed and goes back to the kitchen. She is not too worried. Marie will come back in an hour.

When Mama returns, her face voice is stern, her chest is puffed up and she looks angry. The berries have boiled over. I have ruined Mama's jam making time. She yells at me to stay in the bed and "Stay awake!"

I know I am not the best kid. I get into trouble with Mama. With Dad, never. He enjoys me. I make him laugh and smile. He sings and plays music, so I dance. Together we are joy.

Another time that Mama was irate with my shenanigans was the day neighborhood gossip about her smoking and drinking came back to her through my girlfriend's mother. My friend and I were talking as we ate cookies out on the lawn. Her mother poured us milk and, while doing so, overheard our conversation.

My friend said we had to eat store-bought cookies because her mother never baked homemade cookies like my Mama. My friend said her mother did not bake cookies because she needed time to rest.

I said my Mama smoked because she got free cigarettes. I boasted to my friend that Mama drank liquor in a fancy glass with her cigarette. I did not realize smoking and drinking whiskey was forbidden in some people's eyes. I was showing off about the pretty drink glass. It was a girl-to-girl talk about our lives with our mothers.

My friend's mother marched right over to my house and questioned my Mama. She asked Mama if she smoked because she did not want her daughter to see a woman smoking.

My Mama called me into the house. She grabbed the wooden yardstick out of the kitchen closet and whacked me. To be truthful, neither the hardware store stick nor Mama were too strong. The wooden ruler broke in half when she hit me. My Mama's next choice for punishment was the locking me in the attic closet.

Mama grabbed me by the arm and pulled me up the staircase. Shoving me inside the closet, she locked the door. Mama was crying. I was banging on the door. I knew I was too much trouble for Mama.

It was scary inside the attic closet. I could barely see my arms and legs in the darkness. When I listened between my fits of pounding on the door to get out, I heard my Mama sobbing loudly. Wailing in the polio ward overtook my mind and I found myself putting my hands over my ears to block out her crying.

Mama rocked her body against the attic closet door and the wall next to it. She screamed in anguish. She told me the things I had done wrong.

Then there was quiet. Mama got up and left me to go smoke a cigarette.

Silverfish lived in the attic and crawled all around. I was trapped in the closet with them. The bugs crawled between my bare toes and thighs while I slapped furiously at my skin to make them go away.

But inevitably I would always come to the same conclusion that there was no use in crying. She was gone. I would be silent. *You can hurt me. I will not tell. I won't cry.*

Faulting Mama was of no use. I knew nothing would have changed if I spoke up. When you grow up with an illness that requires rest, you have loads of time to observe others all around you. I had time to think about what people were doing and why.

Everyday life made Mama exhausted. She couldn't ignore the situation. There wasn't the prospect of a different future. Having a cigarette and drink was her way of stepping away from the reality of the situation for a while. She saw no good prospect for a less stressful life. Mama could only take so much.

Age brought me even more time to reflect on my attic closet punishment times. My Mama's sobbing was not just for my most recent misdeed, but also was Mama's reaction to the loss she felt when polio took away the life that she had imagined for herself. Her tears were a cry of grief. They were not anger toward me. Mama was mad at the circumstances of life that left her feeling alone and judged by society for something over which she had no control.

Research shows that parents lead happier lives if their children are healthy and have easy temperaments. Economic stress also takes its toll on a parent's mental well-being and their subsequent response to children. Social isolation, as my Mama experienced during the polio epidemic, worsens a parent's feeling of stress. The polio virus deeply affected Mama. As a child, I could understand that anxiety provoked her actions to gain control over life at home. Mama and I lived on our own island which most people never saw or understood.

Polio separated Mama from others. It determined Mama's picture of herself and her relationship with those around her. She ruminated over people's opinions about her inability to prevent her child from contracting polio. Her demeanor became one of anxious nervousness. Polio tore Mama apart inside and pushed her into trying to take control over what she could not. There were days when she had to separate herself and take a break from her polio child.

Mama's story of loneliness and sorrow is not unlike others. Sharing of her life and times I hope moves people to gather up their compassion and with grace bestow it on others facing similar situations. We are all vulnerable. Everyone does better when supported not blamed. Tragedy requires we be present for those who like Mama experience loss. If we are silent, we leave people feeling alone and frightened, and at risk of striking out to feel alive.

Warren Zevon sang in *Ain't That Pretty At All* that sometimes when people are angry and feeling life is unfair, they may want to hurl themselves at the wall. Zevon reasons that they do this because feeling pain is sometimes better than feeling nothing at all. We see this played out in real life.

As a nurse, I never met a parent of a dying child who did not replay events leading up to the illness and death of the child. They ruminated over what action they could have taken to prevent what happened. Parents of ill and dying children picture their child's face each day and each night wishing the nightmare would be over. *It never is.*

Mama came back and let me out of the attic. We didn't talk. *Silence was a way of speaking we both observed.*

I took my crunched-up, sore knees outside and laid down on a blanket in the front yard under our lone tree. Reading about India, I dreamt of where I might go someday.

Other closet incidents for misdeeds which in my mind were unfortunate accidents:

I carved my name in my dresser. Mama did not realize I had taken a knife from the kitchen drawer. I thought giving a name to a piece of furniture was a way of organizing things.

I knocked a ceramic figurine off the wall of my bedroom. It chipped when it and hit the floor. I threw the broken piece in the garbage. Saying nothing, I hung the figurine back up. Mama noticed. I refused to say I broke it although there was no one else to blame.

I wore Mama's best sweater to school because I wanted to look pretty. She caught me when she found it returned to her dresser drawer folded inside out.

Susie • 1953

I walked despite doctors' predictions to the contrary. Following my parents' instruction, I got back up on my own when I fell. They had me walk the talk of the principle of *use it or lose*. Doing so propelled me to become stronger and more confident. I walked right out the door, and gradually into the neighborhood and eventually into the city.

When I tumbled inside or tripped outdoors, somehow my brain controlled my body to land in ways that prevented me getting broken bones. My parents cleansed my wounds, bandaged me up, and sent me back out the door into the world. There were some days I sported a lot of Band-Aids.

When I could stay upright with a degree of certainty and Dad and Mama allowed me to go beyond the yard with my brother, I was not afraid. Together the two of us had free rein in the neighborhood which at that time meant the length of three streets converging in a triangular shape and a wide expanse of cemetery grounds across the boulevard opposite our front yard.

The Triangle

Neighborhood Cemetery

Home

The dozen kids who lived within the triangle were a group. We played ball in the alleyway. Since I was lousy at running, my brother taught me that the only way I could be of any value on a basketball team was to ace scoring free throws. "You don't have to be a star forward," he said. "You can be a steady free throw shooter. You can be the player to be counted on when points are not adding up for the team." I learned to be spot-on with free throws.

Mike teaching me to play to my strengths, while facing my limitations was a lesson that helped me forever. By high school, I made the basketball team as a guard that did not need to move around the court as much as a forward but who never missed a basket when on the line. Mike taught me to be good in a role that did not require too much racing around, but that team members valued because my skills increased our team's final score.

My brother will read here that he taught me quite a bit about being a good nurse leader. Like in basketball, Later on in life, I became a team player when working in roles as a Director of Nursing or an administrator. I was present on the units giving those I supervised (nurses and nursing assistants, dieticians, social workers, physical and occupational therapists) "free-throw" advice to solve patient care issues. This not only boosted our success in improving the healthcare for patients but also reminded them how important they were because all our skills woven together made for the best possible team outcome of better care for patients and their families.

My parents' mantra to keep moving was reflecting in the many activities I participated in that involved physical activity. No longer was my polio leg covered up with a blanket to hide my brace. I now walked out into society as if polio had not happened to me.

I danced on a big stage at the Milwaukee Auditorium. I was a ballerina one day and an Irish dancer the next. Mama never sat in the audience. She stood in the front part of the auditorium next to the stairs that led up to the stage. She could have used an evening enjoying just sitting back and watching the dancing performances, but her protector Mama instincts kicked in and she didn't dare leave me too far away. *My fault. Everybody will talk about us. I must be in control.*

The ballet line up at The Milwaukee Auditorium

There were parents who suggested to the performance photographer that the *polio girl* be moved to the back row for group pictures so my skinny polio leg would not be noticed in the photographs. Mama overheard the other mothers who pointed at me and whispered, "The photographer told her to stand in the first row. Look at the *polio girl*. Her polio leg is ruining the picture."

In response to the mothers who suggested I be out of view in the back row out of view, Mama reminded me, *Smile, so others do not feel so badly*. The photographer, setting up a camera within earshot of the mothers' talk, heard the voiced displeasure at how he arranged the dancers. He raised his voice and instructed us girls to split out of the two rows and line up in one single line. There would be no back row. I smiled at him. He smiled at me. I learned quite young that if you give a smile, you usually catch one back.

On stage, I was a not-so-good baton twirler because you had to move quickly to catch the baton after you tossed it high into the air. The instructor choreographed me in the costume of a tree so I could stand still while twirling and be part of the performance. The twirlers who could move well danced around me in fairy costumes. Some teachers play to the strengths of their students. My Mama was grateful.

My mother took me to weekly dance practices. She sat watching with the other mothers who were not facing going to work in the evening. But she did not complain. She pushed herself to the limit in order that I have opportunity to be like a child not labeled as a disability.

On non-practice or performance evenings, Mama sewed my costumes in the few hours leftover from working and running a household. She availed herself of cigarettes and an after-dinner drink while she stitched. Even if she had the time and money, yoga and meditation were not yet popular as relaxation methods in the United States. The first yoga studio on U.S. soil started in the 1950s in California. Meditation groups started in the 1960s.

Mama's hand sewn Irish dance costume

In choosing her attitude imbedded with the behaviors of not griping about what life deals us and responding in positive ways to make a difference in who we become, Mama role modeled that a person's manner of being can help them get through whatever unexpected circumstances they face. I leaned on this lesson many times in life.

Getting out the door into the neighborhood meant I could hang out with the kids on the block. When dusk fell, we roamed. All the neighborhood kids understood that when I stopped walking, it meant I needed to rest a bit. No one walked ahead and left me behind. They halted when I did and waited with me. Children did not question or judge. They all called me by my name not the *polio girl* like many of their parents. Children taking care of one another came naturally. The oldest boy made sure we all got home safely. Our parents waited on their porches to greet us. This was the way life rolled in those days.

Adults acted quite differently than the kids on the block. They often stared when I walked by and then, seeing I saw them, averted their eyes showing me that contact with me made them uncomfortable. These were pandemic times, and they were rightly scared of catching polio. I heard my mother's voice saying, *Smile, Susie, so they will not feel so badly.*

Although smiling when my leg was sore was not necessarily what I wanted to do, I did as I was told. I learned that adults did not necessarily want the truth. I figured out that to keep others happy I had to keep the truth inside. Hiding feelings became a way of being a "good girl."

I learned to smile while walking as best I could in my sturdy ugly (much disliked) red orthopedic leather shoes. Smiling while walking was a feat of inner strength as I was so often in intractable physiological pain that I had to concentrate on keeping each one of my footsteps moving along safely. I cannot imagine what it is like to walk without worrying about falling.

Red hated orthopedic shoes

Susie • 1953

As a grade schooler, I was outside every day in all kinds of weather no matter how much snow had fallen and including times when the temperature dropped to below zero temperatures which it did quite often in Wisconsin winters. Cold temperatures made my polio leg hurt more than usual. The pain lasted beyond the exposure to cold. Even when warmed up, it took time for my damaged muscles to relax.

My Dad reminded Mike and me that playing outside was therapeutic. Nurses at the isolation hospital told him fresh air was essential for good health. Serendipitously, the outdoors environment wore me out leading to me napping and providing my parents a spell of relief from the otherwise constant surveillance of the whereabouts and condition of a child with a chronic illness.

I loved the freedom to look all around me that riding my bike gave me. When walking, I was looking down at the ground for objects that might trip me up. When biking, I could look forward and dream. My bicycle piloted me out of the neighborhood on my own for new adventures.

Milwaukee provided playgrounds for which I will always be grateful. In the 1950s, it was a city alive with endless possibilities for a kid who wanted free fun. I biked on safe sidewalks and streets to daytime park activities. Our city's mayor was Frank Zeidler, a socialist who promoted the accessibility of parks and playgrounds for all. In the summer, high schoolers and college kids staffed neighborhood playgrounds. They supervised activities for children.

My Dad worked at the *Milwaukee Journal* in the 1950s through retirement. The Journal sponsored family events like summer picnics, zoo outings, a performance by Roy Rogers and Dale Evans along with their horse, Trigger, on stage at the Milwaukee auditorium, and an annual spectacular 4th of July parade down Wisconsin Avenue, complete with Clydesdale horses. It was a fun time to be a kid in Milwaukee. My parents would always carry a blanket to gatherings, and I would take a nap. They recalled that people passing by and seeing the only sleeping kid at these events, would comment, "Oh, there she is—the *polio girl*!"

Awakening from nap at Journal event

Every evening, except those when we went to the lake, Dad took me for a walk. As I became stronger, walks grew longer. There were two routes. One led to an ice cream store. The other dropped us right in front of a custard stand. Our ritual was full of sweets, songs, and storytelling. These observances distracted from the pain of walking far. Shared rituals bond people.

Music was a big part of my life growing up. My Dad's extra jobs were playing electric guitar (Al Schoen Combo) and teaching guitar at a Wauwatosa music store. He taught me to play the guitar. My mother and I played piano. Mike's instrument was the trumpet. Our tiny living room filled with a *wall of sound*.

The beat of live music has always calmed me because it was in the background of my every day as we played our instruments.

Susie • 1953

My Dad went out each Saturday evening and performed at weddings, dances (including two of my high school proms), parties, and **Nike** missile base gatherings.

Nike (named after the Greek goddess of victory) was a nuclear missile base. In the 1950s to early 1970s, there were eight missile bases in Wisconsin during the Cold War with the rising **Soviet Union**.

As a member of the Wisconsin Musician's Union, Dad volunteered once-a-month on a Saturday evening playing his guitar on wards at Milwaukee County Hospital. Each Sunday morning after such a performance, he reminded me, "Be grateful for the strengths you have." I carry his words with me always.

As I matured the effects of polio stayed with me living in all my waking hours as well as in my sleep when I should have been getting needed rest. The polio virus wreaked its nefarious effects on multiple organ systems making me learn more pro-active ways of dealing with the damage.

I needed to be an organized person. To be well-rested enough to get daily studies and work done, it was important to pace. My Dad, then a stock clerk who had every box in our house labeled, every cabinet organized, and every tool lined up, taught me how to write daily lists of what I needed to do that day and check things off when I completed the tasks. I would have not survived without this training. I followed his motto: *Work, study, play, rest.*

I realized I could picture things in my mind and later recall where they were. This photographic memory saved me steps. I could visualize the lists I made so I did not have to keep checking them.

I wrote things down that I needed to remember because picturing the writing later was an invaluable tool. I re-wrote repeatedly the information I needed to know for class tests, and during the tests, pictured in my mind the places where the answers were in my notes.

I was always devising step-saving methods. The polio virus weakened the nerves on both sides (upper and lower extremities) of my body. Somehow my brain figured out that ambidexterity was the best way for me to function. If I could carry two objects across a room instead of taking two trips across a room, I did so. This cut down on wear and tear of my polio leg and evened out the work of my arms.

Mama learned nutrition from reading books she checked out of the library. She told Dad who could not read well what foods would be best for me to eat. To ensure I would not be taking in any germs, the only fresh fruits, and vegetables they allowed me to eat were those that you could wash very well. This limited my choices. I was given an apple a day, carrots, asparagus, onions, homegrown peppers, tomatoes, beans, and potatoes. Mama didn't like to scrub dirt out of ridges in sticks of celery so that was not often part of her recipes.

My parents became "preppers." Then we were not facing doomsday. Their reasoning for stocking up was their limited income. They worried about running out of essential foods, supplements, and medicines for me. Their basement was a stockroom of canned goods, and bottled water bought in vast quantities when on sale just in case Dad did not get enough music gigs to bring in extra cash. Mama made homemade jam, and canned applesauce and pickles. The fight to survive against polio marched on.

Each morning I stood at the refrigerator door as Dad pulled out the Geritol bottle and gave me a spoonful along with cod liver oil. We would go to the local milk store where Dad instructed me to drink the cream off the top of each gallon of Wisconsin milk we bought. Dad added wheat germ to my breakfast cereal. My parents restricted me from eating white bread because it got stuck in my slow gastrointestinal tract. They fed me Roman Meal bread because it contained plenty of fiber. The rest of the family ate white bread because it was cheaper.

A closet in the downstairs' hallway held a large stockpile of medicinal treatments. Its shelves contained bottles of supplements, Vicks, suppositories, Band-Aids and other first aid supplies, peroxide, rubbing alcohol, and a thermometer. Children's aspirin was stored in a kitchen cupboard.

Dad and Mama stocked two types of skin antiseptics to clean up minor scrapes. One was mercurochrome wound cleaner that would turn skin red. It is no longer available because of its high mercury content. In 1998, the U.S. Food and Drug Administration (FDA) declared the product unsafe. The other antiseptic was Tincture of iodine.

I remember my mother's tears, reflecting her heartbreak and exasperation, when city workers tacked up another quarantine sign on the front door. No weekly trips to the library. No school for me during quarantines.

Mama was sequestered with her shut-in little polio survivor. Neighbors, friends, and family again distanced themselves. Mama shut the curtains. I peeked out the window to look for Milwaukee County police patrols looking for any *polio kids* outside their yards.

The quarantine rules prohibited neighborhood kids from getting near me. Books substituted as friends. I became interested in India because Ms. Demand read us stories based there. The characters fascinated me. Her ability to make them come alive inspired me much later to visit the people in that part of the world to give immunizations.

Vaccinating in India

Drawing up vaccines

IndiGO airways

My next-door neighbor was an exception to people who kept their distance during quarantine time. We would connect a pulley system between our bedroom windows and send notes back and forth on clothes pins. This did not technically violate the quarantine order. We would also play card games while sitting at the lot line. This unquestionably breached the rules.

When I was not home-bound due to quarantines, my friend and I crossed over the boulevard to the cemetery. We talked the grave diggers into saving us the satin ribbons that were part of discarded graveside bouquets. Workers had the job of tossing the decorations into a huge trash pile.

My friend joined me in ways which were fun and not taxing on my body. We washed the graveyard ribbons. We designed dress patterns while they dried on the wash line. Then we sat and hand-sewed doll clothes out of the pieces of fabric. We were decades ahead of the reclaim/reuse/recycle movement.

Sewing became a passion that satisfied my creativity and additionally alleviated the extreme fatigue which is an often-hidden side effect of polio. Pain during the night hampered my sleep. Pain during the day added to my exhaustion. My brain shut down. *Hitting the polio wall* was not coined until decades later but my body knew it intimately as a child.

Sewing balanced my tiredness by giving me a hobby wherein I could sit and create with no pressure to follow an agenda. I could practice *mindlessness* and rejuvenate my mind, body, and spirit.

My friend and I designed our doll clothes. There was no pressure to sew something exactly according to pattern. It is not easy to be with people preoccupied with perfection. She accepted me as I was. I am so grateful.

These were the edge years when there was no vaccination and people still dreaded polio. I was fortunate to weave into a neighborhood where I had friends, and hobbies like basketball, dancing, biking, reading, and sewing.

Susie • 1954

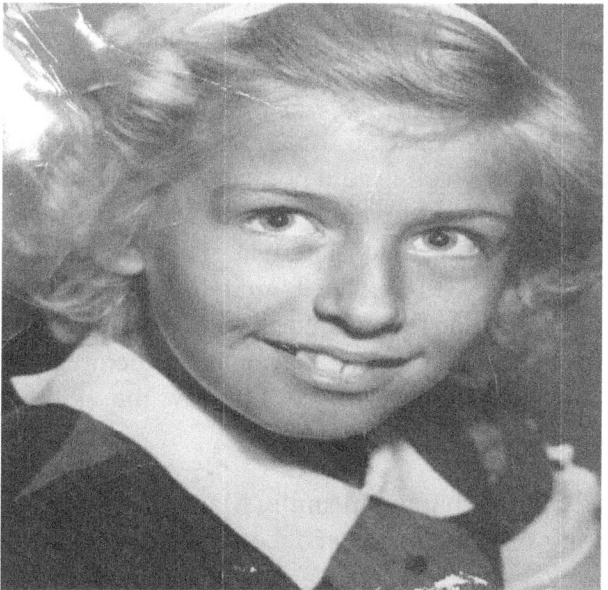

Polio Poster Child Portrait

Through her friends at the charity shop, Grandma heard there was a contest for polio poster child of the year. The March of Dimes, a non-profit organization which supported Jonas Salk's vaccine research, sponsored the event. She marched me right downtown to the interviews. .

Grandma looked at this event as a way of getting attention for herself. She was shameless about wanting everything to center around her. I knew that I was just the means to her real goal of being known as the grandma of the polio poster kid.

I was scared in crowds. It did not matter to her that the contest was set at a downtown hotel where I would have to make my way on sidewalks brimming with busy shoppers. Being in groups of people pushing and shoving made me panic about getting off balance and falling.

Grandma had already lost me once on an outing. She took me to the fireworks at Washington Park on a fourth of July and when the crowd surged to leave, someone in a hurry bumped me, I fell, and Grandma not noticing, left me behind. It took her a while to figure out that I was missing. I could not get back up on my feet amidst the stream of legs of kids, parents, and dogs that blitzed by dashing to get out of the darkened park. When grandma found me, I didn't cry. *You can hurt me. I will not tell. I won't cry.*

From the start, my feelings did not factor into Grandma's signing me up for the polio poster child competition. That I felt awkward when a crowd of people stared at me did not concern her. Grandma put a new-to-me, used, pretty dress out on the bed, and told me to put it on. I wondered if winning the polio kid poster contest depended a lot on my appearance. I pictured my polio leg sticking out for everyone to see. She saw me as the image the judges wanted. .

I muscled up my courage to smile. Mama had drilled into me to that looking happy was better than being real. *Act like you are walking on the sunny side of life*, was one of her mottos. Actually, I know she got this from a song because I heard Dad singing it. I put on the dress and smiled in the mirror.

Grandma thought she had a winner! In her mind, I was the happiest child survivor of crippling polio. I was more active exercising, swimming, dancing, riding a bike, than her own twin children who were only a year older than me. Dad ingrained in me the "*Use it or lose it*" principle. And I did it all with a smile.

She didn't understand the fakery. Mama and Dad did not burden her with the truth about what polio still did to us every day. Grandma would have called them complainers. I guess it was not all her fault that she did not understand that we as a family were still rolling along with polio. A lot could be hidden behind a smile.

The March of Dimes sought a beaming poster child with just enough debility to gain the sympathy of donors. A photographer took portraits of contestants as we alternated turns sitting on a raised stool. The photographer's assistant pranced puppets around to inspire us to make a happy face.

But the polio child could not be too chipper. To garner donations, The March of Dimes Poster Child had to be good-looking and have an ample story of struggle to pull at the heartstrings of the public making them willing to donate.

It was getting on in the day. I had my photo taken and waited in line for the formal poster child interview. I saw my grandmother sitting ramrod straight up, clutching a purse on her lap, listening, and watching the man who was asking the questions.

Then it was my turn. The man could not have been nicer. He wondered when I had polio. He wanted to know how it felt to wear the heavy steel leg brace.

The interviewer asked if I fell down a lot. I answered that I walked good. I told him if I had a spill, I got right back up. All this was accurate.

When the man interviewing me questioned if I was able to walk to school. I looked him in the eye and said, "Yes." My grandmother seated across from me crumpled her face into a cringe like someone had just twisted her arm tightly behind her back and would not let go.

I told the interviewer my friends, my brother and I walked to school together. We sometimes played a game. We would bet on the number of times I would fall on the way. I had the advantage in this game especially in the winter when cold that brought pain and snow that was slippery added to my chances of running up the fall total. On these days, I was the only one who knew I had leg cramps due to the weather and was more likely to stumble and fall. This edge increased my winning the game.

The March of Dimes man smiled quizzically at me. He said, "Isn't it too hard for you to walk to school?" I emphatically replied, "No. I do it!"

Upon hearing my answer, I could see my grandmother shift in her chair and give me her "You're in trouble" stare. She pulled back her shoulder rigidly and looked like she was heading into one of her huffy moods.

I confess I could have lied if I thought lying was what was required to win. I lied all the time to people about my pain and tiredness. That was because others expected me to be a cheerful, nondisabled, crippled child. I had learned the ways in which people expected me to hide how the polio virus damaged me.

If you asked me if I was hurting. I would look at the ground and shake my head to indicate "No." If you would see me limping and wondered aloud if I wanted to sit out an inning of a ball game on the playground, I turned my lips up in a pout, and placed my hands on my hips, while shouting, "No!" There were many times when my stubborn streak refused to admit any weakness.

The man gave me another question, "Why don't your parents drive you to school?" I said they both worked. It was unusual for a mother to work then. His eyebrows went up as he wrote that down. My brother was the one who got me out the door and to school. We were *latchkey* kids before it was a vocabulary term.

At the end of the afternoon, the man who interviewed us announced the name of the contest winner. I was not The March of Dimes Poster Child. Swiftly, my grandmother grabbed my arm and pulled me to my feet. She said we had to get on the next streetcar to her house. Shoulders hunched over, purse gripped tightly to her chest, lips closed firmly, she ignored me. Grandma did not speak at all on the way home. I was a little sorry I disappointed her, and she would have to tell her charity friends I lost the contest.

"Pa," Grandma shouted when we returned, "Susie could have won that contest if she just told the people she could not walk to school. I don't know why she did not just fib a little."

I know why. My parents taught me that lying about everything except all my polio deficits was wrong and that not all stories have happy endings and that's okay. Dad taught me you just must try harder and get the best ending for your story you can. My dad always said, "Every time you fall down, you have the choice to get right back up."

Or maybe, I inherited a bit of the pride gene from my Grandma. I was awfully proud that I could manage walking to school. You know pride is an undercurrent in all of us. It can go this way or that. We control its depth and flow. Narcissists (who tend not to have friends) grab pride and use it as a tool to showcase their importance, whether real or not. Their over-the-top pride hides their inner insecurity and leads to them bullying others to make themselves feel good.

My pride about walking to school was tethered with enjoying time with lots of friends and becoming part of a group. Although needing to pace and nap, I kept up the walking no matter how much my polio leg hurt.

I moved on from the poster child contest, but Grandma did not smile at me for a long time. I guess I wasn't her ticket to fame. Although she would have wanted me to say I was a little more disabled than I was, I could not. It was a complex time in history. The nation did not want to hear about the complicating ways the polio virus maimed its victims. Frightened, people did not want to see or hear about the reality of polio.

Franklin Delano Roosevelt and Polio

Franklin Delano Roosevelt (FDR) (1882-1945) could pretend just like me. Polio struck FDR in 1921 when he was thirty-nine years old. He became ill in the hot August summer. Roosevelt experienced slight fever and fatigue. He retired to bed. Within days, he could not move his legs. They were paralyzed.

When he came down with polio, FDR was a national figure having served as assistant secretary of the Navy under Woodrow Wilson in WWI. In 1921, he was the vice-presidential nominee on the losing Democratic ticket.

FDR was the only president who was elected four times in a row (March 4,1933-April 12, 1945). He was the only president to serve more than two terms. He died prior to completing his fourth term in office. FDR assumed a leadership role in the fight against polio.

With the financial resources to attempt all known treatments, Roosevelt experimented with massage and electrical current stimulation therapies. He went to Warm Springs, a naturally heated spring in Georgia where he had hoped to find a cure for his paralysis and deformed legs. Roosevelt enjoyed the soothing waters and camaraderie of the spa where he exercised undamaged muscles which supported those weakened by the polio virus. Warm Springs did not cure polio.

Warm Spring guests were mostly well-to-do Americans. At times, wealthy patients and their families donated monies to help those who could not afford treatments.

In 1926, Warm Springs was having financial issues. As its favored and most famous visitor, FDR would not allow the facility to shut down. He bought the place for $200,000 and transformed it into a rehabilitation center for polio patients like himself. The following year, the American Orthopedic Association designated **Warm Springs Foundation** a permanent hydrotherapeutic center.

Franklin Delano Roosevelt was a dubious symbol of a recovered polio survivor. He required assistance for both standing and walking. In the public's eye, he conquered polio. Boys and girls around the country saw the president as their role model.

Because muscles of his hips and trunk were damaged and weakened by the virus, he wore a corset attached to leg braces, which he called "painful" contraptions. This combination of assistive devices allowed him to stand upright while holding onto crutches.

He could not walk alone. He used a wheelchair in the White House. The public never viewed FDR in one. At times, FDR used a cane and the arm of an assistant, often a son, to bring him to a podium on which he leaned to give speeches to crowds.

FDR's gait was lurching in motion as he lifted one leg forward, put his weight on it, and followed this by swinging his other leg into position. He experienced "foot drop." This condition meant he could no longer lift the front of his feet up. If he did not have the braces in place, his feet would drag on the ground.

The nation started in earnest paying attention to collecting money for polio when FDR took over as head of the **National Foundation for Infantile Paralysis** in 1938. The foundation partnered with the nonprofit Georgia **Warm Springs Foundation**.

After FDR took over the National Foundation for Infantile Paralysis, the organization held balls (over 6,000) across the country. These fundraisers brought in close to $800,000 for research into the cause and prevention of polio and care for patients.

Eddie Cantor and The March of Dimes

Eddie Cantor (1892-1964), a vaudeville actor, singer, comedian, and famed Ziegfeld Follies entertainer led the fundraising strategy to fight polio. He reworked the title of a *Time* newsreel shown in theaters throughout the country called "*The March of Time*," into the "*March of Dimes.*" The name was familiar to radio listeners and catchy, so it stuck.

Cantor understood that a way to get all people involved in donating to the polio fight was to coin a slogan that spelled out the everyday person's ability to make a difference in the fight against polio. The catch phrase *March of Dimes* drew in people who would need no medical understanding of polio but would be driven by fear of the disease and the human instinct to be a part of something bigger than themselves. The *March of Dimes* slogan was first broadcast over radio airwaves in November 1938.

Cantor announced, "Everyone can send in a dime." He was right. Everyday Americans sent in dimes and more. People mailed more than 2,600,000 dimes to the White House. President Roosevelt went on the radio to say "thank you" to the country for their donations.

Projecting hope was the foundation for building the success of the organization. People joined their neighbors to fight a dreaded disease. They chose to battle polio by supporting scientific research efforts.

People gave dimes because they had the belief that individuals doing so could change things not just for themselves but for others whom they saw suffering. People in the 1950s expected that collectively they could have a positive influence over disease. They believed they had a determinative role in society. They are our heroes because their collection of dimes led to eradication of polio in the United States. Their hope—knowing they could contribute to something greater than themselves, changed the world.

Door-to-door campaigns popped up to raise money. *Porch Light Nights* sprung up in Milwaukee and throughout the country. Families would put the front lights of their homes on to alert *March of Dimes* volunteers to knock on their doors and pick up dimes and other coins. People could get *March of Dimes* cards at local stores to fill up with dimes and turn in at businesses that delivered cards back to the organization.

In 1979, the National Foundation for Infantile Paralysis officially changed its name to the **March of Dimes Birth Defects Foundation**. Underwriting the development of vaccines by **Dr. Jonas Salk** (1914-1995) in 1955 and later **Dr. Albert Sabin** (1906-1993) in 1962, quelled polio epidemics.

The March of Dimes is one of the best remembered American nonprofit foundations. Putting forth the image of a cheerful, struggling child who was smiling while overcoming deficits caused by the poliovirus, inspired people to give money to the foundation.

March of Dimes card

President Franklin Delano Roosevelt's Correspondence with Polio Survivors

FDR connected with the fears, struggles, and hopes of polio survivors by answering polio survivors' letters sent to the White House. While Roosevelt's replies were just a line or two, they were treasured by the recipients as words of encouragement.

Daniel J. Wilson (1949-2021), historian and polio survivor, read copies of FDR's correspondence and concluded the notes "usually urged the recipient to follow doctor's orders, and to have courage." Wilson noted that during WWII, due to an overwhelming number of letters to FDR, the White House secretarial staff helped prepare and sign letters.

FDR concluded that his own will power and exercise helped him defeat polio. He endeavored to transfer this message of hope to other polio survivors.

Black People and Polio

Polio was a disease that could affect anyone no matter what age, race, religion, or status in society. However, Warm Springs did not admit Black polio survivors until September 1945 and The March of Dimes did not choose a Black child as poster child until 1947 (Rita Reed from Illinois).

The head of the March of Dimes, **Basil O'Connor** (1892-1972), held the belief that Black people were less susceptible to polio. This incorrect assumption was not based in fact. Unequal access to healthcare under Jim Crow laws played a part. Polio epidemics at the time took place more often in the North and Midwest than in the South. Cases of polio amongst the Black population were uncounted due to medical racism and neglect.

In 1939, the March of Dimes provided funds for a segregated **Tuskegee Infantile Paralysis Center at Tuskegee Institute** in Alabama. **President Franklin Roosevelt** marked the opening in January 1941 saying it was a "perfect setting for a hospital unit to care for infantile paralysis victims." However, Tuskegee did not have the capacity to care for but a fraction of Black patients that needed its services.

In 1941, Texas although practicing racial segregation, opened a polio center serving White, Black, and Latino patients in Gonzales, Texas. Houston hospitals opened two integrated polio wards. Texas healthcare at the time was not moored to the support of racist voters.

First Lady Eleanor Roosevelt Jostles for Polio Treatment for Black People

First Lady Eleanor Roosevelt (1884-1962), wife of FDR, was a woman of conviction, often ahead of her time, and a voice in support of civil rights movements. In the 1930s, she joined the **National Association for the Advancement of Colored People (NAACP)** and later became a member of its board of directors.

At a 1938 meeting of the Southern Conference on Human Welfare, she defied segregated seating choosing to protest by sitting in the aisle. Roosevelt gave up her Daughters of the American Revolution membership upon the organization denying Black singer **Marian Anderson** (1897-1993) the right to perform in their segregated concert hall. She campaigned against the poll tax. She advocated to end racial discrimination in the armed forces. The First Lady met with activist, **Rosa Parks** (1913-2005), and civil rights leader and union organizer, **E.D. Nixon** (1899-1987), during the Montgomery bus boycott.

Eleanor Roosevelt's admiration for minister and civil rights leader, **Martin Luther King, Jr.** (1929-1968), is recorded in her prescient comment remarking that his 1957 statement that there be "no hatred in this struggle," was "almost more than human beings can achieve." Eleanor Roosevelt wrote: "The people of the world will condemn—not Georgia, unfortunately—The United States for treating as a criminal a man who is looked upon with respect."

Eleanor Roosevelt recognized as false the assumption that Black people were not susceptible to polio. She believed that most Black people suffering polio received no treatment or substandard care.

Eleanor Roosevelt found it disturbing that Black people were not admitted to the Warm Springs rehabilitation center. She pressured the president to address this medical racism.

In 1941, the **March of Dimes** opened the Infantile Paralysis Center at Tuskegee. This provided separate and not equal treatment.

The First Lady encouraged her husband to admit Black polio survivors to Warm Springs. By 1945 Black children were being treated at Warm Springs. Black people were housed in one of the center's residential cottages. A separate pool was designated for their hydrotherapy.

In response to Eleanor Roosevelt's support of civil rights and an anti-lynching bill, the Ku Klux Klan put a $25,000 bounty on her head. **J. Edgar Hoover** (1895-1972), first Director of the Federal Bureau of Investigation, assigned agents to surveil Eleanor Roosevelt's activities.

Charles H. Bynum, Black Educator
And
Civil Rights Activist

Prior to joining The March of Dimes, **Charles H. Bynum** (1905-1996), was a high school biology teacher, Dean of Texas College in Tyler, Texas, and an assistant to President Frederick Patterson of **Tuskegee Institute** in Alabama.

From 1944 to 1971, Charles Bynum served as Director of Interracial Activities for the National Foundation for Infantile Paralysis. He traveled on behalf of the **March of Dimes** throughout the United States, including the segregated South.

Bynum asserted that polio care was a civil rights issue. He sought to equalize polio care for all races. He organized fundraisers bringing in millions of dollars to provide rehabilitation care and vaccination programs. Bynum promoted inclusion of Black children in the **March of Dimes Poster Child** contest. Collaborating with civic leaders and the National Medical Association, he ensured March of Dimes monies were spent equally on people regardless of race.

March of Dimes & Vaccination

In 1958, after the vaccine trounced polio cases, the **National Foundation for Infantile Paralysis** changed its name to The **March of Dimes Birth Defects Foundation**. Its mission became to support research, education, and advocacy for children's health.

The March of Dimes Birth Defects Foundation now addresses the vaccination equity gap in the United States. The **Centers for Disease Control and Prevention (CDC)** collected data showing that kids who are underinsured, in lower income families, Black or Hispanic tend to not have recommended vaccinations.

During the **COVID-19** pandemic, vaccinations have declined. Forty percent of parents/caregivers report that their children missed vaccinations due to the pandemic.

The Facts

Children born in 2017 and 2018 have a 70.5% completion rate of recommended vaccinations.

Children with no health insurance have a 48.3% completion rate of recommended vaccinations. This rate is lower than children with Medicaid coverage (65.5%) and with private insurance (78.3%).

Black, non-Hispanic and Hispanic children are the least likely (64.7 percent) to have completed recommended vaccinations. This rate compares to White, non-Hispanic children (74.7 percent) and Asian, non-Hispanic children (74.2%) vaccination rates.

Children living below the poverty level have a vaccination rate of 62.5%.

https://www.marchofdimes.org/vaccines.aspx;
https://tinyurl.com/3k3kvrj7; Last accessed 3 26 22

Marjorie Clare • 1955

Margie: Al, I need to talk to you. Last week at the auditorium where Susie's ballet class is practicing for the recital, I overheard the stage manager calling Susie *polio girl*. He told the dance instructor to get the *polio girl* out of the way of his sweeping. Susie was taking a rest break sitting on a crate that he wanted to move to continue his cleaning up.

Susie cannot conceal that she had polio. Her disability is not going away. But why can't people see her as a kid first of all? She is not polio. She is Susie.

I wonder how people calling Susie *polio girl* will make her think of herself. Will she be affected negatively when people view her someone who had a contagious, awful disease? Susie needs to know herself and all her strengths just like other kids do as they grow up.

Does calling her *polio girl* make the person doing so feel superior or is that person just too lazy to take the time to find out her name? I do not want the stage manager's labeling to make Susie feel badly.

How long will this go on? Will she outgrow people first focusing on her polio leg? How do we teach her to deal with people who call her a disease?

Al: Don't be afraid, Margie. Life does have a rugged terrain and not just for Susie. She really is no different or less than others. Susie has built up strength others cannot even imagine. Watch her.

Even if someone treats her unkindly, she is not mean back to the person. Most people cannot be like that. Susie saw the fork in the road.

Perhaps Susie carrying polio along with her in life, has helped her understand everyone wants to feel accepted by others. Susie can sit back and listen to others. You've seen her be all ears when Pa tells his war stories. No one is more polite than Susie at the farm when Gladys tells how sad she is about an animal dying. She has the patience to let a person talk on and on. She doesn't judge. You want to know why? Because she realizes that no one truly knows another person until they listen to that person's story. She knows that showing interest in a person is a part of being a friend.

Max Hintz always welcomes Susie by calling her name when she comes into his office. First thing he asks about is what she has been doing. He sits a minute and listens before starting treatment. Susie's life is woven together with polio virus damage. But Max first shows interest in her life outside of polio. He loves Susie. Maybe Susie has picked up a bit of her way of showing interest in people from Max.

All the neighborhood children call Susie by name. They never tease her. To them, she is just another kid on the block. I have hope and reason to believe that how others—like Max and the kids— treat Susie is the strongest influence on how she views herself.

We all bear scars from what life has thrown our way. We all carry with us the circumstances of our childhoods. Margie, we all have disabilities. Not everybody recognizes their deficits. Some weaknesses are more obvious than others.

Susie • 1955

The tragic separations when I was hospitalized, and the disconnection from her family due to fear of polio, reverberated in Mama. She questioned if she was a competent mother. Rejection even for good cause is hard to accept. But her exclusion from groups for something she could not prevent was a burden that vexed her. Her self-protective reaction was to bury her true feelings.

Mama was like having two mothers. My *"first Mama"* was scared, anxious, worried, and perpetually over-tired. She lost her daughter once. Getting again close to me as she had been as a new mother would mean opening herself up for becoming hurt again. Trying to numb herself against potential loss, she left the door ajar to a warm relationship with me.

It is human nature to put up barriers to prevent being hurt. Mama built a wall around her feelings. Driven by unremitting fear of losing me again, she held back her emotions. She did not put her arms around me and hug me like Dad. Mama kissed me was on the top of my head. Maybe she thought if she held me close, I would bust apart and be sick again.

Mama's behaviors were probably not noticed by most people. She was open to joining in the good parts of my day. She smiled and clapped at my dance recitals. But when bad things happened as inevitably, they do, whenever possible, Mama stepped back and let my Dad manage the situations. She closed the conversation not wanting to listen to me.

When I was not feeling well or got injured, it was usually Dad who stepped forward and opened his arms. Mama showed up only when Dad wasn't home. My being ill made Mama nervous. She felt insecure. In order to soothe her escalation of excess energy, she picked up a cigarette, crossed her arms over her chest, and stared out the kitchen window.

Mama built up walls to communication. I didn't learn a lot from her about how to traverse uneasy conversations in life. Like daughters often do, I unconsciously learned to mimic her. I repressed my feelings too.

We were both innocent about hiding our emotions. Caught within the polio epidemic, it was the way we both came to feel safest. Unfortunately, closed off discussions prohibit learning healthy communication methods. Not sharing how we felt interfered with our emotional growth. Not talking over my feelings with Mama led me to not truly know myself until much later in life.

I could play the role typical of polio survivors. I am obedient. I am cheerful. I can help. I will overachieve. I can perform.

Just as he had not become an angry man after the death of his brother and mother, Dad displayed no bitterness toward polio. He said facing bad circumstances was a universal experience. *No matter how hard it gets, you will survive. Feel sorrow and let it go. Keep reaching for your goal.*

I did not grow up feeling like I had to be mad at the world for my disability. Being a girl people constantly referred to as the "sweetest" went over very well in school and social arenas. I was always being nice to others to make up for my obvious physical deficits. But taking on this persona was at a cost of not truly expressing my own needs and having them met. I became the perfect match for someone who was needy but not giving.

Susie 1953

My *"other Mama"* was supportive and proud. Holidays were times when I could behave in ways that made her appear to enjoy herself. She looked happy. When someone gave me a gift, with my linguistic aptitude, I could spit out words to thank the person profusely. I rambled on describing the awesomeness of the gift giver. The other children seated around me looked down and said a meager "thanks" after tearing off the holiday paper covering their gifts. Mama looked over at me and smiled. She was proud of me. My performance shined a light on her.

After festivities ended and we returned home, household rules dictated no child could go out and play until all their thank you notes were written. Because I always sought to please, my cards were exceptionally detailed. I might have disliked the gift, but the reader of the note would not be able to guess my real feelings. Mama always read them over before she put them in the post.

Mama was typical of the parent of polio child when she pushed me into activities and intellectual pursuits to make me appear less crippled. She understood the less disabled that people thought me, the more they would accept me.

As a child with polio, I remember standing at the swimming pool entrance and being told to leave because I had an atrophied leg which made parents panic that I could spread polio to their children. Milwaukee County routinely posted signs restricting polio survivors from city swimming pools.

Polio Precautions

Mama knew when to accept defeat. My parents responded to pools being inaccessible to me by loading us kids into the car and heading to Pewaukee Lake where I readily became a strong swimmer pushing the weedy flora aside with enthusiasm. I loved swimming because with each stroke I could move fast without worrying about falling. I learned to swim better than I could walk, and my parents would have to coax me out of the water.

The Beginning Work of Scientists to Develop the Polio Vaccine

In 1908, **Dr. Karl Landsteiner** (1868-1943), and **Dr. Erwin Popper** (1879-1955), established the pathway of transmission of polio from human to monkey. Polio virus taken from the spinal cord of a boy who died of polio was injected into a monkey that then developed infection.

In 1951, the **National Foundation for Infantile Paralysis (March of Dimes)** confirmed there were three forms of wild polio virus. These wild viruses are labeled type 1, type 2, and type 3.

Jonas Salk who developed an influenza vaccine from killed virus, led the way to polio vaccine development by establishing ways to grow the three types of polioviruses in cultures of live Rhesus monkey cells. Salk grew large quantities of the three types of polioviruses on cultures in monkey kidney cells. He used formaldehyde to kill the live virus. Salk believed use of the killed virus safer than use of live virus which could accidently cause polio.

The enormous number of monkeys needed to produce the vaccine in monkeys prohibited production. The work of three scientists paved the way for replicating the virus without injecting monkeys with the polio virus. In 1954, **John Enders**, (1897-1985), **Thomas Weller** (1915-2008), and **Frederick Robbins** (1916-2003), were awarded the **Nobel Prize** for their research in demonstrating that the polio virus could be grown in human embryonic skin and muscle tissue. Their experiments also showed that poliovirus could infect not only nerve cells but also other cells. The research findings of Enders, Weller, and Robbins indicated that the polio virus affected both the gastrointestinal tract and central nervous system.

This discovery paved the way for Salk to develop the first polio vaccine. In 1952 Salk began testing the vaccine in humans, starting with children who had already been infected with the virus. He measured their antibody levels before vaccination and then was excited to see that the levels had been raised significantly by the vaccine. On April 12, 1955, Salk's vaccine was declared safe and effective in protecting against polio.

Inactivated (containing killed virus) polio vaccine is now the only polio vaccine used in the United States. Three doses provide at least 99% immunity. The United States is currently polio-free.

Albert Sabin, an American physician, and microbiologist believed that only a live virus would produce human immunity for an extended period of time. Sabin believed an oral method of producing immunity to polio was preferred because it was easier to administer. Sabin's vaccine was given in drop form placed on a sugar cube. His work built on the prior vaccine work of **Hilary Koprowski** (1916-2013).

Koprowski, a Polish virologist and immunologist developed the first attenuated (live, weakened form) polio vaccine in 1950. He, like Sabin, thought that giving a live virus had advantages. He believed a live virus vaccine provided lifetime immunity and was less expensive. The cost and ease of administering an oral vaccine is less than for an injectable one. Koprowski conducted trials giving himself the vaccine and also giving injections at the **Letchworth Village**, home for children with disabilities in Rockland County, New York.

Sabin received an attenuated virus sample from Hilary Koprowski. In 1957, Sabin began trials of his oral vaccine in the **Soviet Union** because he was not able to find support for his vaccine in the United States. In 1960, the Soviet Union trial declared the live attenuated oral polio virus safe. In 1961, the **United States Public Health Service** approved the vaccine for production and use in the United States.

Because there is risk for vaccine-derived polio from Sabin's oral polio vaccine, the United States no longer uses the vaccine. The **World Health Organization** (WHO) encourages countries worldwide to switch from administration of oral live attenuated virus polio vaccination to inactivated killed virus injections.

Israel reported a case of polio in 2022. Ukraine recorded two cases in late 2021.Two countries, Pakistan, and Afghanistan, continue to host cases of polio. The **Taliban** actively bar immunizations. Health workers administering polio vaccinations have faced violent attacks. In 2016, a doctor giving polio immunizations in Pakistan was shot and killed by persons associated with the Taliban. Pakistan has the most outbreaks of polio and is the chief exporter of polio virus.

Today one person in two hundred people who develop polio infection, become paralyzed. Five to ten percent of these people die due to paralysis of the respiratory muscles. Children in poverty who lack access to clean water, good sanitation, and immunization along with other healthcare services are more vulnerable to polio virus infection.

Victory Over Polio

The People's Vaccine

Jonas Salk was born to a mother who immigrated from WWII-devastated Minsk, Belarus and a father born in New Jersey. He grew up in East Harlem, the Bronx and Queens, New York.

At thirteen he entered a high school for the talented and gifted. He was known to be a perfectionist and avid reader. Salk graduated after three years of study.

Salk then attended City College of New York, a public college that is part of the City University of New York (CUNY) system. In 1847, it became the first free public higher education system in the United States.

Admission to City College of New York was by academic merit. It became known as a working-class school providing access to offspring of immigrants and the poor who were turned down by other institutions. City College of New York was called "the poor man's Harvard." Women were admitted to graduate programs in 1930 and in 1951, the entire school became coeducational.

Other notable graduates of City College include **Abraham Maslow** (1908-1970), psychologist, educator, and author of *Maslow's Hierarchy of Needs;* **Ira Gershwin** (1896-1983), lyricist; **Alfred Stiglitz** (1864-1946), photographer; **Daniel Patrick Moynihan** (1927-2003), ambassador to the U.N. and senator representing New York; **Ralph Morse** (1917-2014), youngest war correspondent in WWII; and author/journalist **Bernard Kalb** (1922-2022).

Salk graduated in 1934 and went on to New York University (NYU) School of Medicine. Although tuition was relatively low compared to schools such as Columbia and Yale, Salk worked as a lab assistant and camp counselor to make ends meet during his studies.

Salk's goal was not to practice medicine although he qualified to do so. His focus was on biochemistry and bacteriology. His stated goal was to help humankind rather than single patients.

During his last year of medical school, he conducted research about the influenza virus. Salk carried out experiments related to virus infectivity and immunization. Building on this experience, Salk did post graduate work in virology at the University of Michigan under **Thomas Francis** (1900-1969), who discovered type B influenza virus.

In 1947, he became a professor in the School of Medicine at the University of Pittsburg where his academic work centered on the varied polio viruses. In 1948, he moved on to work for the National Foundation for Infantile Paralysis.

By 1955, **Albert Sabin** studied weakened live oral polio virus vaccines. Although there was an urgency among Americans for a safe vaccine against dreaded polio, Salk chose to use a safer killed form of polio virus for his vaccine.

The first Salk vaccines were injected into laboratory animals. In July of 1952, Salk's polio vaccine was administered to children at the D.T. Watson Home for Crippled Children in Pittsburgh, Pennsylvania.

In 1953, Salk vaccinated his own children. In 1954, the vaccine was tested on one million children. It was announced safe on April 12, 1955.

The National Foundation for Infantile Paralysis with its March of Dimes campaign financed the final research to bring the polio vaccine to the public. The Salk vaccine began its widespread use in 1955. Domestic polio was eliminated in the United States within twenty-five years.

In 1955, Congress passed **The Polio Vaccine Assistance Act**. The bill was signed on August 12 by **President Dwight D. Eisenhower** (1890-1969). This act provided federal grant money to the states to purchase polio vaccine and to conduct vaccination programs.

The Salk vaccine continues to be listed on the **World Health Organization's List of Essential Medicines**, which are the safest and most effective medicines needed in a health system. To provide distribution globally which is essential because *one is not safe if not all are safe*, Salk chose to not patent the vaccine. Salk received no profit from his discovery. He gave the polio vaccine to the world.

Jonas Salk was offered a tickertape parade to honor his work. He requested that money collected for such celebration instead be used for student scholarships. *The Salk Scholarship* at City College of New York is named in honor of Dr. Jonas Salk.

Salk believed that vaccination of children against disease such as polio was a "moral commitment." He called for mandatory vaccination.

The Cutter Incident

The April 1955 **Cutter Incident** marked a time when people recognized that enhanced government regulation of vaccine production was necessary. Due to faulty inactivation of the live virus, a batch of vaccine was tainted with potent (live) polio virus.

Out of the 200,000 children who received doses from this cluster of vials, there were 40,000 cases of polio. Two hundred suffered paralysis. Ten children died.

The manufacturer, based in California, was a family firm called Cutter Laboratories. It had failed to inactivate the virus with formaldehyde. Inspectors did not catch this flaw in processing.

A June 1955 congressional hearing determined that the problem occurred due to the lack of scrutiny from the **National Institute of Health (NIH) Laboratory of Biologics Control** and its excessive trust in reports of the **National Foundation for Infantile Paralysis.**

In Fall, 1955, after government oversight of laboratories was expanded, Cutter Laboratories continued production. Other companies produced safe polio vaccines.

The Cutter incident led to more use of Albert Sabin's oral vaccine. Ironically, later it was discovered that the Sabin formula allowed the polio virus to sometimes be reactivated in the gastrointestinal tract. Sabin oral formula has not been used in the United States since 2000 because of this danger.

The United States currently has the safest vaccine supply in its history. Several systems monitor vaccine safety and conduct research on vaccine-associated health risks.

The **Vaccine Adverse Event Reporting System** (VAERS) is an early warning system that monitors for potential vaccine safety issues.

The **Vaccine Safety Datalink** (VSD) is a consortium of nine healthcare organizations and the CDC which conducts active vaccine safety monitoring and research.

The **Clinical Immunization Safety Assessment** (CISA) Project is a partnership between the CDC and seven medical research centers. This group provides expert consultation along with conducting research on vaccine-associated health risks.

> **Winston Churchill stated,**
>
> "The longer you can look back, the farther you can look forward."
>
> Vaccine development and safety is a case in point.

HeLa Cells - Contributions of a Black Mother and Two Black Tuskegee Scientists

HeLa cells are a type of cell that do not die like regular cells do in response to normal aging, called senescence. These "immortal" cells keep undergoing division ad infinitum.

Before the polio vaccine could be injected into a human, **Jonas Salk** had to make sure the vaccine was safe. He needed a cell group in which he could inject the blood from a patient who had received the polio vaccine to determine if antibodies were produced in response to vaccination. The cell group would be observed under a microscope to validate the antibody response.

HeLa cells were taken without her permission from **Henrietta Lacks** (1920-1951), a Black woman. Lacks was a 31-year-old woman who died of cancer. Her cancer cells were sent to the lab of **Dr. George Gey** (1899-1970), a researcher studying cancer cells of women who died of cervical cancer. Dr. Gey found that Lacks' cells were unlike those of others retrieved during biopsy after death. Her cells doubled every 20-24 hours. He nicknamed Lacks' cells "HeLa" after the first two letters of her first and last names.

The HeLa cells were mixed with a small dose of polio along with blood of a vaccinated patient. When the blood contained the desired amount of antibodies, no damage was observed. If the HeLa cells became misshapen, the correct number of antibodies to fight polio was not present. Jonas Salk needed millions of HeLa cells.

Dr. John Chenault (1904-1965), who led Orthopedic Surgery at **Tuskegee University's John A. Andrew Memorial Hospital** conducted a study to determine the rate of occurrence of polio in Black people. His research reported the belief that the incidence of polio was somewhat lower in Black people, but the fatalities were higher. Dr. Chenault believed lack of quality treatment facilities for Black people due to Jim Crow discriminatory practices led to this finding.

The Chenault study showed that Black people suffered approximately 20% of the crippling cases of polio. When the vaccine became available in the 1950s, "Jim Crow medicine" continued. Delayed vaccine access left Black communities' vaccination rates lagging behind the rates of White people.

With the support of **Basil O'Connor** president of the **National Foundation for Infantile Paralysis (NFIP)** along with **Charles Bynum**, the Director of Interracial Activities at the NFIP, **Tuskegee Infantile Paralysis Center** opened in 1940. The National Foundation for Infantile Paralysis recruited two Tuskegee Black scientists to develop the cell culture.

Drs. Russell W. Brown (1919-2013), and **James H. M. Henderson** (1917-2009), created the conditions for the growth and preservation of millions of HeLa cells for Salk's vaccine trials. At Tuskegee, cells were grown in incubators, placed in tubes, and transported around the country. **Norma Gaillard**, cell culture supervisor at Tuskegee, designed systems to ensure the integrity of cultures when transported. The Tuskegee team dealt not only with culture production but also quality control for shipment to laboratories in other states.

HeLa cells continue playing a significant role in scientific inquiry. They have been used to evaluate the effects of radiation and poisons, and to study the human genome. HeLa cells continue to advance the effort to combat viruses such as **COVID-19**.

John Hopkins University has never profited off the discoveries around the nature and use of HeLa cells. They are shared free with researchers. John Hopkins University acknowledges that the family of Henrietta Lacks should have been informed of the use of her cells. This would not be an accepted practice today.

President Dwight D. Eisenhower and The Polio Vaccine

Salk honored at The White House

https://www.eisenhowerlibrary.gov/research/online-documents/jonas-salk-and-polio-vaccine;
https://tinyurl.com/4c7nfkm4

New U.S. cases of polio in 1954 totaled 38,741 with 1620 deaths. This was the third highest incidence of polio in U.S. history exceeded only in 1949 and 1952. Polio most often struck children ages four to six. It was a summer disease with the highest number of cases occurring April through October.

On April 12, 1955, church bells rang to celebrate completion of successful trials of the polio vaccine. Facing increasing rates of poliomyelitis in children, relieved parents ran into the streets crying. Newspaper headlines read: *Victory Over Polio*.

On April 22, 1955, **President Dwight D. Eisenhower** held a White House Ceremony to thank **Dr. Jonas Salk** for saving the world's children. Reporters observed that President Eisenhower choked up as introduced the man who developed the polio vaccine. Within two years, U.S. polio cases dropped 85 to 90 percent.

On April 26th, 1955, The Public Health Service received reports of cases of polio contracted by children after vaccination using materials from Cutter Laboratories.

On April 27th, 1955, the Surgeon General instructed Cutter Laboratories to withdraw its vaccine. Eisenhower's White House staff met with wire service and Washington reporters *within ten minutes* of notification to explain the details around the suspension.

In an April 29th, 1955, cabinet meeting, President Eisenhower instructed staff that no child be denied the vaccine for financial reasons. He said Federal funds, including the **President's Emergency Fund**, would be made available. On May 2nd, 1955, a cabinet meeting was held to develop a formula for equitable distribution.

President Eisenhower released a statement on May 31,1955 stating that a committee of scientists screened the polio vaccine and would release it within days. He noted that scientists who were gaining new knowledge about the vaccine, built in more safety checks and safeguards.

In this *Statement by The President*, Eisenhower cautioned the American people:

To not forget that no vaccine is 100% effective.

To be patient with manufacturers who needed to "retool" as more information came out and production standards were revised.

To be grateful to the scientists who worked tirelessly in the fight against polio.

Susie • 1955

> *To hope* that the vaccine will be made available to our children in a manner in keeping with our highest traditions of cooperative national action.

Vaccination shaped the future of children growing up in the 1940s and 1950s. Life changed for me and my family too. It gave me freedom. After the polio vaccine began its protection, people were not so afraid of me transmitting polio to them. Mothers of other children on my block began inviting me inside their homes for cookies and milk at their kitchen tables.

Still, I was a handful. There were times, my parents needed respite from caring for me. Grandpa Emil (Pa to Mama) provided that in a couple of ways. On Saturday mornings, he would pick me up in his green Chevy saying he was taking me for a ride. He took me to a rag and paper collection station.

Grandpa had piled newspapers (left behind on the train), and rags (old family clothes) in a wagon. He carried me out of the car and put me atop it all. He rolled the wagon into the station where the man behind the scale would weigh what we brought in and pay Grandpa for it. Maybe we got a penny a pound.

Old rags became new paper. The scraps of cloth were made into paper by beating the fabric into pulp. The pulp was laid on screen to dry. Rag paper quality depended on the type of material used.

The old newspapers were passed on for folks to use as toilet paper or re-used as fire-starters. By tying them into log shapes, they could be ignited easily to get coal burning.

Whatever change we got from selling newspapers and rags, Grandpa pocketed for his "boilermakers" which were alcoholic beverages first drank by steam locomotive workers in the 1800s. Lore has it the men who worked the rail lines toasted at the end of each shift with the combination of a shot of whiskey (downed in one gulp) followed by a beer to ease their pain.

Mama often sent me on train rides when her Pa served as an engineer for The Milwaukee Road. Grandpa would seat me in the beginning of the passenger section before the train seats started filling up. The fire had already been lit by the time Grandpa got aboard to direct the firemen who would keep stoking the flames to heat water and make steam which powered the engine.

As engineer, Grandpa was in charge of the men. From the car behind the engine, he arranged for the firemen shoveling coal into the boiler to keep an eye on me. When my grandfather gave the okay, the shoveling of coal would stop and with a fireman by my side holding my arm, I would gingerly walk past the hot, flaming coal furnace into the engine room.

As a child, I witnessed the firemen bent over shoveling coal during the long rides. It was hard and dirty work. I could tell by their grimaces, low murmurs of aching, and hands splinting their backs at the end of rides, their job brought agony.

The men did not gripe. In fact, they joked a lot with Grandpa. But their stooped postures and dry, wrinkly skin told the story of railroad drudgery that wreaked soreness and misery. A boilermaker eased the pain. It was like Dad said, you do what you need to do when faced with life circumstances. *No matter how hard it gets, you will survive.*

Once safely escorted up to the front of the train and seated on a tall chair with cushions atop it in the engine, Grandpa would tell me the specifics of the whistle call I would give when he gave me the signal. I did not really blow a whistle. I pulled a cord.

Whistle calls told people what was happening. I had to pull the cord when the train was backing up or we were crossing another rail line. Grandpa coached me to pull when he put on the train brakes. It might be three short yanks or four long yanks. There were many codes. Grandpa had them all in his head. He would tell the exact number of times to pull the cord according to whistle code.

After I completed a good whistle call, Grandpa would look over at me and grin. He was always proud of me. I felt good with him.

At the end of each train trip, Grandpa and I would invariably end up in a bar. He paid me off in Baby Ruth candy bars to keep quiet about him drinking boilermakers. I don't think Grandma knew about the paper and rag collection fund or the drinking. I never said a thing. Heck, I had gotten the message from Grandma at the polio child event that she didn't want me to tell the truth.

Just like he had done many years before with my Mama, my Grandfather Emil read with me. Family gatherings, which increased after 1955, when everyone was vaccinated, numbered near thirty people to include all my mother's siblings and their families.

After a big dinner which always included a German dessert, my grandfather would excuse himself from the table, take my hand and lead me to his special small closet where a lone lightbulb lit up his shelf of beloved National Geographic magazines.

Grandpa sat on the ledge and I on the floor. We read and rested in our shared quiet space. Grandpa Emil had watched and observed me. He figured out I was tired from polio. When he came to our Westside home for dinner, we did much the same leaving the cacophony of the large group and finding a quieter place to read encyclopedias together.

Having served in France in WWI, Grandpa knew our fight against polio was against an enemy like the one that brought a load of unseen wounds to warriors. He sensed that people might feel different beneath the surface. He taught me that being understood gave a person a warm feeling inside. Grandpa Emil was one of my best supporters and a hero to me.

It was a happy scene when all the family could be together more often after the polio vaccine was invented. Mama changed a bit then. She laughed a lot with her siblings. She was enjoying life among people.

Susie • 1956

I felt him tap my shoulder and whisper, "Susie, time to go." The rustic cabin our family rented every year for vacation, was quiet. A wintry-like cold hovered although it was summertime in Northern Wisconsin. The smoke of pine logs filled the air. Dad got up early and stoked the stove. I could smell the coffee. Dad warned me, "Don't get out of bed until I tell you it is warm."

Dad's preparations in warming the cabin came from his observations over time that when my polio leg got cold or tired, it hurt. He noticed many times when chilly air coupled with too much morning swimming triggered my damaged calf muscle to spasm. Dad would periodically walk back from the beach where other kids were taking an afternoon swim and check on me. I was laying on the pier reading again. There was nothing he could do at this point to relieve the pain. My pretense that I wanted to finish a book did not convince him. He knew me too well to believe I was fine.

On early fishing mornings, protecting me from the cold morning air, Dad handed me my clothes after first helping me put on two pairs of woolen socks so that when I stepped out of bed my feet would not feel the ice-cold floorboards. I knew our routine. We did it often. No one but me wanted to get up and take the boat out with him to fish at dawn. I hurried rolling back and forth in bed to tug on layers of slacks, shirts, a winter jacket, a hat, and gloves. I was excited. I loved fishing with Dad.

For weeks before our annual vacation, after he soaked the lawn with water to make the angleworms that we needed for fish bait to come up to the top, we walked hunched over in the backyard. Our steps repeated a steady cadence when our shoes squished the wet grass. With flashlights to guide us, we picked up the worms' slimy bodies surfacing amid the grass blades. We deftly grabbed them with one hand and dropped them into an old soup can we held in our other hand. After an hour or so, Dad collected the cans from Mama, Mike and me and took them to the basement where he kept a box of moist dirt mixed with used coffee grounds taped all around so nothing could seep out. There the worms waited their time until they met the hook.

My oatmeal, sprinkled with cinnamon and sugar, was ready on the table by the time I was dressed. I ate quickly while Dad had a second cup of coffee. Mama and Mike slept on as we crept out into the darkness.

Dad held my hand as we walked to the outhouse. Then, he gathered up the long-handled net, hanging basket for our catch, cane poles, a can of worms, and a coffee can to pee in. Last, after we walked down the stairway to the dock, Dad picked up the boat oars stored in the brush along the shoreline.

He held me around the waist as I climbed in the boat. The wood creaked but no one heard us because it was just getting light…the perfect time to lure pan fish to an earthworm breakfast. Dad always repeated the rules about sitting still and being quiet. I could do that. Anyway, it would have been tricky for me to change positions in a moving boat. Dad was rowing at a steady, quiet pace. I shivered passing through the morning dew.

When we got to the bay where the lily pads lay at the edge, Dad anchored the boat. He reminded me the lily pads were protected. I was not to get my line tangled in them. He handed me the hook at the end of a line on a cane pole and told me to put a worm on it. I could do this as I had done hundreds of times before. I grabbed a squiggly worm out of the can and pierced its length firmly several times onto the barbs. It wiggled so I knew it was a lively one. I was happy because it pleased Dad that I could do this.

Susie 1950

My pole had a short line. I flipped it over my head gently into the water and heard the familiar "plop." I was ready to wait as long as it took for the bobbing that signaled a fish was biting. Dad did the same.

We waited. If we got no bites in the spot, Dad rowed a bit down the bend, and anchored again. I trolled as he rowed. Dad said trolling was illegal, but he knew I would not catch anything that way because it was impossible for me to turn in my seat and pull a fish in while the boat moved.

When we got lucky, and the sunfish started biting, I would see my bobber dip and I pulled the cane pole up evenly just like Dad taught me. Feeling the fish was hooked, I brought the line up into the boat and Dad netted my catch.

It was harder to take the fish off the hook than to put the worm on it. I learned that some tasks take stronger hands and I yielded to Dad helping me. He plunked the fish over the side of the boat into the net basket of fish that were accumulating. Blue gills, perch, and sunfish…a good supper for our family.

All this time, Dad and I worked like a machine…rowing … anchoring…baiting…unhooking, placing the fish in the basket. These mornings were quiet excepting for the sounds of beavers entering the water from their shoreline dens.

Occasionally, I broke our silence because I had to pee in the coffee can. That led to a pause in our fishing when if we had caught enough for a meal, dad sat back and opened up with some stories.

In a soft voice, he looked in my direction. He talked of old times speaking like he was unwrapping a burden and through its revealing, shedding an ominous weight. He spoke about serious stuff. I got the feeling that you have to let some bad things go in life to make space for good things to enter. Talking was his way of doing so. I listened.

Dad said, "You don't remember this but…" and then he told me about things he thought I could not recall. He described the hospital where I was a baby in the iron lung in the isolation ward. Dad said he looked through a small window at me. He talked about how my mother suffered a lot not being with me during that time. Dad told me she wanted to be with me. He said she cried for her baby. I guess he wanted me to understand she loved me. I don't think he ever doubted I knew he loved me.

With our catch in the mesh basket, we held hands walking up to the cabin. Mama smiled seeing all the fish we caught. She had baked kuchen while we were gone. The warm pastry was a ritual she had for welcoming us back. We sat down together for a family breakfast. My polio leg hurt just a little. But I didn't tell. Who would want to spoil this family time? Dad had a good story to tell Mama and Mike about our great dawn catch of three perch, four bluegills, and five sunfish. We had the present to celebrate.

Marjorie Clare • 1959

Susie told me she didn't feel cold walking with her neighborhood friends to middle school in the middle of winter. I know better than to believe her. That's how she is. She only tells me so much.

Milwaukee has been lucky to hit 50 degrees for a high and we are hovering at 30 degrees in the early mornings on these wintery days. Every year we have a day or more when it is below zero.

With Mike being in high school now, Susie has to get going to school on her own. Al and I have to be out of the house early for our drive to work.

There's a bus stop just a block away. On cold mornings, I have to put out of my mind that her polio leg is hurting because of the temperature outside. It would be nice if Susie could take the bus on all the frigid days, but we don't have the money for her do that.

Miss B., a teacher at the middle school who lives in the apartments behind our alleyway, always catches the bus there each school day morning. The teacher gets on the bus as soon as the driver opened the doors and quickly sits in the front row. A gruff older woman, she routinely clears her throat with a loud "harumph" as Susie takes a bit more time pulling up on the bus railings to climb the steps of the bus and drop her change into the box.

I have been saving up to buy Susie a new winter jacket. It will keep her warmer on the walk or at the bus stop. She wears two pair of Al's hunting socks inside her boots. She hates dressing in snow pants but knows the consequence of not doing so is more pain. I know she wishes she had a matching woolen jacket and pants snow outfit like is the fashion today. *My fault. Everybody will talk about us. I must be in control.*

I have a second drink with my third cigarette. My worry about Susie walking to school in the freezing weather has been eclipsed by a note she brought home in a sealed envelope from Miss. B. The teacher wrote that Susie disrupted class.

It all started when one of the customers who routinely comes to my teller window gave me a holiday gift of haircuts for Susie and me at her salon. In the past, I cut Susie's hair, so this was the first time a professional trimmed her hair. I set up the appointment for just before her birthday. I picked her up at middle school.

The haircut appointment took only an hour, but the fallout lasted longer. When Susie returned to class and slipped into her assigned desk, girls and boys passed her notes telling her they liked her new hairdo. Susie smiled. The teacher did not.

Miss B. forced Susie to stand up in front of class and apologize for being "a light." The teacher scolded Susie saying she was taking everyone's attention away from the lesson.

Susie had not complained to me that the teacher made her stand up and say she would not be a light that shined. When I asked her what happened, she said, "You taught me to smile at people who stare at me." Her classmates were looking over at her new hairdo, so she smiled. Susie did not know what their notes said until she got home because she had stuffed them unopened into her red book bag.

How do you explain to someone who has not been through the darkness we experienced that Susie's glowing smile comes not from trying to steal attention but from wanting to take away the sadness of others?

I take control and write:

> Dear Miss B.,
>
> I received your note. It's my fault. I taught Susie to smile when people gawk at her limping, so they do not feel awkward for looking. Shaming her in class will never take away Susie's smile. When the attention is on her, she shines it back on the people around her.
>
> Sincerely,
>
> Mrs. Schoenbeck

I sealed the envelope and gave it to Susie to take back to the teacher.

Several school days later, Miss B. sent a second sealed envelope home with Susie.

> Dear Mrs. Schoenbeck,
>
> I am sorry I made Susie stand in the front of the class. I am a strict teacher. Other teachers say I am "an old bag who should retire." Students do not like me or obey my class rules.
>
> I stand out on the bus stop corner on freezing days waiting for the bus and I do not smile back at your daughter. I rush on the bus first because I am cold and old. I get angry because Susie moves so slowly getting on that it delays the driver from shutting the door to the wind.
>
> My only explanation is that I was a little jealous that day when all eyes were on your daughter. I did not grow up in a family where anyone smiled. I never learned how to make friends.
>
> Your daughter is well-loved by her classmates. I never found people who liked me.
>
> I should have known better. I wish my mother had taught me that a smile brings more smiles. Your daughter is fortunate.

> Sincerely,
>
> Miss B

I gave Susie an envelope with reply:

> Miss B:
>
> Thank you for your kind note. Your thoughtful words made me smile.
>
> Sincerely,
>
> Mrs. Schoenbeck

Susie • 1961-1964

Erik gave me a campus tour on our weekend date. The university was celebrating its annual ice carving competition in Michigan's upper peninsula. We ended up our long walk at the hotel where I was to share a room with another visiting girl who had yet to arrive.

Erik was happy to meet me at the bus station. Polite as usual, he gave me hug and kiss and told me he missed me. We had been dating for years. He was a college freshman. I was still in high school.

When we got to the hotel room, things changed. Erik's actions became forceful. He continued his sweet talking but held me down on the bed. He was way stronger than me. It was a tussle of arms and legs and clothing ripping. Then, we looked into each other's eyes and knew the deep bond we cherished for two years cracked. This scene served neither of us well.

I asked him to walk with me back to the bus station. "*I will not tell*," I assured him. His eyes welled up with tears and wetness splattered down on his chest despite him trying to wipe the drops away. He let out a coyote-like wail from deep inside him, crying, "I never wanted to hurt you." We both felt shattered and frightened. We were smart kids in circumstances over our heads.

Erik carried my suitcase as we walked in silence down the middle of the college town street neither of us knowing what to say. Snow plowed to the side and piled ten feet high lined the curbs and created a tunnel that echoed the fall of our boots each time they hit the asphalt pavement. Holding mittened hands in silence with our heads staring down at the pavement, we made our way forward.

At the bus station, I called a high school friend to pick me up back in Milwaukee. The boy and I enjoyed dating with the understanding that Erik was a significant part of my life. This other boy was quiet, a trait that my Mama said made her uncomfortable. She believed silent type guys were the sexy ones. She did not want that right now for her daughter. She felt more at ease with Erik who always engaged her in conversation.

I took a window seat on the bus back to Milwaukee so I could turn my face toward the outside. I hoped to hide my tears from fellow passengers. The long hours of the bus ride gave me time to think and plan.

My thoughts were fixed on how I could parse my words to spare Mama knowing the details. I knew being honest was not always best around her. Mama would rather not get the particulars of what happened. I understood if I told her, she would only wish I had not. Daughters glean a good picture of what to tell their mamas.

Somethings should not be said. I didn't want to hurt her. Mama's feelings over the years had washed over me and slipped into me. She protected me. I tried to shield her also.

Together, Mama and I kept the picture of me as an incredibly untroubled girl alive. It was the way with polio children. If we were not happy, you would never know because we would not let our misery show.

When I arrived on the front porch of our home in Milwaukee, I concealed my feelings deep down inside. With my eyes staring at the ground and a fabricated placid face, I rang the doorbell. I lived the mantra I learned in the isolation hospital: *You can hurt me. I will not tell. I won't cry.*

No one expected me home now. I had not taken a house key with me. "How did you get home?" Mama asked seeing me on the front stoop when she answered the doorbell. She looked at me and then at the car pulling away from the street curb.

Her young high school daughter was supposed to be at the college campus in Northern Michigan until Monday. It was more than a seven-hour bus ride back to Milwaukee's bus station and then another hour to the house. Mama could quickly do the calculations.

"My friend drove me from the bus," I shouted over my shoulder. I kept moving past my mother, huffing, and puffing with my suitcase so it seemed like hurrying up the stairs to my bedroom was due to its heavy weight.

My Dad came into the room. I knew he would not like hearing anything about the juxtaposition of the two young men. Previously, he had cautioned me that a nice girl did not date more than one boy at the same time. Roses had arrived for me on my last birthday from both the young men. I never liked roses again after that conversation with my Dad because I associated the flowers with his disappointment in me. His good girl let him down.

Honestly, I thought to myself: Dad had a 1940s guy's point of view. Explaining to him I had an agreement with the college young man that I would go out with others would get me nowhere because he was from a different generation. I understood being quiet was the better path. I couldn't change his history. *I am obedient. I am cheerful. I can help. I will overachieve. I can perform.*

Mama asked no further questions. By coming home early I had just ruined her temporary respite from oversight of me. Mama's mantra was called back into action. *My fault. Everybody will talk about us. I must be in control.*

Mama had not worried about me on this weekend away. She trusted Erik who was polite, smart, respectful, athletic and church-going (*None of which corral teen hormones.*) kid like me. He would come over and spend the entire day at our house, joining also on family trips.

When we dated, Erik would read aloud on the back stoop and explain to me the lessons in books teachers had assigned him for homework as an upper classman. We kept active walking, biking, sledding, and skating. Both of us loved swimming on high school teams.

We wore matching plaid shirts, the turquoise color of both our eyes. On homecoming and prom nights, we were inseparable. My Dad twice got to break in for dances when his band was playing the music for the proms.

Mama pictured a future for Erik and me. She honestly believed God set up Erik and me to date, marry and live happily ever after. If so, I disappointed God.

Perhaps if Mama had known what happened she might have understood. But, with all she had already been through with me in life, I did not want to saddle Mama with this situation too. I bailed. Our relationship was a kind of structured disclosure.

So, I sat on my bed and cried, muting my sobs by stuffing my face into my pillow. After all, I thought Erik did not deserve my parents' thinking badly about him. He was, at nineteen more grown up and ready for a deeper relationship than I was at the time.

The early 1960s were a time when girls did not engage in sex with boys without fear of pregnancy. There was no birth control pill option. Although the **Food and Drug Administration (FDA)** approved the drug in May 1960, it was not widely available. Everyone knew which girls got pregnant in high school.

You needed a prescription from a doctor to get the birth control pill. That may sound simple, but it was the main barrier preventing a young woman from obtaining birth control in the 1960s. And it was not only teens and young women who wanted control over their pregnancy timing. During the years between 1961 and 1965, twenty percent of births to married women were unwanted.

Mama had been through enough. Dad loved Erik like a son, spending time fishing with him on our vacations in Northern Wisconsin. I did not want to ruin that by a pregnancy. My role as an obedient, good girl, set up for me by polio was too strong a presence in my psyche to abandon now.

I remember the girl scout lesson about sex. It was mostly a hodgepodge of diagrams like the driver's manual showing the gears and gauges. The scout troop leader required each mother to come to the meeting. A girl could not attend on her own. Sex facts were secreted.

I found a resource at home. Mama and Dad's marriage guide was tucked away in a strongbox on their closet shelf. I reached up for it while Mama and Dad were at work. I relaxed on their bed and read. I found Mama's diaphragm below their bed one day when mindlessly exploring while confined to my parents' bed to rest after one of the falls I had down the stairs. I saw the device pictured in a chapter on contraceptives in their worse-for-wear paperback book.

I learned more about the boy-girl world from my girlfriends with whom I went to adult drive-in movies. Our close-knit group also drove to bars outside the county to drink beer outlawed for people under twenty-one years old in Milwaukee County. We wanted to meet up and dance with older boys. We plotted high school pranks never acceding ownership or staff ever catching us in the act. We kept a serious demeanor in front of our teachers which kept us off the usual suspect list. But we were a bit naughty.

I knew I had to move on with life which meant getting through each new day. I did not want my high school friends to know the extent of my polio damage. Although some of my symptoms were noticeable, no one knew about pain and its partner fatigue which affected all my waking hours. Trying to achieve the biggest goal of a teen, which is fitting in, I became more pro-active in keeping polio's nefarious effects hidden from view.

Family responsibilities focused me on what I could accomplish rather than what I could not do. There is nothing like practice to ingrain in a kid the knowledge that work broken down into parts and shared is more easily done.

Each weekend day, Mike and I could find Dad's chore lists for us on the kitchen table. Mike got the ones that took more muscle power. He never complained about this. He pushed the lawnmower. I trimmed blades of grass along the edges. Mike washed the car hoisting buckets of warm, soapy water and a hose. I cleaned its windows. He washed the high kitchen cupboards squeaky clean. I made the silverware and towel drawers neat as a button.

Mike and I grocery shopped at the local A & P together, gathering up last minute items Mama needed for cooking when she got home from work. We walked to the store and did not carry back a heavy load. Mama would not let us take the wagon. Then, our shopping might have been more noticeable. Neighbors might have disapproved of us latchkey kids shopping. But we liked doing this particular chore. We gladly went to the bakery for German potato rolls and, if we had a little extra change, a cruller (treats not on my regular diet).

Mike and I shoveled snow as a team. My parents expected us also to be the snow removal team for the elderly neighbors next door. Shoveling for us always meant at both places. That's the way life worked in our household. If people were in need, you stepped in and helped them. It was obvious to us not all families were playing by the same rules because we were the only ones shoveling at the neighbors.

Early on Sunday mornings, chores included me assisting Mike deliver the *Milwaukee Journal* newspaper to doorsteps, rain or shine, snow, or freezing temperatures. The deal was I did what I could although I was not nearly as fast as Mike. He treated me like I was a normal, albeit slower helper. He never criticized me for lagging behind his fast pace.

Mike loaded the newspapers into his wagon, I walked as fast as I could back and forth to the wagon. In cold temperatures, this wreaked havoc with my muscles, causing excruciating pain lasting for hours or days. I learned I could keep my mind on work despite pain.

Mike running as fast as he could yelled over to me where I should place the next newspaper. Customers had their preferences. Mike kept a list of his client's directions for delivery and followed them without error due to Dad's training on responsibility for pleasing others.

Some people wanted their newspaper inside the outer door. Others wanted it on a porch. Mike delivered all the papers designated for inside the door as latches could be hard to open and proper closing had to be ensured once the newspaper was placed behind it.

I was not the best helper as Mike had to keep an eye on me and give me constant instructions about where papers should be delivered. But Mike reinforced with me the everlasting understanding that I could be part of a team. Mike wasn't alone on his route. I got the picture that I counted, and I could contribute. Mama had hot chocolate ready for us upon return on wintery days. All felt right in our world.

We always had pretty much the same chores. The lists gave us the joy of accomplishment when we crossed off each chore. Mike and I had concrete evidence of our hard work. The sequence of Dad's *Work, Study, Play, Rest* motto penetrated our lives.

My high school was one of the top ten in the country. With all my home training at getting tasks done, I was ready for a challenge.

A great part of the student body was more intelligent than the teachers. But teachers had other highly valuable, admirable qualities.

I learned from teachers that being the smartest is not always best. You have to be able to get things done and to accomplish things alongside others. They taught that a key trait for being successful in the work world was being supportive of co-workers. The teachers were not looking at the bottom-line profits. They taught how to make the environment a place where everyone would succeed.

Girls commanded spaces at the top of the class. I am grateful for friendships with students who did their homework before they partied. The group I spent time with put work and study before play just like Dad's motto.

At home, the TV was blaring 24/7. Every school night, I would be screaming from my upstairs bedroom to turn down the TV volume so I could study. Family labeled me the kid who always had her nose stuck in a book. Reading was rest.

As it turned out, despite being bookish, I was popular at school. Polio schooled me to be nice to others to fit in with students at my high school. *I am cheerful. I can help.* My girlfriends were supportive of each other and zany. Boys often asked to walk me home. I was on prom courts and went to homecoming dances.

Everything at school fed into my polio personality. High school offered a stage on which I could function exceptionally well. *I will overachieve. I can perform.* These years soothed away my flashbacks to the loneliness of the isolation hospital and early quarantines.

I plunged myself into academics and extracurricular school activities. I grabbed onto all the activities that high school had to offer because I had assumed the polio personality.

For my Mama, this was a blessing. She could finally sit back. The parents of children with polio would have given most anything for people to accept their children into society. I fulfilled my parents yearning for my inclusion. They enjoyed the pride of my achievements. I gave Mama a hiatus from her feelings of: *My fault. Everybody will talk about us. I must be in control.* Daughters protect their mamas too. I took charge and became leader of student organizations.

I would get the A grades. When the science teacher told the class we would be dissecting a frog and most girls screamed, I stepped up and asked to do it first. Dad had already taught me how to clean and gut fish at ten years old when I could finally see over the edge of the fish cleaning table set aside at the woods' edge. He showed me the art of fish filleting. He explained all of the fish organs to me when he cut them up. I was prepared not scared.

I liked dismembering and analyzing the dead creatures at which other girls cringed. They called lab specimens stinky and smelly. I was familiar with the scent of fresh caught fish, and shot, skinned, and chopped up squirrel and rabbit. The gamy smell of de-feathered duck and pheasant from my Dad and Grandpa's hunting was commonplace to me. So, I did not get all squiggly-legged and faintish in class dowsing the hopes of boys in the class to run over to help me. I was a good slicer and dicer. I organized and labeled all the parts.

Susie and morning catch

Scoring grades at the top of my class while taking biology, chemistry, physics, and trigonometry, I knew I was good at the sciences. I almost failed home-economics as I was using the frying pan as a chemistry pot, making my own concoctions to get the attention of the boys in the class. Ms. P., the teacher, always had a scowl on her face and her hands on her hips when she came up to the stove on which I was cooking. Making up recipes is for me the joy of cooking.

The principal called me into his office to report back to me my high math scores on placement tests. With his eyes turned on the floor, he said that my spatial intelligence ranked with boys. He did not say, "Congratulations." He instead steered me quickly out the door. The principal made a girl feel like a nuisance.

Since I was a serious student, I was tasked with responsibility to take charge of study halls, Boys periodically stood up and sang, "*Runaround Sue*" and other songs with my name in them until a teacher would overhear the ruckus and intervene to stop the noise.

I was president of Latin Club, probably because no one else cared to be head of a group that was considered nerdy. When **Virginia Levin**, the Latin teacher, needed someone to tutor, she called on me because my polio personality led me to love helping others.

She also encouraged my creativity to show. At an oratorical recital, she coached me to sing in Latin, surprising the audience but giving me praise that my personality craved. Making it through singing an oration in Latin, heightened my ease in front of a crowd. Mrs. Levin's belief that I was good at public presentation awakened me to display my inner potential.

There are people like Virginia Levin that help you identify your strengths and encourage you to build on them. Growing older gives the opportunity to look back and wonder why certain people came into your life.

Getting involved was like giving sweets to me, the over-achiever. I became president of the Girls Athletic Association. I swam freestyle and played basketball remembering all my brother taught me about being a team player. I continued to practice in the back alley with Mike. I remembered his tutoring me that I could be a mediocre guard who scored free throw shots to help drive up the score. I did not have to run fast to be a team player. I understood the philosophy behind team play.

I was a captain on the pom-pom drill team whose director had to be the kindest woman in the world for giving me a spot considering my gait was never in sync with others and my limp always noticeable and worse some days than others. **Joyce Klarner** had an important life lesson to teach me. *Kindness matters more than winning.*

Drill team on Wisconsin Avenue

She embodied the axiom that *helping people is the best thing a person can do in life*. I learned from her that you need to figure out what you value most in life and let your principles guide you for these may make a difference in the lives of others. I will never forget that she chose me for the team making it a certainty we would not win any drill team competitions. The lesson she bestowed was kindness counts.

My Dad would photograph the drill team as we paraded down Wisconsin Avenue. He was one proud father. My legs hurt so much while marching I wondered how I could go on. But then my mind would travel to what he taught me: *No matter how hard it gets, keep reaching for your goal.* I kept on moving.

Mama never saw the performance side of drill team. However, she worked hard at the bank so we could afford the fees associated with this after-school activity. Her weekend time when I was marching with the drill team was her precious time alone. After Mama got household chores done, she played the piano. I would come home from competitions and find her, sitting either at the piano singing songs like *Tenderly* and *Autumn Leaves* or at the kitchen table with her pack of cigarettes, waiting for Dad to make her a drink.

I was probably the worst member of the debate team. Part of debating meant standing. That was not my strong suit. (Even in grade school, I would rather sit down, due to pain in my legs, during spelling bees than stand up a long time and win.)

I dropped debating and joined the school newspaper. I found an outlet for my love of writing, statistics, and athletics. I was the only girl who wanted the role of girls' sports editor and lone poet. All that time I spent with books, a pad of paper and pencil laying under the front yard tree as a kid was a garden for the growth of wordsmithing, and poetry.

My first exposure to women's rights came when mathematics teacher **Charlie Bilek**, hauled me into his classroom during a class break. I had been passing by in the hallway wearing a boy's letter sweater, a custom of the time. Since I swam for the girls' swim team, he explained that it diminished my accomplishments to wear somebody else's letter, not my own. Mr. Bilek was advising me to stand up for myself. He believed in me. It got me thinking. I gave the boy's sweater back although I could not afford to ever buy the letter I earned.

The high school years were fun for me, but I needed to contribute to the household budget. If I wanted new clothes, shoes, or cosmetics, I had to pay for them.

Girls were wearing "flats" which in my budget range had little support for my polio foot. My right foot dragged and my calf spasmed in flimsy, inexpensive shoes. I became self-conscious when people watched me walk down the street. I looked around at school at girls with more expensive shoes. I wondered what it would be like to have enough money to buy better shoes like the girls who came from families of doctors, dentists, and lawyers.

I started working part-time on my 16th birthday. My Dad sat me down at the *Milwaukee Journal* circulation switchboard to answer phone calls from people complaining their newspaper carrier did not deliver their paper. When I became a senior, I worked for the *Milwaukee Journal* full-time and went to school part-time.

I was leaving high school behind and expanding my world. I was dating older fellows. Movie dates were my favorite because I could get some catnapping while the film ran on and be more rested to socialize afterward. My friends would laugh and tease me when I could not tell them the movie plot. Honestly, I cozied up hugging the guy's arm and dozed off to ease my polio fatigue.

It was not pleasant taking the bus downtown from high school and walking the blocks from the bus stop to the *Milwaukee Journal* building. By the afternoon, my legs were overtired and the calf muscle in my polio leg spasmed unceasingly. On cold and rainy or snowy days, the pain took over my thinking. I wanted to cry. But, of course, I did not. Polio children do not cry. *You can hurt me. I will not tell. I won't cry.*

I still picture the difficulty I had climbing the steps of the city bus and plunking in my change. The bus driver's smile and hello kept me going somedays. He may have never realized how his attitude of patience while I took time to pull myself up the steps by my arms, helped me. This kind stranger boosted my spirits. Later, as a nurse when I entered a patient room and put on a smile, my mind often wandered to that good feeling the bus driver gave me. He reinforced how a smile may affect how someone else feels in a positive way.

Loving Bach, I regularly sang solos in church at this time. I learned to play classical piano and guitar, which my Dad taught me. My piano teacher was coaching me on the *Warsaw Concerto* when midway through I pounded out *The Jelly Roll Blues* that I learned from my Dad's *Hit Parader* magazine. Her face showed profound disgust. Thinking back, I wonder if I had not experienced feeling at times like an outsider due to polio, would I have taken the risks I did to do crazy antics?

My classmates treated me like anyone else at school as we jostled rushing through the mob of two thousand students getting through the hallways from class to class. Only once do I remember winding up with a problem after struggling getting from one end of the building to the next.

I signed up for typing class which was not located in the part of the building for the college prep course classes where I usually hung out. Typing was for girls who were destined to be secretaries. Mama said I had to take it extra just in case I needed to type someday. The bell rang and a crowd rushed the hallway. I could not keep up with the fast movement and had to stop and rest along the way.

I arrived last in class. The only typewriter left was one that did not have any alphabet letters or numbers inscribed on the keys. The tops of the keys were blank. I learned to type without looking at the keyboard. Serendipitously, this increased the speed at which I crank out the words. *Blessings.*

Taught through millions of minutes of reading, and by the finest human beings, I thrived as a scholar. Although I was in the top two percent of my class and a National Honor Society member, no one on the advising staff at high school encouraged me to go to college. I was a sweet girl. School counselors figured my family did not have the means for sending me to college. They encouraged me to go to nursing school. This vocation was a respectable one for a smart girl at that time.

I graduated from high school and got my appendix taken out the next day. Postop a young nurse grabbed away the pillow I had placed over my eyes to block the annoying glare of overhead lights reminiscent of my stay in the isolation hospital. She shouted at me, "You can't have a pillow over your face!"

I did not bother to explain that hospitalized as a child I had to lay flat on my back with glaring light bulbs above me. I could not sleep with lights. They were reminders and gave me flashbacks. She was too young to have done nursing during the polio pandemic. Nobody cared about polio now. In their minds, polio was over.

I hid my emotions, rolled over on my incision, and buried my eyes into the mattress. I alone still had to deal with polio. I had to make a future that took the damage polio caused me into consideration.

Count your lucky stars if you had parents to guide you through how to go to college. I made so many mistakes figuring it out on my own. College was an unknown to me except for that one trip to Northern Michigan. It was like a Rubik's cube puzzle, and I was not even familiar with the big pictures.

I wanted to be a costume designer. This love was born all those days sewing graveyard ribbon into gowns for dolls. But such a dream I knew did not come with free schooling and a job the day you graduated. So, dash that major. I needed a degree that guaranteed work.

The Palmer School of Chiropractic offered me a scholarship and I would have taken it except my polio condition did not allow me to stand for prolonged periods of time and manipulate backs without falling over and needing a chiropractor myself. Max, my chiropractor, probably arranged the whole tuition-free ride.

I grabbed a brochure for nursing school from counseling office. It described a three-year diploma program ending in becoming an RN. I sat for the admission tests.

A concerned and kind counselor at the school called me back for an interview. She said, "You should go to college. Your knowledge far exceeds our expectations." I looked at her and said, "I can't. I don't know about college. My parents haven't been. We do not have the money." She took my hand in hers and patted it, telling me, "You have to figure it out because you are college material." I walked out holding the tears back. I was so afraid of not taking the easier path.

I had promised to marry Erik. Mama expected me to do so. He had been waiting for me to graduate high school. He would be finishing college soon.

I was confused about what to do next. My automatic pilot defaulted to my comfort place, the library. The library was the place that gave me one of the biggest gifts of my life…love of reading, and also access to the wider world.

The school library had college catalogues and information on who to contact. I followed the leads and chose to go to a university that had a nursing program where I could use all the science I loved.

To pay for college, I cut back my classes in high school to just two, worked full-time for the *Milwaukee Journal*, and picked up a part-time waitressing job at a pizza place on evenings for a year before college. I doggedly took every shift I could get. My goal was to stockpile money in the bank.

I would walk a mile home at midnight from my waitressing job with tons of change from tips in my pockets, fall into bed, and rise early to get to the *Milwaukee Journal* by seven in the morning. I did not have time to ruminate about life circumstances.

When I had to present at the University of Wisconsin-Madison for entrance exams, I found myself falling asleep after a night of pizza slinging. Jolted awake repeatedly by my head bobbing, I was relieved to finish the tests.

Information about dorms came with my letter of acceptance to campus. I was like a rabbit running around the desert searching for a hole. I had to wait to apply for a dorm room because I needed the down payment for the year to go with my application. Mama would eventually help with the money, but I had to earn my share.

My acceptance into the University of Wisconsin-Madison was a big deal as it was one of the finest university campuses in the world. The first term tuition (Fall 1968) was $125.00. I applied for a job two evenings a week working at the university hospital as a nursing assistant to help pay room and board.

Dad dropped me off at the dorm with a suitcase, typewriter, guitar, and popcorn-maker which doubled as a soup tureen. Pressed against the elevator doors with giggling girls and their possessions, Dad, in a world before unknown to him, forged on to help me. He carried my stuff into my room. That was that. I was on my own. My Milwaukee homelife was over.

Your childhood travels with you. I was grateful mine was a fun one and fostered me building strength of body, mind and spirit, love of people and books, exercise and the outdoors, firm determination to succeed at many things, politeness, and a curiosity for what I had not yet experienced beyond my home and school life.

My going to college was medicine that alleviated some of Mama's worry for me. Although it did not please her that I would not marry Erik, I would have a career. Two young parents who gave more than anyone could expect, despite what doctors called the futility of their efforts, were overjoyed their child was going to college.

Al • 1962

From the bandstand, I watch her dancing in Erik's arms. Another prom...time has passed so amazingly fast. I hold back tears of happiness.

The beloved blue second-hand dress

Susie looks like Margie did when I first met her. They each have a smile that that invites a person to smile back. Margie beamed in the early years. But her smile dimmed when polio grabbed Susie away.

The doctors said Susie would never walk but here she is dancing and smiling. She is following the dance steps I taught her while listening to vinyl records in the living room. She tends to lead not follow. I told her so.

Susie is wearing a dress Margie altered for her. It was the matron of honor, blue swirly one, Margie wore for her sister's wedding. Susie does not seem to mind that the dress is secondhand.

After the photographer finished prom court pictures, Susie came over to me to ask for a dance. I wish Margie would be here too just to see that everything has turned out all right.

There is something about hope. I never wanted to dream too big. I did not want to get Margie's hopes up and then feel her heart broken. But here we are. *No matter how hard it gets, you will survive. Feel sorrow and let it go. Keep reaching for your goal.* Despite all the polio damage, Susie dances and is much loved.

Susie • 1964

Mama and I wrote each other letters. More than words, they were a connecting thread between our two disconnected worlds.

Our correspondence was factual. I did not share all the that was going on. I had taken on the role to protect her from unpleasant happenstance. Her part in our mother-daughter dance was cheering on the overachiever and performer in me.

Mama's correspondence detailed Dad and Mike's hunting trips. She kept me in touch with news from the Sundays when they got together with her Pa, Ma, and siblings who still lived at home. She reported when old relatives died and were buried. Letters held reminders of upcoming family events. As I warmed my legs under the electric blanket Grandpa gave me to keep my polio leg warm at college, I penned cards to those I would not see on their birthdays. I was the dutiful daughter.

Mama always asked me how I was doing on money. Without exception, I said that I was fine. I knew the home budget was tight. The details I shared were lean.

The bookkeeper of our family was Mama. Account reconciliation was her job at the bank. There never was a penny unaccounted for at our house. I always knew exactly the amount of cash I had in my pocket albeit not much. When Mike and I would come home from an errand to the grocery, she looked over the cash register receipt and checked off every item, making sure to the penny the amount we paid was correct.

Susie • 1964

Mama perseverated over money. Her night job recounting the bank ledgers led her to a position as a daytime teller. Most evenings she would stay at the kitchen table for hours after dinner going over in her mind how funds balanced at her window that day. She did not need a pencil and paper to check herself. She was a math genius and backtracked all the calculations of her day in her mind. No one interrupted her time staring out the window, smoking a cigarette, and sipping on a drink Dad made her.

In my letters to home, I did not mention the potent smell that overwhelmed my dorm when the wind blew. Since Mama had not seen campus, she did not know that I lived downwind from the university pig farm. The manure, a mixture of nitrogen, sulfites, phosphorus, and ammonia, had an intense, frankly disgusting odor. The only window in my dorm room faced the pigs.

I learned the hard way that when you got your dorm room down payment in last of all the applicants, college admission personnel assigned you to one of the only rooms available. This for me was on the top floor of a lakeshore dormitory on the outskirts of campus with a window overlooking the school of Animal and Dairy Sciences barns and classroom buildings.

But the dorm had its good points. My assigned roommate was from South Africa. Beth's parents were missionaries. Being in America was a jolt of new reality for her.

Beth and I were the only ones on our dorm floor who could not afford to go out to dinner on Sunday evenings when dining halls closed, and students flocked to local bars and restaurants. Over soup heated in my crock pot and a sleeve of wheat crackers, we shared our backgrounds. We talked about how strange college was for the two of us who had no family who had gone to college to give us a glimpse ahead of time and guide us.

Every time I went home, I packed up and brought back a dozen cans of soup, Triscuit crackers, apples, and homemade cookies which became the "Sunday Special" we ate while she talked of faraway places all over the world where she had lived. For me, a girl who only once had been outside Wisconsin, Beth's life was an adventure. How her family helped others in foreign countries inspired me. A flame was lit. I wanted to experience the world.

Beth did not have an easy time making friends. She was soft-spoken. The groovy girls in the dorm walked by her without saying hello. Beth dressed in clothes not shown in 1960s fashion magazines. I could not lend her mine because she was very tall and thin, and I was not.

I look back on this time now and wish I then had the skills I learned in nursing school: to make people feel welcome, okay about themselves, and understood by someone else. At this time in my life, I had no reckoning of how to do that for Beth. I only knew the snotty, stuck-up girls were wrong. But my voice was too uncertain and scared to speak up to them. This was a conundrum for me. I wanted to be good in everyone's eyes: *I am obedient. I am cheerful. I can help. I will overachieve. I can perform.* I could be Beth's friend, but I did not know how to help her integrate into social life on campus.

My communication with Mama did not include that the walking distance to main campus was more than a mile. Fall, when the term started, was beautiful with all the elm trees turning bright yellow. But in Wisconsin's biting cold winters, I was slipping on ice and snow when cautiously plodding along to my first class of the day, *Greek and Latin Medical Terms*.

I painted for Mama a picture of school life obscured with other detailed information to hide that the immense amount of walking on the huge UW-Madison campus wore me out. By the time I got to class and spread my binder out for notetaking, I was exhausted. My extreme fatigue showed.

One early morning, the Greek and Latin professor walked from the podium over to where I was sitting, looked at me and said, "Are you awake?" Polio exhaustion...sometimes you can hide it from your mother but not from someone sticking a pointer in your face from the stage in front of you. I had to concede that I had nodded off.

I worked out ways to compensate for my tiredness. On Mondays, Wednesdays, and Fridays, I accepted the arm of a boy going to the same class. He wanted to be a friend and at least I moved faster hanging on to him and kept upright all the way to class. Other days, I would set an early alarm and start out walking using a flashlight to guide me before it got light outside. This allowed me time to stop at benches or lean against buildings to rest along the way. The bonus was, when I got to class, I had time to rest before the professor started speaking.

Mama and I corresponded each week. I described where I studied which was either in the basement of a dormitory or in a study carrel at the Memorial Library. One day, Ronnie, a guy who also worked at the *Milwaukee Journal*, yelled across the library mall, "Hey, Susie Schoenbeck, stop!" I met up with him and told him I was surprised he could pick me out in the crowd. He said, "I know your walk." He had a wonderful way about him. He did not say, "Well, duh, you limp!" Instead, he addressed me as a person. My happiness to see him made me forget I did not blend in.

I did not mention to Mama that at this mall students were protesting the action of the United States in Vietnam. In 1965, faculty held a teach-in to educate students about the "Vietnam conflict." What started out as a peaceful protest escalated.

In 1967 demonstrations against **Dow Chemical Company** took place on campus. These protests preceded the March on Washington in October of 1967. Students challenged Dow for producing a chemical called napalm used by the United States in Vietnam.

Napalm is a flammable gel that maims its victims. Napalm burns at an unimaginable 1500-2200 degrees Fahrenheit. When napalm falls on a living being, the gel sticks to skin, hair, and clothes. It causes severe burns, at times down to the bone, and as it does, also generates extreme acute and later horrible chronic pain. A direct hit with napalm can bring unconsciousness and asphyxiation, and lead to death.

The hot temperature of napalm causes fires that deplete the oxygen in the air. People in the area not directly hit by the napalm may also suffer and die due to inhalation of smoke, and carbon monoxide produced by its use.

The most famous photograph of napalm victims from the Vietnam War —winning a Pulitzer Prize for Nick Ut—pictured a nine-year-old girl, Phan Thi Kim Phuc. In 1972, she, along with others fleeing her village at Trang Bang, were mistaken for the enemy and a napalm bomb was dropped on them by the **South Vietnam Air Force**, officially the **Republic of Vietnam Air Force**, which relied heavily on photo reconnaissance for identifying and pinpointing targets.

Working as a nursing assistant, I knew firsthand the agonal screams of burn patients when nurses changed their dressings. Their guttural sounds made me understand my polio pain did not measure up to theirs. Napalming the innocent was not an issue I could step back from. I was growing up with new awareness that there were world events that shaped other people just like polio affected my every day.

The Commerce Building where students were blocking Dow job interviews was on my route to the hospital where I worked my evening shifts twice a week. Protesters at first numbered in the teens and then grew into a crowd of hundreds and later thousands of students amassing at various sites on campus.

Being in a crowd with people pushing terrified me. I could not walk well in the mass of students and police officers. I could not join in peaceful protesting carrying a load of schoolbooks in my arms.

My first thought was to be sure I kept to the group outskirts. Police spraying tear-gas left my eyes burning and my vision blurred limiting my studying for the day. I realized quickly that I had to know how to get away from the crowd hurling objects such as shoes, sticks, and stones. I was frightened of stumbling over debris.

Setting aside the polio survivor paradigm of being good and obedient to join the protesting was going beyond my lifelong good girl persona. Demonstrating against atrocities was part of my coming of age. I joined the protests. I could not set aside the damage done to my insides by the polio virus. I realized I would have to participate in moderation.

I felt caught in a dilemma that many people face in life: How much would I push beyond my comfort zone? Importantly, what would my body absorb and keep standing within a jostling crowd? Everyone decides what to offer to others and the world. What we give defines us. *Polio limited how fast my legs could move, but I could yell. I could follow my Dad's example to embrace the truth and change a life.*

Instead of worrying my mother about my activism, I told her about classes. My science classes were both theory and direct laboratory experiences. I was fortunate my professors were world renowned and loved teaching. Mama got a glimpse of the quality of the university education. She liked learning about **Abraham Maslow** and **Bruno Bettelheim**. She loved hearing about **Harry Harlow's** .experiments. We enjoyed a repartee of me pouring facts out to her, and she exclaiming her amazement.

Once I completed the challenging pre-nursing coursework, I made the cut off requirements and entered into the junior/senior portion of the nursing program. I let mama know I could afford to buy my two blue (*Thank goodness not white.*) nursing uniforms, shoes, and cap with money from my nursing assistant job. Mama was proud of me.

Professors followed an informal reporting system alongside the academic one. When given a post card by a student taking a final exam, they would jot down the earned course grade and mail out the card. Professors posted my grades to my Dad at the *Milwaukee*

Journal where he pinned them up on a bulletin board in the stockroom. He may not have understood what it took to get those scores, but he was proud to line up the As.

The nursing program was not easy. Textbooks often gave case examples that were complex at a time when we junior students were just starting to learn the basics about diseases and how patient responses varied. It was difficult to take book learning and apply it to our clinical work.

I formed an alliance with another student to meet the challenges. I was good at theory and had direct experience at the bedside from my part-time job at the hospital. She was superb at figuring out ways to practice and perfect our procedural skills. Our studying together as a team gave us an edge.

We would always put our hands up volunteering to be first in our cohort to perform a nursing skill. Doing a bedside treatment in front of an instructor, and getting it checked off the course list, made me more confident. *I am cheerful. I can help. I will overachieve and I can perform.*

There were teachers who set the scene up so students might have a tougher time succeeding. I remember my first assigned patient. My Nursing 101 instructor told me to get an apical (located above the heart not at the wrist) pulse on a patient. I held aside the patient's gown to uncover unbeknownst to me (but known to the instructor), that the patient had no breasts. The patient recently had a double mastectomy. The left breast was the landmark I was supposed to find to help me proceed. The situation was quite anxiety producing. I let my study partner know before her turn so she could be better prepared.

Watching faculty teach was a lesson for me. *Bad examples can be good teachers.* I realized I learned more and loved nursing when nurse educators demonstrated their understanding and respect for student nurses. I could tell that learning occurred more readily when students who naturally have anxiety approaching new and often frightening procedures, know their instructor has their back.

Later, as a nurse educator, my goal when teaching clinical procedures was to prepare students very well, so they would not fail. I had an agreement with each student that, at the last minute, they could take two steps back from a procedure to signal me they wanted to postpone performing it to the following day. I would just step up and complete the treatment. The patient got the care needed and I kept up my practical skills up.

As an instructor who assigned students to patients with complex procedures, such ventilator care, tracheostomy suctioning, chest tubes and intravenous lines, and extensive, sometimes hour-long, wound management assessment and redressing needs, I believe this not only gave the student nurse additional time to observe a procedure being done, but also showed them that nurses are called to recognize anxiety for what it is and care for each other.

Everyone feels anxious at one time or another. To reach out to a person who is nervous and fears what might happen next not only may create comfort but also validates that such feelings are within the common thread of being human.

To unburden myself of school stress, I partied a lot as was tradition at the university. There were advantages to living in the furthest out dorm on the face of the campus. Far from central campus activities, students in lakeshore dorms made their own fun. We had to use our ingenuity. We gathered in groups prowling the landscape and lake around us. We hiked up to "picnic point," hunted for berries, in winter skated on and in summer swam in Lake Mendota.

Splitting into teams we pulled off pranks like tying a student to a tree at dark. After dancing around, singing, and yelling, we left him alone, hid nearby, and watched. A bystander must have viewed the scene from a dorm window and called the police. We saw the cars topped with red lights coming through the trees. We scattered but not far. We looked on and could see the police officers talking to the young man. He never told who bound him. He was moving his hands to let the police know he was all right. He understood that we never would have left him long attached to the tree. Our pranks never led to harm. We all headed to a bar to buy our fellow prankster a beer. That was friendship in the farthest out dorm area.

I was flighty and flirty with guys. I did not want to get involved too deeply with anyone because that might ruin my goal to graduate college. I went to frat parties to increase the pool of prospective dates. I wasn't successful at shaking off the memory of 1962. I felt ashamed remembering my disobedience. I became a firefly among the boys, sparkly for a minute, but quickly gone and onto the next. I promised myself I did not want to again face getting out of a dicey circumstance.

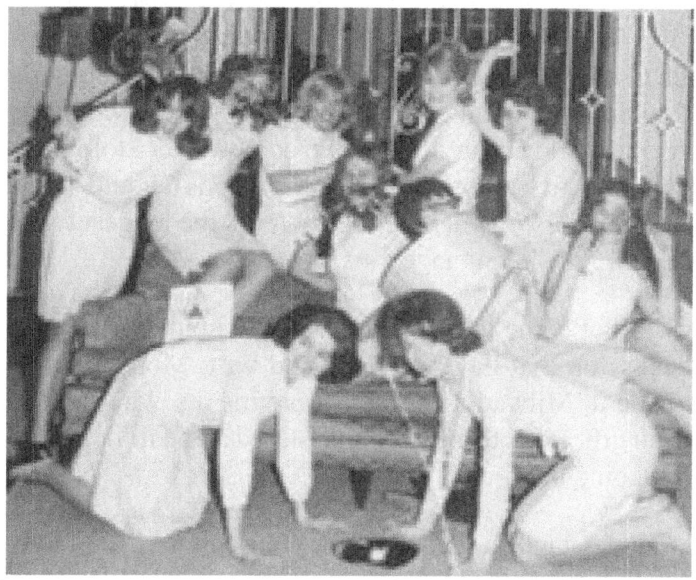

Sorority fun

Our lakeshore "games" were endless. We absconded with food trays from the cafeteria and used them as sleds. Young men roped me to a toboggan pretending they would send me down a steep, snowy hill when adults intervened to tell the young men this might not be a clever idea. A girl in a high-rise dorm threw a bucket of water out the window not knowing she would soak our housing advisor when the water landed on her head which it did. Motorcycle exhaust burns on ankles. Bathtubs full of alcohol refreshment. Frat boys climbing up balconies to enter our sorority houses. Unique memories. Serious students. Party college. We let off steam and energy, and then got back to studying.

Thinking Badger football would be a big draw, I worked extra shifts at the hospital as a nursing assistant to buy football tickets so my family could see a game. *Mama's letters* indicated she and Dad would come. I stood outside the stadium at our designated meeting place until I conceded with the roar of the crowd at half time, they were not showing up.

I should have realized that my Mama, always anxious about how people would judge her, would avoid new people and places. She had been to only a few cities outside Milwaukee. I later wondered *if* I had taken time to talk up in more detail what it would be like in Madison, would she and Dad have come? Or *if* I told her I was scared when I first came to live on campus, would that have shown her I understood her feelings? "*If*" is the longest two-letter word in the English language.

Family did not come to my undergraduate graduation. My sense of aloneness on that day was deep and vast. Months later, on a visit I made to Milwaukee, Mama gave me a sewing machine, a graduation gift. I was thrilled. Mama stared at the floor as she said, "I wish it could be more."

I did not understand for decades that your children, although they never really leave you, may move on to places you may only hear about, read details in correspondence, or imagine in your dreams. It is how life goes on generation by generation.

Susie • 1968

I never ever was angry at my Mama for saying, "Marry him." She did what she felt she had to do. The truth was she just wanted me to be safe. Polio crept into every pore of her and made her always feel vulnerable. She planned to outsmart this burden by having me marry someone she thought would take care of me.

Mama was hostage to her memories of quarantines and shaming. She never was able to shake her feelings of *My fault. Everybody will talk about us. I must be in control.*

Even though I did not share with her the half of it, Mama knew polio compromised my physical strength. She had glimpses into my daily machinations to get around all the destruction the virus wielded. Mama was grateful the college house cook supplemented my diet with foods that addressed neurological damage related to polio.

Other people could only see the limp. But Mama and Dad knew there was so much more wrong with me. The consequences of polio required foresight, planning and resources to meet all the daily long-haul effects of polio.

Although I did not talk about my pain, tiredness, and the myriad of other annoyances due to polio damage, Mama knew the effects of polio were ever present. My silence did not reassure her. *You can hurt me. I will not tell. I won't cry.*

Mama hoped marriage would provide security for me. She had endured twenty-one years of worrisome responsibility for child with polio. She could endure no more faking being in control when really there was no way of containment of symptoms as they marched on. The virus was not giving up being in charge.

Smoking brought Mama chronic obstructive pulmonary disease (COPD) with a nagging non-stopping cough, just like her Pa's. Her health was waning. She underwent emergency surgery for stomach ulcers. She had aged, and became a weary, skinny, and tired woman.

Did Mama ever forgive herself for not defending me from getting polio? Never. I would surreptitiously glance at her from a place around the living room wall. Peeking into the kitchen where Mama sat after dinner, I saw her gazing out the window, her faraway thoughts hidden from prying eyes, tears pooling in her eyes.

Mama kept reviewing the events of 1946. She wept, haunted by the sights and cries of a struggle not won. Like memories of war tormented her Pa, Mama grasped a cigarette in one hand and a drink in the other and recommenced reviewing what happened asking herself, "How did Susie get sick? Was I the one? It only takes one to infect another person with a virus." Mama was smart but also unforgiving of herself.

When I look back at the many instances when Mama pushed the stroller to get books to read to me, stood up when people wanted to exclude me, taught me how people act when they are feeling afraid, and let me go to experience the world, I knew she did not just love me a little. Mama loved me a lot.

People might look askance at the ways Mama coped with my mischievous behaviors. I do not. Mama did her best under very trying circumstances.

I always picture Mama twisted tight as a pretzel her arms crossed over her chest displaying that she was not letting anyone in. Escalating tension wound her up tight because it took understanding and courage to be kind to those who offended her.

I look around and see many people who, although they live in less demanding situations than Mama did, are not kind to others. Being kind to others, something not always afforded her because of being mother to a polio child, was a trait she valued and an action she lived.

Mama showed great strength to consistently display her way of being in the face of scorn and stress. Bullies view kindness as weakness. But, despite them, I observed Mama in situations wherein she dug deep to not let others change who she was. Mama was stronger than those who would make her feel less.

From her own life experiences growing up in a crowded home with verbal and physical fighting commonplace, never feeling financially secure, and stuck in polio epidemic circumstances beyond her control that devoured her adulthood, she figured out that people act according to their needs. I had to take a college psychology class to understand this when I learned Maslow's Hierarchy of Needs.

Mama lived what it was like to be the person others viewed as different. She felt the scorn of people who cupped their hands over their mouth and whispered to each other about her child. She was no fool.

Mama wished me to be in a place that was as far out of harm's way as possible. She knew that in life anything was possible and the unexpected could step in your way and hurt you. Mama thought marrying the guy would put me in a more protected space than that in which I got sick.

The guy, wanting to meet my family, came home with me for a weekend. He had attended undergraduate at the University of Wisconsin-Madison. He was about to graduate from law school in another state. He hoped to live in Madison, a place he felt more comfortable in than the big city where he grew up. He was older than me, a self-professed world traveler, and experienced in ways unknown to me. Naïve me thought these circumstances something admirable and exciting.

Susie • 1968

Only through chance and my friendship with Kitty had I met this guy. My friend asked me to go to a party with her off campus. I explained that I already promised to go out with someone else. Kitty begged me to change my commitment. Trying to be a good friend to Kitty, I rescheduled plans with my date.

It was one of those parties where people pour alcohol in a bathtub, and everyone dips their cup in. Kitty was quite the star of the party. I remember sitting on a kitchen table uncomfortably waiting for any decent guy to show up. Kitty was not as fussy.

I became apprehensive surrounded by people who were drunk. I wanted to head back to campus. Kitty and I had taxied to the party. The guy arrived and presented himself as a serious person at a party that was getting out of hand. We talked some. I never met a person who went to law school. He offered me a ride home. I accepted.

The guy talked a lot about *big city life*. That was alluring. He constantly complimented my looks especially, my blonde hair and clothes I designed and sewed myself. We dined in restaurants, something I was not familiar with doing. He never cooked for himself. We spent hours at bookstores. I was attracted to him because he could bury himself in a book for hours leaving me time and space to rest in peace and quiet. I unexpectedly found more emptiness than solitude.

The guy said he was applying to graduate school. His schooling would take him to Africa. His voicing a sense of purpose in helping the less fortunate charmed me. I envisioned nursing where Beth, my first college roommate, grew up. She told me stories about the desperate plight of people in need of healthcare. I believed there might be a chance to take my nursing skills to the places I learned about from Beth and books.

One of my closest friends in nursing schools had just married an academic and they were leaving for his home country, Honduras, upon graduation. Penny was excited about the opportunities to nurse where there was a great need for healthcare. I had dreams to help the less fortunate in faraway places. I thought the guy could be a key piece in making it happen. I was too optimistic and unsophisticated enough to believe our coming together was other than destiny.

There were clues that this might not be the best match. The guy stood apart from my friends, not joining much in conversations. I loved sociable people, and he did not take to parties. He leaned on the wall watching from the sidelines. I ignored the sign that he was not eager to have fun.

I reasoned that his aloofness was a sign of his advanced education and maturity. I talked myself into believing I just needed to grow up. Later, I realized his standoffishness was a homegrown trait, a sense of superiority imbedded in him by his upbringing.

Our families were so different. I loved my family. The guy voiced hating his own. That should have been a red flag. Dating me whose religion was outside his family's seemed to be part of the attraction. In hindsight, I think he unknowingly was pushing the buttons to trigger a volatile parental reaction using me as a wedge to open the door of freedom from his parents.

The guy's family disowned him in retaliation for asking me to marry him. I did not know parents could discard their kids. They speedily confiscated his car. They cut off his financial support for graduate school. The drama bewildered me. Of course, this only made him want to marry me sooner than later. By then, I was feeling sorry for him being all alone. I mistakenly thought he was waving a white flag indicating the need for help. We nurses are prone to being rescuers.

In contrast to the guy's family, Mama did not think a person's religious upbringing was a good barometer of who that person was at heart. She believed her Pa's view that religious books abounded in stories of bloody wars which often took the attention away from the simple teachings of wise people and prophets about how to live gently with others. Pa had seen downfallen war buddies in recurrent dreams way too often.

Susie • 1968

Mama was like her Pa in believing that the greatest religion was kindness. The church people after all did not welcome her when watching me limping to Sunday School. They asked Mama, "How did your little girl get it? Why didn't you get her vaccinated? Mama believed that just because you went to a place of worship did not mean you were a kind person. She said you have to be careful what you worship.

Mama would only attend church on Easter morning and Christmas Eve. We family sat all in a row in a pew toward the back of the church. She did not look around but kept her eyes fixed on the front of the sanctuary still believing, *My fault. Everybody will talk about us. I must be in control.* She never stopped believing people were judging her.

Dad ushered in church every six weeks and always came to hear me sing. But most Sundays, he stayed home too tired out from strumming his guitar when performing with the combo the night before. He would give me a dime to put in the payphone at the drugstore across the corner from church. My instructions were to call our home number, let the phone ring twice, and hang up. The two rings would let my dad know church was over, and he could drive over to get me. I would get the dime back and return it to him. We saved money any way we could. It was the 1960s and I still had the only working mother on the block.

So, I was at a loss to believe the guy's family would reject me because of religion. Everyone loved me. After all, I had the polio personality*: I am obedient. I am cheerful. I can help. I will overachieve. I can perform.* I was always popular with people. I rationalized the guy's parents would come around. I learned later that rationalization is often self-deception.

When I brought the guy home for the weekend to meet the family, I slipped across the hall at bedtime to canoodle. Mama was waiting at the bottom of the stairwell and called me down to talk to her. She was not pleased. She grew up in the era if a girl gave herself to a guy that meant they got married or the girl was a floozy. Worse yet, the young woman became pregnant.

She called me on the carpet and asked roundabout questions about my sexual activity. I avoided answering. But Mama was not going to accept her daughter ruining an education by becoming pregnant. She persisted in questioning me.

It was 1968, so I could let Mama know that girls could get birth control pills at college. There was one physician in the city of 140,000 people who prescribed them to young women. A girl just had to be confident when picking up her prescription at Rennebohm's Pharmacy because, as the pharmacist came to the counter, he would announce loudly to everyone within earshot the name of the girl and the fact he had readied her "birth control prescription." People in line turned around to stare.

I had been through worse, so the pharmacist's bullying behavior did not dissuade me. *You can hurt me. I will not tell. I won't cry.* Every month, with a stoic face, I waited in line as the pharmacist tried to scorn me. I can still picture the inside of that store. At the time, the pharmacist was not required to ask for identification. My roommate would give me money to go back and pick up her birth control prescription to spare herself the embarrassment.

"The girl of his dreams," the guy called me. He surprised me by asking me to marry him. I said, "Yes." Being swept off one's feet by someone from another, alluring world is magical. The timing seemed right. In my naivete, I did not understand he was looking for someone entirely not like me.

Of all the guys I dated, the guy was the most educated. Mama respected education. No one, besides Dad, could have been prouder that I was finishing college. I thought college education changed your life. I learned much later that education gets you somewhere, but wherever you go, you take yourself with you.

The guy and I were married just before my last term. The dean of the school of nursing called me into her office. She asked questions: How was I feeling? Was I up to the final term? She probed. No, I was not pregnant, and I was looking forward to this last term. I was excited that I would be learning in critical care units, places the dean had never been.

It was a busy year. My nursing instructors matching me up for intensive care units (ICUs) was key. They said they were confident I would do well in critical care because I was so darned organized. *Thanks, Dad.* Interestingly, the instructors never themselves came into the ICU to teach me because they were not educated in this clinical area. Instead, I was fortunate that dedicated diploma graduates mentored me.

The university instructors met with me weekly. I would present a chart of what I had done. The teachers guided my thinking. They brought me research articles to supplement my learning. The instructors taught me listening to a student is an important facet of teaching.

John Dewey believed teachers take students down paths, share information, and most importantly, help them to understand how to learn. The world relies on people who can continue to pick up knowledge as it changes. Dewey knew a person's education did not occur at one static point in time but was a lifelong way of being a functioning member of society. A community depends on its people being able to sift and winnow current information and update their knowledge base.

In the ICUs, I could nurse without walking a lot. I would be at the bedside of the sickest patients who needed constant monitoring and care. Some were on ventilators. Each had chest tubes draining blood which we administered back into them.

Nurses' minds had to be sharp and alert. Their hands were always poised to resuscitate babies in incubators who had anomalies in their hearts repaired and adults post open-heart surgery for valve replacements and artery bypass procedures. In the midst of the cacophony of technological gadgetry, nurses extended compassion and hope to those who counted on us for their physical, emotional, and spiritual well-being.

Rest was essential for me to be a good nurse. My pacing and organization ensured this. Since the guy and I had no social life, I could get all the sleep I needed so I was always ready for work.

The chief surgeon and head nurse were attentively supportive of all nursing staff. When a baby was not doing well or plainly not going to make it, it was not unusual for a surgeon to sit beside the nurse caring for the baby.

Our ICU surgeons and nurses cared for babies from around the state with a condition called Tetralogy of Fallot. This anomaly consists of four structural defects in a baby's heart that impair the pattern of flow and oxygenation of blood. Infants and young children had blue-tinged lips, nailbeds, and skin. Older kids often presented with clubbed fingers due to long-standing poor oxygenation.

Causes of infants' heart defects varied. Mothers exposed to rubella or other viral infections during pregnancy had higher risk of delivering babies with Tetralogy of Fallot.

At that time, the CDC warned women of childbearing age who might become pregnant to not get MMR (measles, mumps, rubella) vaccination because it contained a weakened but live virus. Women exposed to measles in their communities during pregnancy were advised to contact their medical provider.

While almost all of our open-heart surgery patients survived, and went onto healthier lives, the head nurse realized nurses who were mothers felt most emotionally battered when taking care of the sickest children. There was a unit rule that no pregnant nurse or nurse who was a young mother would take care of a child unlikely to live. Until I became a mother, I did not know what a wise a rule that was.

There were days when all our team's critical care expertise could not make a patient better. I always remember the chief surgeon of the open-heart intensive care unit pulling up a stool and looking at me with my hand poised to again resuscitate the baby in the incubator in front of us. Tears welled in his eyes. He had made a promise to every parent to do his best to heal their child. He said, "Susie, I think I need to call the parents and tell them their baby will not make it." There was only so much we could do. It was hard to let go.

His heartfelt statement reminded me of the "White Coats." I thought then of what must have been their similar feelings of frustration and helplessness during the polio epidemic when they could not save us all. The virus was in charge not healthcare workers. They could only do so much. It was frightening for them too.

On graduation day 1968, I stood outside the athletic stadium where students and families were shouting and singing. I sent my family a map showing where to park and the place I would meet them to attend the ceremony. I waited alone until I had to go in to line up to get my undergraduate degree. No family showed up. Feelings of abandonment trampled my heart.

At least the guy was there. I had moved into marriage because Mama told me this is what a good girl would do. Many good things came about because of her directive. After the graduation ceremony, we went straight home. No celebration. The dining out we did during courting stopped once we married. I was a wife, no longer the girl of his dreams.

My dream, however, of helping people with intensive medical-surgical needs was a reality I embraced and loved. I would be collaborating with nurses and doctors I admired. I felt fortunate and grateful.

Increased Risk for Outbreaks of Measles

The **World Health Organization** and **Centers for Disease Control and Prevention** (November 2021) released a report showing a worldwide decline in measles vaccinations during the **COVID-19** pandemic.

Measles is a highly contagious viral infection. The disease is almost entirely preventable through vaccination.

The measles-mumps-rubella vaccine prevents spread of viral disease that may adversely affect babies of women exposed to viral infection. Women contemplating pregnancy are encouraged to receive the measles-mumps-rubella (MMR) vaccinations **before** pregnancy to prevent complications. The vaccine is contraindicated during pregnancy because it contains live, attenuated viruses.

Women who contract rubella (German measles) or other viral illnesses while pregnant are at higher risk to deliver a baby with Tetralogy of Fallot.

In 2020, measles vaccination decreased by more than 80 percent. This translated into more than twenty-two million infants not receiving their first in a series of measles vaccines.

Pockets of measles cases spring up yearly. The CDC reported thirteen cases in the United States in 2020 and 43 cases as of November 10th, 2021. Travelers coming in from abroad can bring in cases to further the spread of unvaccinated populations in the United States.

The expected outcomes of decreased MMR vaccinations are serious complications and deaths for babies and children.

Susie • 1984

You cannot outrun the damaging effects of a virus. Polio echoes. The changes it makes in your body continue every day the rest of your life. The virus does not care how busy you get. The virus does not mind if it turns your life upside down. I tried ignoring the aftereffects of the virus. This did not work.

The years moved on. I was now thirty-eight years out from acute poliomyelitis. I was enjoying a vigorous family life raising three active children and participating in swimming, skating, and other family sports. Carpooling for athletic and dance practices and events, grocery shopping, cooking, cleaning, and doing laundry for a family filled all my time.

I finished graduate school learning statistics by studying the subject using notes on index cards I carried around to kids' sporting events, set on the kitchen windowsill to study during dish clean-up, and put on the dashboard of the car when slumped over the steering wheel waiting for kids as "carpool mom" in parking lots. Sometimes I planned child pick-ups, so I had an extra fifteen minutes to nap in a car parking lot.

The polio virus taught me early on to cluster tasks to save energy and ward off fatigue. I never walked more steps than needed to get to a destination. Becoming ambidextrous had grown out of a need to save steps. I continued to live following the motto that if carrying one object somewhere offered the possibility of dropping another along the way, my arms were full.

Bedsheets in my mind never required folding. Who looks at the folds when they sleep? It was faster to roll sheets up and toss them in the closet. During several years, sleeping bags served as my children's bedding. Sleeping bags required less time and motion on my part. Beds did not need to be made and were cleaner as less dust mites could settle in when bedcovers were not tightly pulled up.

I cooked in large batches. I never made a dozen brats for a meal. I made twenty-pound boxes of brats and froze them in the buns single-wrapped, ready to be reheated at mealtime. I doubled the lasagna recipe so the extra pan could be frozen saving on overall preparation and clean up time. At least one hundred veggie rolls passed through oil during a stir fry session. My teenagers took turns tossing the egg rolls in the wok. I doubled cookie recipes in size for efficiency in batter production. Why take the energy to get out the flour, sugar, and chips more often than necessary?

When I arrived with five children (Two were playmates of my kids.) in tow to my graduate statistics professor end-of-term meeting, he chuckled and said, "You made the top in the class with so many children!" Happy with my grade, we all walked to the Memorial Union for an ice-cream treat made by students in the university's agriculture program. Half-way across the mall, a young man put his palms high in the air stopping us. He shouted, "I suppose you live in a shoe, too!" Campus culture always had room for clowning around.

I figured out how to cope with a growing family. Each child kept a book and a ball in tow to entertain themselves when we would proceed to drop off another child at an event. Life marched on. I knew movement and rest were essential to my health and that of my children.

In 1984, I began falling more. I tripped over my polio foot that dragged as I walked. When the kids were doing their homework in the evenings at the dining room table, I was alongside them writing, correcting papers, and planning for my teaching nursing at the University of Wisconsin-Madison. I commonly went full speed ahead all day and exhausted, made my way to bed sometimes before the kids did. My head hit the pillow and I was asleep, with my polio leg tremoring (fasciculations).

I was pushing an aging body that suffered numerous injuries from the polio virus. The changes the virus brought were not new to me. But my ability to effectively respond had changed. Naps had always been my fallback to keep my walking stable. Now there was less time to sit down and take a short break.

My level of pain from muscle spasms due to an overworked polio leg escalated. I tried my best to compartmentalize pain and ignore it. My use of non-steroidal medication led to gastric ulcers.

My extreme tiredness was indescribable and brought me to my knees. The kids started to help with the laundry. I appreciated that the soccer coach encouraged all the players to scrub the dirt out of their uniforms. The children were willing to do anything asked. Each cleaned their own room. They took out the garbage, cut the lawn, and did snow removal. They carried in cases of groceries: Why spend time buying just one pack when it takes less time in the long run to grab a case and put it on a shelf in the basement? They kids did the heavy lifting chores. Their days however were also full of school, sports, and other activities.

After falling down a flight of stairs twice, I could no longer deny I needed a more focused approach to intervene to stop falls and to offset my pain and fatigue. I feared breaking bones.

Talking over my situation with a colleague, we met to discuss options. As an orthopedic surgeon, he offered me a couple of surgeries he could do in a unique way. Surgery was scheduled for an early morning during Spring break from my classes at the university.

A psychologist trained me in self-hypnosis for post-operative pain. This proved to provide good distraction and boosted my ability to be comfortable during the post operative rehabilitation time period.

One team of surgeons opened a hip and took out a block of bone along with a syringe of bone marrow. Another team extended my Achilles' tendon which had shortened. This team also opened my polio leg ankle. A two-inch block of hip bone was set into my ankle so that my foot could no longer drop down. This procedure is called an ankle arthrodesis. The use of my own bone—an autologous bone transfer—left me with the bonus of no pins or metal devices.

I came home on crutches with a knee to toe cast on my polio leg. I needed help bathing and dressing which my youngest child provided in addition to later also plucking out stitches under the supervision of the surgeon. One of the hardest parts of recovery was managing walking safely using crutches through slushy Wisconsin snow to make my way to classes and other activities.

Not able to engage anyone at home besides the children for participation in housework, although I begged for it, escalated my distress. *You can hurt me. I will tell. I ask for help.* My graduate school friends stepped up to the plate. They knew I was no longer the dream girl, but now the overwhelmed manager of the household and working wife.

A colleague came over with meals and did shopping. Friends drove the children places. I pulled back from attending the children's activities. These gestures all helped immensely as I was battling walking with a heavy cast reminiscent of my steel polio brace and fighting pain along with anxiety that came with not knowing if these surgical changes would for sure improve my stability.

The ankle arthrodesis was not an easy surgery from which to recover. Surgical changes altered my gait. Because the unique way I had of balancing changed, my spine had to accommodate. It took my spinal cord a while to settle down (adjust and be less painful) and accept the new way of walking.

Walking downhill with a fixed ankle pulled on the tendons in my polio foot. I could no longer wear shoes with a heel higher than a half inch which pitched me forward when I walked. I gave away shoes that no longer fit because of the fixation. I had to make an accommodation of my self-image. I learned by trial and error to avoid inclines such as hills. I asked questions ahead about access and ramps in buildings and parking lots so I could plan routes. My surgeon insisted I get a handicap parking license plate saying, "I do not want you in a parking garage, being unable to run from someone." I swallowed down another image revision.

I had to employ all the step-saving tools I developed since I was a child. My nurse and doctor friends and I pooled all our rehabilitation knowledge to sketch out ways to keep me safe. Facing the aftereffects of a viral disease such as polio can be daunting. I was grateful I had a village to help me again fight the virus.

Marjorie Clare • 1984

The way I have known about Susie's adult life is mostly from her letters. From the time she went away to college twenty years ago, Susie wrote home every week. Her letters were factual not overflowing with emotion. I knew what she was doing, but not what she was thinking. Occasionally her feelings bled through the words.

Like every parent who believes their kid is over a stomach bug until the child opens their mouth and pukes again, I hoped her years of polio consequences would be at bay. Her letters spelled out telltale signs they were not.

As she grew up, Al and I kept telling Susie she was one of the lucky ones because we believed this to be so. The newspaper reported that around the time Susie had polio, case rates were high. Sadly, many children did not walk afterward. Because she had polio at such a young age, Susie has known no other way of life. Susie understands her days will always be reliably difficult. That is her everyday reality.

As a young child Susie accepted that polio had given her weaknesses. She took whatever came without whining or writing home about it. Not once did she complain to me about polio. In her younger years, polio shaped her to become feisty about overcoming obstacles.

From the time she was a young child, Susie took time for what she called *"mindlessness."* She described what she called her brain getting foggy and coming to a place where she was so tired that needing to concentrate too much, or outside chatter and interruptions made her anxious.

When she was little and her blue eyes glazed over, I knew she needed her *mindlessness* state to relax and rejuvenate. During these times she wanted to be alone with her thoughts undisturbed by others invading her space.

If you didn't realize this was time for her to be in her own space, she put her fingers up to her pouty lips and whispered, "*mindlessness time.*" She didn't mean to be rude. We got used to her prompting us when we didn't get the cues.

We bought a fan, put it in her bedroom to block out noise, and shut the door. *Mindlessness* didn't mean she wasn't accomplishing something because I think even in her naps and dreams something was going on in that head of hers.

Sometimes when she was in the state she called *mindlessness,* she might draw patterns for clothes she wanted to sew. The *Milwaukee Journal* press operators sent home with Al scraps of paper they would normally toss. They bound the paper into tablets for Susie. She would lay down on her stomach and sketch designs. Or she might lay down under the tree in our front yard to shut out the outside world by reading a book that took her away from the present time and place.

Susie believed that distraction through *mindlessness* gave her the ability to rebound. It was a slippery slope downward if she did not take moments for *mindlessness.*

Susie wrote in her letters that she felt lucky to grow up in a hardworking family. She told me working different shifts, with difficult people, in varied situations made her realize she could get through tough times. She said these experiences helped her become a person who does not give up easily. Her letters told of students failing because they were less accustomed to demanding expectations. They could not organize to succeed. Susie said soft lives may not cultivate hardiness.

She followed Al's attitude of looking at the bright side of life. Her sunny personality attracted people just like his did. He enjoyed his second job playing the guitar and leading his band. Susie was like Al in her way of being self-assured and positive. Al taught her to smile for his camera. She knew her smile connected her with people. I used to picture her smiling after reading one of her letters. Now, not so much.

I never saw the campus when Susie got her undergraduate degree. I wish Al and I had made the effort to go there. She wanted us to come to her undergraduate nursing graduation. She sent a map along with the invitation. We did not go. I thought about her all that day.

At the time of Susie's first graduation, I believed (and I was wrong) that Susie had outgrown the life she once had in Milwaukee. I thought she had moved on to a world unknown to me. Susie had accepted herself as she was, but I could not do the same. She didn't change as she grew into nursing and motherhood. She took the lessons of her childhood and used them there.

I was uncomfortable about attending Susie's undergraduate ceremony. My life had existed within the boundaries of Milwaukee. I did not know people who went to school after high school. I was smart— at the top of my Riverside class. I moved up the ladder at the bank later becoming an officer in international banking. But I was uncomfortable mixing with college people. How could I talk with other parents? I did not want to embarrass Susie with something I said.

I don't know if Susie realized our reason for not attending her graduation was that I did not think I fit in the crowd. I hope she did not think we did not love her enough to come.

Susie had less time to write in detail about classes when she entered graduate school in the 1970s and again in the 1980s. With three little kids, I wondered how she managed. Al taught her organization methods. I am sure that helped her get more things done in a day than most people. I hoped she was getting her naps.

As she got older, Susie realized she had to keep mounding up maneuvers to control her symptoms. I could see how she did this when we began in the 1970s to visit the college town where she now lived with her family. Each child was quite the adorable little person. Susie doted on them and loved her time with them.

I know it was not easy for her being a mother, full-time student, working, and running a household. The challenging times of her youth instilled a resilience into her nature. I sensed she did not think writing about her pain or tiredness would accomplish anything. She had set goals she was determined to meet. She wrote Al and me about accomplishments not the annoyances of polio.

We visited when each child was born. I stayed a week after the first birth as Susie was more exhausted than I had ever seen her be. But otherwise, Susie and family returned to Milwaukee for all holidays. And, in between, she faithfully wrote.

She wrote of bartering for services. She gave a college girl room and board in exchange for help with the children. She thanked the neighbor for helping her sons make Pinewood derby cars by hosting a surprise birthday party for him wherein her three-year-old daughter popped out of a cardboard cake while singing *Happy Birthday*. Susie would tutor students and they, in turn, watched her kids while she studied. She mended and altered clothes for a friend. The woman helped her by taking the kids *Halloween trick or treating* in the dark where Susie felt uncomfortable walking.

Susie wrote that her life was full. I could read between the lines that people counted on and loved her. Susie kept a sense of humor that attracted other people to her.

When Al and I visited, we could see Susie organized with no expectation polio would lessen its hold on her or go away. She would never be able to overcome polio, but she could put into place ways to live as best she could with it.

We saw the homemade calendars that she pasted up on closet doors visible at kid height in the kitchen. Each child had three months of their own calendars with their personal schedules posted. Everyone knew their commitments and the whereabouts of everyone else.

Where other mothers had cookbooks, Susie had steno books lined up on her kitchen counter. Each was marked by topic and broken into sections like *weekly, monthly*, and *yearly* schedules. There were notebooks labeled for the holidays with reminders of the tasks and datelines associated with each. Susie had her way of breaking things down into simpler formats so she could not only accomplish the tasks but have the reward of scrunching up that piece of the notebook when done.

At one visit, Susie told me that one of her well-meaning neighbors commented to her that it would be a great day in the next life because there Susie's bad leg would become whole. Susie knew a deeper reality. She would be the same person no matter what happened beyond the grave. Susie knew she was okay.

In her weekly letters, Susie described her patients' conditions. People from all over the state needing specialty surgeries came to the university hospital. She said it was like Al told us after he played with the band at the county home: Be grateful for what you have. There are people who endure worse.

She was one proud mama. Her letters explained what each child was doing. At three months, sweet girl smiles and charms! Her three-year-old *"little psychologist"* showed empathy, always helping, and sharing his toys with other kids. The eight-year-old was very decisive, kicking a goal through spongy grass in a downpour! Susie's letters always had good news about the children.

Because Susie wrote in cursive, I read the letters to Al. I read each letter aloud more than once. Every word was precious news to us. I never told her that. She was a star. Her accomplishments exceeded our expectations. Reading the letters made Al sure he was right in taking her out of the hospital and bringing her home.

Sometimes when she had deadlines to meet, Susie would drive the youngest child into Milwaukee so we could care for her for a week at a time. Al and I had such fun alternating days with that little girl. We would try to outdo each other in how we entertained her. That child could reveal interesting tales of adventures with her grandmother and grandfather. Al and I loved her company. We spoiled her.

The child was so exuberant and positive in spirit that she reminded us of the days when Susie was little. When we were young and scared of what would happen to our kid with polio, our own anxieties overshadowed days and nights. This precious child gave us times of joy without the feelings of worry we always had when raising Susie.

Then came 1984. When she wrote that she was having surgery to stabilize her polio leg footdrop, I worried. Susie described two teams of surgeons and an extended rehabilitation time in a cast. I knew she wouldn't go through this unless it was necessary. Susie did not like being a patient. She admitted she was falling. I could understand why as she did not have help around the house.

Her letters had been giving me a sense of not only the kids' extensive activities but also about her growing acknowledgement that she could not do it all. I know writing about this was not easy for her to tell us. Not being able to do everything well was not her nature to share. She kept her hurts inside. She is like me in that respect. The guy was busy with his own work life. He had set expectations believing Susie should take care of the children, run a household, and work without help.

At her 1984 graduate school graduation, Al and I saw Susie struggling. We sensed she was completely awash with fatigue.

We thought she would have felt exhilarated. She graduated with highest honors, which we only found out by reading the program at the ceremony.

1984

Al and I were delighted that we got to have the youngest child squirm on our laps during the graduation ceremony. The older boys ran around grabbing all the champagne corks they could find on the stadium floor. A friend of Susie's helped with the after-party food and watching of the children.

She would not share her concerns that day, but we could see she was not only tired but also anxious. She downplayed her good news that she would be teaching nursing at the university. When she started to talk about the position, the guy cut off the conversation, demanding she go and reprimand a child for doing cartwheels.

I knew something was wrong when the letters stopped coming every week. She had never been too busy to write. I could only guess that Susie was very fatigued, or circumstances were too painful to share. I saw her in physical pain throughout her childhood, but this was different. This change in our correspondence made me wonder how much she was struggling. It is a mother's prerogative to forever worry about her children.

Susie had learned in graduate school to better express her voice. She was giving community talks. She was becoming a recognized leader. She liked collaborating with people of all religions and joined an ecumenical group of the city's spiritual leaders.

Now the lack of letters was telling me that something was wrong. Looking back on graduation day, when should have been so happy, she had been quiet and on edge.

I remembered when I was ashamed and afraid. I did not know how to take care of a child with polio. I would stare blankly out the kitchen window as I smoked and drank. If there had been a guide, a book about being a good mother of a child with polio, I would have read it…devoured it. But there was none. Al and I were guessing about what was best to do for Susie.

I ignored Susie's middle of the night cries. I pretended not to hear when Mike would loosen her heavy leg brace and it would fall to the floor in the middle of the night. I was relieved Susie wasn't whimpering after the brace slipped off her polio leg.

In the later years of her childhood, I heard her scampering down the stairs in the middle of the night and go into the kitchen cupboard where we kept the aspirin. I listened to her open the bottle and take a couple tablets. I watched her go by but stayed in bed and said nothing. I did count the number of tablets left each day to make sure we had enough for another round of her pain. I couldn't directly face the pain that I could not take away.

I could not connect with Susie's polio experience. I disconnected myself. Al did the hands-on work, rubbing and exercising her leg. I stood by.

In the past few days, I have often looked at our copy of the in-house *Little Milwaukee Journal* article about Susie as a student nurse. Her polio hospitalization gave her ideas about how to make the hospital less frightening for kids. She made a game board for pediatric patients. As the child moved their token on the board, they talked about their experiences. She remembered how scared she was in the isolation hospital. She created this game to let hospitalized kids talk about being at a hospital far away from their parents. Susie listened to show the children she understood their feelings.

Susie playing game with hospitalized child

Now I cannot stand by and watch Susie hurting. I have decided to write her a letter to let her know I am listening. I know I could be wrong in sizing up the situation. But I am not willing to take the chance of missing out again on stepping forward to help her.

Dear Susie,

A mother senses when a child is sad. There is a private channel, perceivable but unseen, from mother to child. I stood back many times feeling helpless when you were a child with so much pain, countless challenges, and uncertainty in your life. My hope is that a child can never become too old for a mother to act when feeling her child is hurting.

I recognize myself in you. Your face cannot hide your lost dreams. I flash back to the vacant stare I once had when I was at a loss as what was best to do for you. I know it hurts too much to see your way forward in the world sometimes. I've been there. When you were little, I sometimes just wanted to be anywhere else to get a break from the heartache.

When you were young, I thought no one would help us. I was wrong. There was Pa, nurse Marie, and chiropractor Max. And the librarian who read to you and broke the rules so you could take home as many books as we could carry. The Milwaukee Road guys who always were happy to take you on the train and the Milwaukee Journal press room men who saved ends of paper for you to draw on all took a part in helping.

I was not good at letting others know I was drowning...feeling helpless. You are so self-sufficient. I know asking for help is hard for you to do too. I was too ashamed with all the stigma around polio. I know this place of loneliness and the fear of letting go of the facade of being in control.

Time has brought me to the conclusion that the finest achievement we can make is to be who we want to be despite circumstances. I know you have walked through painful times. You have lived through one of the worst times.

Life is messy. You alone cannot change that. I am writing to say I am beside you now wanting to help. Tell me what you need. Do not be embarrassed. I erred in life letting my uncertainty block me from new opportunities.

You will never be alone like when you were a baby and young child. That you must believe. I know your experience in the isolation hospital makes you anxious. You hide so many wounds.

Life can be an endless struggle juggling what we do to keep up with what we face. As a family, we have come through trials with love intact. It is not what you accumulate in goods but the good in yourself you hang on to that counts. That is victory.

The hardest part of a new journey begins with the first step. I am with you whatever you decide to do, and wherever this path takes you. You took steps when no one believed you could. You can do it again. This time I will be there to hold your hand just like dad did so many years ago.

I want to be the one to rub "the cramps" out of your life now. I know I told you to marry him. Maybe that was not the best mother advice. I ask your forgiveness. Mamas just do their best. I know you are protecting your children just as I tried to protect you.

Love, mom

Susie • 1990 Awful

Just one word: *Awful*.

Amidst awards and accolades, 1990 was an awful year. A fire. A marriage abandoned. Exchanges made for emotional and physical well-being. Protecting those loved dearly. Mistakes made. Lessons learned. Patience. A time filled with beginnings.

I was strong, dependable, well-respected in my field and loved dearly. No one could take this away from me. My work with people showed them I cared about their welfare. I would shield good actors from bad ones who ridiculed by others to build themselves up. I would help the underappreciated ones.

Sometimes standing up for nurses brings repercussions. I would go to battle to protest nurses harassed by administrators. This position was a lonely place because others shied away from getting involved or taking any responsibility. I took an unpopular but truthful position when nurses not worthy of recommendation for promotion did not get my support. Both administrative actions had their backlash. Others' jealousy, anger, revenge, and retaliation shadowed my days.

Mama said, "Always have compassion for those people who never have felt loved as a child." She said, "People are shaped by their childhoods. Learn that people may put others through pain because of their own inside suffering. Without intending to, we have all hurt one another. It is important to forgive others and ourselves."

Mama also said, "Never let someone's anger change your behavior. Lead with your smile. Touch with your understanding. Remember you always choose who you want to be. Some people cannot help being drawn back into the pain of their childhoods. They never let old resentments and behaviors go. You cannot change that. Be sympathetic to the pain others feel. Know their fright underlies their anger and revenge. But go on."

Overloaded with responsibilities, I *hit the polio wall* every evening and fell asleep early—way before my children, with a book on my face. I made a point to take more naps. I figured out less steps to get stuff done. The house was not as clean. My car went a year without washing. The garden shriveled and became compost. I leaned on friends who cared. Although, physically, I knew no time without pain and fatigue, I was present for the people dependent on me. *I used my voice.*

Susie • 1990s-2000s

The path we walk in life defines who we are. Like others, the circumstances of polio shaped my personality: isolation, physical and emotional losses, long term consequences of viral damage, family expectations, coping mechanisms, and reactions of the community of people around me. I found meaning in nursing.

The polio experience gave me deep-seated hope along with a smile. I was optimistic, followed the rules, controlled my feelings, and went the extra mile to become educated and overachieve. These characteristics fed into becoming good at the skills required of a nurse.

Critical care was a place demanding strict adherence to protocols. Through teaching critical care nursing, I could follow science-based inquiry, teach procedural competency, and demonstrate compassion. As a nurse administrator, I could be a leader who supported team members to be the best they could be. These nursing roles came quite naturally to me. Polio set me up to be a good performer. I was surprised how much I loved the role of the nurse, educator, and administrator.

Polio gave me the foundation to be the nurse who understood that bringing a brightness to dire patient circumstances mattered. As a young child, I was so very wary of "The White Coats." I found that nurses who smiled and made caring gestures to me as a patient (even if unspoken) led to me feeling less scared amidst the cacophony of the polio ward. Those facing critical illness need nurses to be beacons that light their way when overwhelmed just as I was as a child.

The positive spirited polio survivor nurse: Polio planted a smile on my face and ingrained in me a cheerful outlook which reinforced me connecting with patients and families in an agreeable manner. Approaching patients and their families with confidence, empathy, and reasonable expectations was key.

No matter how dismal the conditions patients and families face, greeting them with a smile that welcomes interaction helps people feel a human connection. Sometimes the only uplifting words I could say were, "Can I get you a cup of coffee?" or "Is there someone I can phone for you?" or "I will sit with you." Connection even without words helps people cope.

Being positive has benefits beyond the immediate interaction. Studies show that nurses forging a good relationship with people, helps patients heal. Patients who feel that their healthcare worker is an ally in their struggle produce immune cells that increase healing.

A nurse coming into a room with pain medication and offering a positive message that the drug will work such as, "I have something that will help you," gives a patient the expectation that the pill will bring relief. Studies have shown that this affirmative statement may reduce pain by over twenty percent which may equal what an eight-milligram tablet of morphine might accomplish, but without the opioid drug's side effects.

The nurse also gains from adopting an agreeable demeanor. Researchers report nurses feel better about their job and experience less emotional exhaustion when they are optimistic, positive thinkers. A cheerful disposition helps a nurse perform in ways that increase efficiency and performance while at the same time improving patient satisfaction. Studies report that patients and their loved ones do less well when their caregiver is stressed and angry.

In The Descent of Man published in 1871, **Charles Darwin** proposed that human survival is dependent on kindness. The author argued that being *kind* was more important than being *fit*. In other words, being responsive to other people's needs, showing empathy and compassion are vital to the health and well-being of society. We live less well without kindness.

Being a child who had polio, I learned to appreciate kind people. I carry those who were kind to me within me as part of my character. The nurse down the block who befriended Mama. Max, the chiropractor, who would not take payment from two young parents strapped for money. The drill team coach who cared more about being kind than winning competitions. The Latin teacher who encouraged me believing I could accomplish something no one else had done before. The math teacher who told me to wear the letter for swimming I earned. The university instructors who believed I could be a good nurse by playing to my strengths of organization, scholarship and caring. Nuns who trusted me, though very young, to teach their nursing students critical care nursing.

We have an ongoing conversation in our household about the difference between being a "nice" person and being a "kind" one. My thesis is that while a person may be nice which implies being congenial, politically correct, and friendly, these qualities do not necessarily translate into the person being kind. *Kind* takes *nice* a further step. It requires movement, i.e., acting in a compassionate way toward others.

The nice person may look upstanding in the neighborhood, community, or professional arena. But when asked: "What has the nice person done for others?" the person who is nice but not kind may come up short of a list. What you do for others counts.

The kind person acts for the benefit of someone else. Going from nice to kind requires movement from a focus on self to an extension of oneself to meeting a need of another. I wish the word "kind" —which in Middle English referred to a person who was 'benevolent" —would be a verb—an action word.

Research shows that nurses who are kind may set in motion good feelings and healing. Studies demonstrate that healthcare given with kindness leads to a decrease in pain, an increase in immune function, lowering of high blood pressure and decreased anxiety. In addition, patients treated with kindness heal faster.

The organized, overachiever polio survivor nurse: Polio developed in me the ability to organize to save energy. I had to always be cognizant of my limited strength and my tendency to become fatigued. I had to accomplish tasks in the most efficient ways. Developing time-saving systems helped me not only at the bedside but also as a Director of Nursing, administrator, and nurse educator.

Every step I took always counted for my health. Keeping in mind exactly where every medical supply was stored on a unit enabled me to be a nurse who was timely in getting patients their medications. Memorizing what was in each drawer of the emergency crash cart saved looking through drawers when a code was in progress.

Creating schematics of buildings and noting where infections were popping up, sent me to bedsides to figure out what was happening to make patients sick. Sometimes it was staff technique. In other instances, how people transported equipment into a patient room and by whom mattered most. I looked at traffic from visitors and auxiliary personnel including maintenance staff. This contact tracing paid off by preventing new cases and hospitalizations and saving organizations money. Good nursing affects the bottom line.

I was making my own pencil and paper spreadsheets with boxes to check off patient treatments and medications when **Dan Bricklin** creator of the first electronic spreadsheet, was just a kid. (Thank you, press operators at the *Milwaukee Journal* for all the leftover scratch paper which allowed me to practice drawing patterns.) Using these "pictures" of tasks allowed me to memorize and cluster my work to prevent fatigue for both the patient and me.

Bricklin noted in an interview, "I came out of the word processing and typesetting worlds, where every keystroke counted." I came out of polio where every step I needed to take counted. I checked off completed nursing care on my handmade sheets like I had done as a child with the chores lists my dad made for me. I saved steps. Serendipitously, this gave me more time to listen to patients.

There is value to being organized. Research reveals that people who plan, make lists, and get to their appointments on time have lower levels of cortisol (stress hormone) and are less likely to have heart attacks. Being organized can lead to improved sleep and productivity.

The listening helper polio survivor nurse*:* My early polio isolation hospital experience gave me time to listen in silence while taking in what was going on around me. Sounds of sadness became familiar to me. I could hear the child in the next bed roll over and sense him hiding his tears before the sobbing began. I was familiar with the dense, heavy feeling of anxiety accompanying the contagiousness of despair and the quickened footsteps of the nurses scurrying to another emergency.

Polio gave me confidence that people could survive traumatic situations. I became a nurse who did not look away when circumstances became frightening. I knew I would walk through them and come out okay. I became a nurse who believed that, despite the horror of disease, people could become well.

My love of patients and their families was endless because I had been in their situation. Like them, I lived not knowing what would come next. Because I knew polio affected our whole family, I became a nurse who listened to the stories of not only patients but also their family members and other loved ones.

My parents and brother had their own personal stories from polio. Disease of one member of a family affects each person in that family in a unique way. I had the experience of a sick child. I surreptitiously watched how my mother coped. I felt my dad's gentle hands and breath as he coached and guided me. I knew my brother as someone who I could always count on to support me through the polio experience.

Polio trained me to wait patiently. Sometimes my voice was still, and I just sat beside patients and family members in quiet until conversation was a place we together could comfortably enter.

So often when something bad happens, a friend or family member will say, "Well I remember when a similar thing happened to me." or "That would never happen to my child because my kid doesn't party like yours," and go on to tell their story.

Interviews with people who have faced loss indicate that telling your own story to someone experiencing current tragedy does not help make their situation feel better. When coming to grips with unbearable torment, those facing loss say they do not want to hear how someone else dealt with similar adversity.

Those who grieve want others to walk softly beside them. Someone else's story just does not matter at this point in time. Studies have shown that sitting down beside the person, saying nothing, and just listening is more comforting.

Some people find it uncomfortable to be present in silence with another person. But sitting in quietness and showing you care enough to put your own world aside and just be with that person, connects people.

As a Clinical Nurse Specialist for death and spiritual care, my days would be long and stretch into the evenings and night. I sat with the dying and their families with only the sounds of the ventilator swishing air in and out, and the IV pump beeping intermittently amidst whispers of conversation of comfort and consolation.

I was cautious about overtaking the dying or loved one's personal space. My polio experience ingrained in me a fear of people unknown to me touching me. As a child, I would withdraw when a stranger came too close to me.

As a nurse who had experienced as a child the loneliness of isolation along with the confusion of being groped by strangers, I followed the research evidence telling caregivers how to respect boundaries. I always say, "Tell me." when I want to know the wishes of patients and loved ones left behind. "Would a hug be comforting?" I ask before embracing. A reassuring or consoling pat along the outside edges of a person's body—the back, shoulder or outside of an arm— are respectful ways of touching.

I also led with respectful silence. An old story describes people who purposely come to meetings chewing on seeds. Why so? Because having seeds in one's mouth, forces a person to take a bit of time to clear the mouth before speaking. This gap provides the brain a filter of time to think before their words spill out saying something regrettable.

Americans overall are speedy talkers, pausing on average only one and one-half seconds in conversation before saying something to fill the gap of quiet. We tend to start to talk before hearing the end of the previous speaker's words. Talking over the last part of a previous speaker's sentence demonstrates not fully listening.

Closing one's eyes and being silent can be a good thing because it creates space in which to consider what the person who just spoke means. Silence is speech and can speak volumes.

How patients when hospitalized in critical care and their family members voice their needs was the focus of my first research. The memory of voices of children and parents crying in the isolation hospital was permanent. I carry with me the fear of being alone. When these same emotions punctuated the lives of those for whom I cared as a critical care nurse, I was ready to study what nurses could do to make the critical care experience less traumatizing. (*Heart & Lung, The Journal of Critical Care* published study findings.)

The times when I moved outside my body into a spiritual world while as a young child in the isolation hospital primed me to listen to patients' stories and take their concerns seriously. Because I took the time to stay a bit and talk with patients after they experienced cardiopulmonary resuscitation, I could confirm for patients they were not alone in describing a realm not recognized by everyone.

My second research project reported patient stories of near-death experiences after cardiopulmonary resuscitation. (*The International Journal of Near-Death Studies* noted study findings, using the Greyson scale.)

The performer polio survivor nurse: Living with the sequalae of polio, led me to choose to first nurse in an open-heart surgical intensive care unit (ICU) for patients ranging from infants to age eighty. A twelve-foot by twelve-foot cubicle around each patient gave me a small space in which to do monitoring and care. This limited the walking I needed to do.

The unit had twelve beds arranged in sets of four around a central nursing station. When I supervised, the walking was not fatiguing because the size of the unit was small. The atmosphere of camaraderie and support helped keep my pain in control. I was fortunate that the head nurse and surgeons smiled often and voiced support for every nurse who worked there.

The excitement of working in intensive care fed my desire for achievement, while giving me opportunity to help patients, family members, my team, and students. I often presented my research about the needs of patients and their families in ICU and the near-death event reports of patients undergoing CPR.

I later moved on to working in a medical coronary intensive care unit (CCU) where the set-up also involved less walking than on a ward. The CCU consisted of four rooms surrounding a central nursing station where monitors relayed information from each room to a nurse's desk. Either I would be in the room with one to two patients or at the station sitting observing screens, charting, and making calls.

My critical care background brought me my first educator job. Sister Myra tapped me on the back as I stared at a computer at the CCU station and asked me to meet her for lunch the next day. Actually, she *directed* me to do so.

Sister Myra told me straight out that she wanted nursing students enrolled in the diploma program at the hospital run by the Sisters of St Mary to learn critical care nursing. The nuns were originally from Germany, first based in the United States in St. Louis Missouri and later in Wisconsin. Sister Myra said she needed me to give up my staff role and teach student nurses.

I began teaching at age 25, with a baby cared for by a friend when I had students learning in the ICU unit, or by Sister Myra when I lectured. This combination of teaching wherein walking was in a confined space and interspersed with breaks to review care with students allowed me to remain energetic. I was beginning to think Sister Myra had connections.

I relied on my study of curriculum and instruction methods in graduate school to help me figure out how I was going to prepare clinical experiences and lectures. Sister Myra gave me only a two-week advance timetable along with the words, "You can do it!"

Fortunately, university coursework gave me the tools I needed. I could apply **Abraham Maslow**'s hierarchy of needs, **Howard Gardner**'s theory of multiple intelligences, **Viktor Frankl**'s understanding of each person's search for meaning in life, and **Bruno Bettelheim's** message about leading with your heart to capture students' enthusiasm for learning the care of patients who unexpectedly land in a coronary care intensive care unit.

General and former **President Dwight D. Eisenhower** demonstrated the art of leadership with a simple piece of string. Pull it and it will follow wherever you wish. Push it and it will go nowhere at all. It is also this way when it comes to instructing students. I followed educator, **John Dewey**'s principle that teaching is about motivating students to become capable of processing and applying current information. Believe in students and learning will follow.

UW-Madison School of Nursing faculty members **Nancy Diekelmann, Karen Pridham, Margaret Williams, Margaret DuRose, David Allen**, and **Barbara Gessner**, demonstrated the role of teacher was to advise and inspire. Their collective vision of faculty as guides rather than critics was critical to my growth as an educator. I hope I have passed forward their understanding and compassion.

Students were quick to learn from the mini-lectures I gave them when we rounded seeing patients on the unit. They grasped the gravity of how both the demeanor and the performance of a nurse affected patient recovery. We all worked hard together. I encouraged them to make notecards so they would gradually build a file of key points for taking care of people in critical care.

I loved teaching students to consider the waterfall of emotions patients felt when first rolled into an intensive care unit and the importance of staying in dialogue with patients about their recovery goals. The nurse giving person-centered care makes a difference.

We know patients and their family members benefit when they participate in care choices and therapies that reflect their conditions, beliefs, values, lifestyles, and resources. There is a better chance patients stick with health treatments if they have picked ones that are compatible with their likes and dislikes and means both money-wise and people available for support.

It wasn't rocket science to go from teaching students to helping staff nurses and auxiliary healthcare personnel when I worked in administrative roles as Director of Nursing or Administrator for a continuum of care. Just as nurses always assess patients and their families before developing a care plan, I knew I had to first understand the people I supervised and take their personal skills and preferences into account.

I was fortunate to meet exceptional colleagues who shared with me their current practice. They were wise in their understanding that patients' medical needs and health goals varied according to the individuals having the illnesses. They took the time to listen to people. This consistently paid off because care plans became not just written documents but realistic pathways outlining what worked and what did not work to help patients achieve wellness.

Not all nurses had the same training and background. Some were licensed as practical nurses. Others held diploma or associate degrees. A few graduated from Baccalaureate schools. It didn't matter. What made the difference was knowing that whatever your strengths or weaknesses, we would be working as a team. No one needed to know it all or be able to do it all. Our meeting together to evaluate situations was critical.

There were certified nursing assistants who amazingly could understand the particular meaning of the two syllables a man with dementia would make. He repeated the sounds with varying cadence and tone. That is all he spoke. Listening and tracking when the patient uttered the syllables led nursing assistants to the discovery that the man had his own language. Their knowledge did not come from books. It was born of caring. With all my university training, I could not translate the man's utterances into any meaning. They could and did.

Anxiety associated with being unable to perform one's own hygiene is universal. People at end of life often label this loss of dignity as the final straw that overwhelms them. Many describe it as a space so cavernous they do not even want to try anymore. And they give up on life. You've heard someone say, "When I cannot get to the pot myself, I'm done."

When bathing assistants asked patients what made them most comfortable and less embarrassed when they had their baths, the people told them. They wanted individualized routines that ensured safety and a bit of privacy. They did not want bath time to be a cold, rushed event. A warm towel. Soft music in the background. Lavender scents. These touches did not cost much and brought joy to patient faces.

When bathing assistants said they wanted to start their shift at four-thirty in the morning, I asked why. Looking around they said, "See all the people who used to live on farms and got up early to milk cows. They want early baths simply because that is when they have been waking up for decades." This city girl with graduate school education could not think of that on her own.

Bathing assistants replaced old routines that did not fit the patients' needs with what did. They designed a system with individual options through listening to the patients they served and re-arranging their schedules.

I knew my advanced degrees might seem threatening to staff members. In the beginning, I needed to explain my teamwork philosophy. Polio taught me you could have weaker parts thrown into a good system and maintain orderliness and success. The sum was greater than the parts. The situation now was just like when my brother Mike taught me that being good at making free throw shots on a basketball team made up for my not being able to run fast. I reinforced the value of everyone's efforts.

Some nurses were better at planning and paperwork. Others were more proficient interpersonally and skills wise at the bedside. If I lined them up, I knew I would not be accurate at telling the education level of the nurse by their performance.

One thing they held in common: They all were kind and willing to do their part. Once staff got to know me, they relaxed in knowing that I did not expect each nurse to be the best at everything. If a nurse could not place an intravenous line, I could step up and do it. Nurses called me in the evenings and in the middle of the night if they needed help.

Staff nurses were not shy about pulling me out of my office to assist them to solve putting a puzzle of dressings and ointments together for a newly arrived patient. My designing of patterns for clothes came in handy. Some wounds frankly were shockingly intricate with pathways we had to explore with long Q-tips to gauge their depth. My not backing off and helping with the worst wounds came from the resilience I learned making it through my childhood hospital experiences. Healing was a vision I embraced instead of giving up hope.

One Fall evening, a patient smashed a window on a patient unit. I heard the glass breaking in the background through the phone when a nurse called me at home. I drove to the care facility to take the pressure off the nurses who had plenty to do without this interruption.

Nurses told me the background of the patient's complaints. He agreed to walk with me to my office where I told him I needed his help to read papers. I turned on a metronome, gave him his own medical chart and we each read in silence. He calmed down by the time the paramedics came to transfer him. The five minutes that passed seemed like an exceedingly long time.

The tall, large paramedics strapped the patient onto the gurney. I felt weighed down by a moment of anguish that I was sending the patient to an unfamiliar place that might frighten him. Then he joked with the ambulance crew that their purple latex gloves reminded him of bruises he gave his wife. A nurse standing next to me felt my angst and said softly, "You did the right thing." This was a team effort for everyone's safety. I knew we could not save them all…even from themselves.

There were people who outpowered me. Dealing with the bosses who bullied and higher echelon administrators who took advantage of workers or students of little means to defend themselves, was an on-the-job education I never expected to need. *I used my voice.*

Both men and women preyed on nurses. Words of a man: "Everything will be all right if you just come for cocktails with me." Translation: If you are *nice* to me, I will let your project go forward." As an administrator, I took steps others refused to take to protect nurses who reported being inappropriately pressured, touched, or trapped in rooms and stairwells with men. Observing personnel in a human resource department turn a blind eye to misdeeds to protect their own jobs, I took my mama's advice to never let the bad behavior of others change my own. No longer did I say, *"I will not tell." I used my voice.*

Veteran nurses who had done things only their way for way too long preyed on younger nurses with novel ideas that actually worked better at getting things done. One head nurse complained that a male ICU nurse was wearing his name badge in the middle of his chest, not according to uniform protocol. She wanted him disciplined.

Because I experienced being trapped in a hospital bed where seeing a kind face up close was comforting, I realized that the well-being of patients in an ICU would be improved when they did not have to strain to see the name of the nurse giving care. Familiarity brings comfort. My Dad putting his face close to mine so I would know from the isolation crib he was there beside me made the place less lonesome. All patients deserved this connection with their caregivers and loved ones.

I used my voice. I had a discussion with the head nurse who sought conformity and did not want the nurse to place his badge where ICU patients could best see it. The nurse was told he could wear his name badge centered on his uniform. He was a smart, efficient, caring nurse and more well-liked by patients than the head nurse.

Standing up against unfair and disrespectful working conditions, increasing of patient to staff ratios, and the cutting of funding for education classes essential for keeping nurses up to date did not always bring justice. In such circumstances, nurses vote with their feet. We leave jobs when administrators sweep bad situations under the rug, and do not make wrongs right, And why not? There are always job opportunities for nurses. Helping staff find new jobs because they felt demeaned and threatened was part of the role I chose to embrace. My community ties brought nurses new opportunities. *I used my voice.*

Being good to nurses happens to be financially profitable. Nursing care improves patient outcomes. Hospitals may be fined for care that leads to patients picking up added illness during their stays. Having a stable and competent nursing staff reduces patient mortality.

For every patient on a hospital nurse's caseload over four, the mortality rate increases. You want a nurse taking care of you who can eyeball subtle cues to avoid mishaps and catch problems before they become disasters. You want a nurse who makes you feel comfortable and supports you to meet your personal healthcare goals.

It is the responsibility of every person who seeks healthcare to treat workers with respect and dignity. Communities cannot survive without nurses. But not all believe that yet.

The staff I led dedicated themselves to group success. Hiring pool nurses (temporary, highly paid staff) stopped at facilities when I became an administrator because regular staff were committed to work the hours to produce the good outcomes we were achieving. It was less stressful for a nurse to continue in a position where they were confident the nurse before them did a respectable job, thus preparing the way for a nonchaotic shift.

I talked to each nursing staff member about my unwritten memo: If you need a day off because you feel you do, call me so I can arrange someone to take your shift. Nurses appreciated a boss who understood that when bedside staff were stressed, they were the best judge that taking time off was appropriate. I took the grace given me by others and tried to give it back through little measures like coaching, praising, and expressing, in frequent personal written notes to nursing and auxiliary staff, my thankfulness for the care they gave. Nurses can better rejuvenate their compassion when supervisors honor their work. Organizations recruited me because being kind helped an organization's bottom line.

Likewise in the educational arena, I knew students became stronger when faculty would create an environment where the teacher talked with students individually, and created space where students felt comfortable asking questions. An educational system that supported varied paces and levels of learning bankrolled students graduating with strong nursing toolboxes.

Nursing is not only a science, but also is an art. Nurses listen to patients and their family members, so they feel heard. Apart from administering therapies based on evidence-based science (which grows and changes over time), nurses know if we take away some loneliness and grief, we are helping heal. Nurses give people a space where they feel accepted and respected without judgment. This does not mean we necessarily agree with them. But nurses can move patients from that terribly lonely place to a seat at the table where their voices are heard, and they find their rightful place as human beings.

Nurses have opportunity to let their own individuality interact with the patient. It starts with just a smile, a touch of the hand reaching out to help, eyes meeting, intentional silence and listening, giving knowledge, sharing understanding, the offering of options, the allowing of choice, and talking over what works and what does not work for the individual. Not many careers offer an opportunity to allow one's individuality to interact so deeply with another. *This dance of souls is the art of nursing.*

My informal role in the community teaching about spiritual nursing care issues and my Clinical Nurse Specialist work for the dying and those who were experiencing loss and grief at a large metropolitan hospital, led me to continue speaking at local and national conferences to nurses, doctors, paramedics, and lay people. This gave me opportunity to spread the word about what patients reported happened to them when healthcare professionals performed cardiopulmonary resuscitation.

Paramedics (both local and national responding to domestic terrorism), doctors, and nurses wanted to know what patients said happened to them during times of emotional and/or physiological stress. Conferees shared their stories. Listening to healthcare responders who had an inkling of what was going on and just needed someone to confirm for them the **out-of-body experiences** those near death or psychological trauma report was rewarding.

Doctors, nurses, first responders, and other frontline healthcare workers believed patients' stories. One doctor recalled his story of collapsing with a heart attack while on rounds. He handed me a sketch depicting his **out-of-body experience**. The doctor said he came back into his body from a high corner of the room where he was watching staff resuscitating him. His wife entered the room and shouted his name. The doctor said he was drawn back into his body by her calling him. He vowed he would in the future always call a patient by name when doing CPR.

An editor and publisher who attended a hospital forum where I retold patient experiences asked to meet with me. Although the focus of this publisher's work was on local history and flora, he requested that I write a book about the stories I was reporting.

Being frank about how I did not have a lot of spare time to author a book, I explained to the publisher how pain and fatigue intertwined in my life. Because of these, I had to pace my activities. To deal with the various outcomes of polio required time. Overdoing brought more pain and increased risk for falls.

I told him that my daily life had a rhythm. It required time to swim every other day. I was already working extra shifts to help finance two children in college. I was saying "no" to proposals of marriage not wanting to become the housekeeper for anyone again. Rest periods were essential to my well-being. I was worried the pressure of writing a book would interfere in getting the naps I needed.

The publisher thought outside-the-box. "How about if you just send me one story at a time?" he suggested. I still envision today the old desk where I would sit down when I had time to write up a story for the publisher who was a very, patient and understanding man. It was his kindness of collating, designing, and editing that produced my first book.

Not long after Final Entrance: Journeys Beyond Life came out, the publisher phoned me. His wife had died unexpectedly. We met because he wanted to talk over what happened. He said, "Now I truly know why I was drawn to publish your work. It is helping me grieve in a positive way." What the man gained in understanding made my time authoring the book worthwhile. Throughout my life with polio, I had read extensively to distract from pain. Now my writing was helping someone find comfort.

Polio ingrained in me performing. Mimicking my high school leadership of clubs, I became president of the university's chapter of Sigma Theta Tau, the National Honor Society for Nurses. I started a local chapter of the International Association for Near-Death Studies. I volunteered as program director for the Northwest Association of Death and Bereavement, a group of professional grief workers.

Each nursing experience led me to a better understanding of human nature and myself. If reading how circumstances around polio molded my life causes you to pause and reflect on how happenstance or destiny steered your path, so be it. I have a mantra: *Be grateful. Hold onto what is good. Let go of the rest.*

Sometimes You Vaccinate for Others

In 1990, a measles outbreak spawned more than 27,000 cases throughout the United States. Public health historians attributed the outbreak in part to public health budget cuts that decreased access to immunizations.

I was caring for a population of young men who survived motor vehicle accidents. Each suffered extensive spinal cord injuries which cause immunosuppression leaving them vulnerable to infection. Due to a complex biochemical reaction occurring within patients with acute spinal cord injury, measles can be life-threatening for this group.

Measles is highly contagious. The virus may stay in the air even though the person emitting it has left the space hours before. Nine out of ten unimmunized children who are in contact with the measles virus will contract the disease.

Common complications of measles are diarrhea, vomiting, ear and eye infections, laryngitis, and pneumonia. One out of every twenty children developing measles moves on to get pneumonia, which is the most common cause of death from measles in the young.

Encephalitis (brain swelling) occurs in about one in 1,000 children who come down with measles. Inflammation of the brain may lead to seizures. It follows that a child may incur deafness or an intellectual disability. Measles kills on average one to three out of every one thousand of the unimmunized.

Hospital administrators requested measles titers on nurses caring for this vulnerable population of patients. My level was on the low side of normal. I had a choice. I took a measles booster vaccination.

Paradoxically, I am one of those people with spinal cord injuries who face bouts of an autoimmune disorder triggered by a variety of factors, one of which may be adjuvants in vaccinations. Adjuvants are substances that strengthen a vaccine, creating a more robust response. Within 16-18 hours of vaccinations, I get chills, shivering, body aches, and a spike in temperature. My spine aches. By the next day, my ability to walk is adversely affected. I am careful to schedule vaccinations to allow my body three days to rest and recover. I realize that the vaccinations give my body the best protection against spreading a disease. In this case, I was upping my game to protect the patients.

Most young men on the unit had tracheostomies and/or were on ventilators and had feeding tubes and intravenous lines. Nursing care was extensive and delivered in a small space at the bedside. My assignment to those with the most critical time-intensive needs met both the needs of patients and my own.

What I learned from going through polio was helpful for these people who like me had damaged nerves. Nonventilated patients would comment that seeing me limping around their bedside gave them hope of resuming a productive life despite their injuries. Patients opened up to me. They poured out their feelings of frustration. They knew it was okay to ask me any potentially embarrassing question because I was like them and knowledgeable and willing to relate to their angst.

These experiences were a reminder of my unchosen but circumstantial place in the stream of life. I had no control over my early life events. I paused, realizing my polio experience prepared me well to help these young men. I am grateful.

I chose to get the measles booster shot for the well-being of others. It was a reminder that life is full of adversity that can unite us should we choose.

Sometimes disease can be a gift.

Al • 1997

Margie and I arrived at the giant bookstore where the publisher of The Final Entrance arranged for Susie to do a book reading and signing event. She was on a book tour of the state.

Margie was nervous. She had a drink before we left. She dressed up in a suit she used to wear when she worked. I wore a suit and tie. People had already grabbed the front row chairs at the talk. Margie and I stood along the side so we could see Susie at the podium.

Susie was our book kid. On summer days, when the neighborhood children were running through sprinklers, she nestled under the tree in our front yard reading. Since her legs couldn't always keep up with the other kids, she found some of her friends in books.

It was Margie who gave Susie the love of reading. She would put her in the stroller and head to the library once a week. They would return with the stroller piled high with books. We did not have a bookshelf. Susie kept the books under the couch.

On days when her pain was bad, Susie would hang blankets from the laundry lines in the backyard to make a tent. There she spent the day surrounded by library books that connected her with people and places. Here, Susie read and took naps.

Early on winter mornings, I could always find Susie huddled against the warm air vent in the living room with her nose poked in a book. She never came to breakfast before stretching out to get her legs warmed up as the heat came upstairs from the furnace in the basement.

I think her memory of hospital staff ordering kids to stop crying influenced Susie to read. A book disturbed no one else. Susie hated when we had the volume of the home TV turned up high. I wonder if the TV blaring in the background reminded her of the noise of the iron lung and other hospital clatter she could not flee. She hated all the sarcastic remarks on comedy shows. I do not know whether this rowdy dialogue reminded her of kids disciplined by hospital staff. Susie liked all things quiet.

Susie could read when she was four years old. If you asked her what she wanted for a birthday or holiday present, she would tell you she wanted a book. She owned three during her childhood: Rebecca of Sunnybrook Farm, Daddy Long Legs, and The Poor Little Rich Girl. Although one might think Susie looked alone sprawled out reading in the yard during quarantine times, she wasn't. In every book, she met new people. She chattered on about them.

When Susie was eleven, Margie splurged buying a set of encyclopedias. We paid a little each month until we really owned them. We kept the books in a low nook outside Susie's bedroom so she could reach them without walking far.

To get away from the loud voices of Margie's family at holiday gatherings, Pa and Susie always snuck away from the table early, huddled together, and read. When Susie was little, Pa read to her. He also loved showing her maps and telling war stories.

Susie grew up wanting to hear about other people's worlds. I suppose that is why she listens to patients as a nurse. I know she is a good listener because this book she wrote is full of the real words of patients.

Susie once told me she thought the best way to teach nurses was by telling a story of how a disease affected a patient she had taken care of in the past. She said that once a student could imagine the face of an actual patient in their mind and hear their personal story, they could better remember the medical facts and practices related to the treatment of the patient and their disease.

Margie and I kept our copy of The Final Entrance centered on the coffee table in our living room. Many afternoons we would sit together, and she would read me a chapter or two. Margie and I cried when she read me the dedication. Susie had written it to Margie and me. That was Susie.

Susie never forgot us no matter where she traveled. She carried our pictures on a keychain around the world. Susie said it was not where you all traveled but what you learned about yourself on your journeys that counted in life. She said that going to places around the world helped her understand that people are alike in having strong feelings about family and traditions.

Marjorie Clare • 2000

Margie kept her feelings padlocked inside herself until she understood she was near dying. She sipped on a watered-down drink Al made her before he went to bed. Susie sat on the couch beside her.

As the sky darkened, there was a pause in the conversation and she asked in a soft voice, "Do you remember the closet in the old house?"

"Yes, Mama," Susie replied.

"I never meant to hurt you," Margie added, quickly looking away into the night beyond the panes of the patio doors.

"I know, Mama," Susie said, "I did not understand it when I was in the closet. I realized when I was older that polio was a challenging time. You were under a lot of pressure. There was no one but Dad for you to turn to when people were afraid of their children or themselves getting polio. When people are running on empty, dead-on-their-feet, they cannot present themselves at their best. Emotions become uncontrollable. People discharge their despair because folks do not have the capacity when so tired out to hold them in. Polio was the trigger."

Margie wanted to say more and continued, "I was scared and very tired all the time. People talked about us behind our backs. Ma was saying I was a bad mother because you got polio. She believed I was not keeping the house clean enough. I loved you even though I didn't always show it."

"Whenever the health department came to put up a quarantine sign, I thought the nurses might take you. I never knew what might happen when I saw that Milwaukee County Health Department car pull up. I would not answer the doorbell. I know that was wrong, but I did not want them to carry you away."

Susie grabbed her mother's hand rubbing it while she said, "Mama, we all survived polio—you, Dad, Mike, and me. I learned things from having polio that helped me be a more understanding nurse. I recognized parents of sick and dying kids in the intensive care unit (ICU) were shocked, concerned, and scared like you."

"Working in the ICU, I saw how hard it was for many parents to get near and touch their sick child. With so many tubes, wires, and unfamiliar sounds all around them, children's parents stood afraid and motionless. I would drag over chairs for them to sit down at the bedside and place their child's hand in theirs. When possible, I would take their infant out of the incubator and hold it near to them. Sometimes words seemed out of place. In a cavern of silence around the bedside, the language was tears."

"Parents who are afraid their child might be taken from them often put up emotional and physical barriers. What you did mama is what lots of other people do when faced with loved ones who are ill or dying. You did just fine."

"I met parents in the emergency room as they were told their child had died. All that happened to me because of polio helped me understand and stand quietly beside them being respectful of their trauma. I let them choose when they wanted to talk. I realized watching you and Dad as I grew up that sickness of a child affects everyone in the family. Parents dread an ill child will worsen and die. To be told your son or daughter has died is the worst thing that can happen to a person."

"I remember waiting hours in a room off the emergency area for a mother to speak. Her infant died of sudden infant death syndrome (SIDS) while being cared for at a babysitter's house. The mother wailed, sobbed and when exhausted, whimpered. I stood by her side. I knew the things going through her head were yet unspeakable because saying them would make them real. I recognized those emotions we felt as a family churning inside of her…shock and numbness, guilt, and aloneness. I was patient. I kneeled on the floor and waited for the time when she could speak. Polio taught me you can help people by staying beside them while they process what has happened."

"Despite times when you could not get close to me, I knew you loved me, Mama. Understanding ways parents cope and grieve was a gift from our shared polio experience that I could use to support others to help them through similar tough times."

Marjorie Clare • 2001

I cannot eat much. Food disagrees with me. What's left of my stomach turns over and I get shooting pains. It is not worth dealing with how I feel after meals. I like to just sip a drink Al makes me.

I am looking forward to Susie visiting today. This weekend she worked extra shifts both Friday evening and Saturday, so she is coming to Milwaukee today. She always brings me fresh flowers and books. I tell her "You don't have to, Susie. Save your money to take care of your kids." But she has always been stubborn.

Susie thinks I do not see her sneak away when I close my eyes as I rest a bit on the couch. I can hear water running and clearly see the bathrooms and kitchen are sparkling after she has been here visiting. In the study, she carefully dusts Dad's beloved collection of statues that remind him of the places we have visited. She acts like I don't hear her. I say, "What a surprise!" Susie knows that having the house squeaky clean and in order makes me feel good. This is a game we play over and over to make each other feel better.

Susie encourages me to eat smaller meals six times a day after my stomach removal surgery. So, I nibble at this and that and don't eat too much that would start my stomach cramping. If it does, I have to take a few drops of paregoric. I get kind of tired after taking the medication, so I do not like to take it much. It's a game of chance. If I do not take enough, I feel sick to my stomach. When I take the medicine, I sometimes feel faint. I am not telling anyone about the dizziness. When Susie asks me, I tell her I am fine. Like daughter, like mother. Susie gives me iron shots to make me less tuckered out.

Every time she visits, Susie brings me tiny cream puffs. She bakes them and fills them with fake cream as the real stuff would be way too hard for my stomach to digest. She wraps each individually. I keep them in the freezer. In the middle of the night, I get up and eat one, sometimes two. Life goes by so fast. I taught her how to bake rolls. Now I am receiving the reward.

A couple of things have been bothering me. Last week, Mike had to carry me to the second floor because I felt too weak to walk up on my own. Al caught me by the arm before I would have fallen. I was tired after being out to the doctor's office for my blood test for atrial fibrillation. I wanted Mike to put me down, but there was no other way for me to get up the stairs. Problems going out or getting around the house are building up. I have lost control. *I must be in control.*

The *9/11* attack was so unexpected. "No one is safe," I told Al. "This is like the years when there was polio." I hope what Susie says about people leaving their bodies when in distress in motor vehicle crashes is true. I picture those who jumped from the burning towers watching themselves fall but feeling no pain because they were in another form somewhere else where we cannot see. My dreams are unsettling. I awaken with flashbacks to polio times. The world is out of control. *I must be in control.*

I am worried about my grandson who visited after being med-flighted back from Peace Corp volunteer work in Honduras. He stopped in to see Al and me on his way back to the village where he served. He stressed the villagers were not responsible for hurting him. The world is changing fast. A growing number of people harm others because their leaders say it is okay to do so. I told him to not change his behavior because others are corrupt. I hope I hid my tears when he hugged me to say good-bye just before leaving for the airport. I know I may not see him again. I respect his choice. Such a good boy.

I sent Susie on a mission to find words for my gravestone and for the message I want her to hand out at my funeral. Susie likes visiting graveyards. She sits on the grass in front of grave markers copying off inscriptions.

Late at night, when Al is asleep, Susie and I talk over the words she has found. Sometimes we get silly. Then we straighten up to the task. I have chosen what I want her to type up. The words make sense. I will say thanks to all who helped Al and me when the times were the toughest. Their faces are etched in my heart. I carry them with me.

Susie has a friend who volunteers at a women's shelter. I have clothes to donate. It is time to part with the toys I had set aside for great-grandchildren visits. I have kept a soccer ball my oldest grandchild gave me when he played professionally. He signed up with a team here in Milwaukee so we could see him play. Such a good boy. Time to pass it on to a child who needs it now. Susie will drop everything off on her way home. I want to feel like I can do something for someone else. My heart is not dead. My body is just weak.

My watch tells me Susie will be here soon. I haven't lost my marbles. When Al is scared, I am going downhill, he calls her to come. She can drive the seventy-five-mile trip in less than an hour. I have talked to her about this speeding. She needs to follow the law. I forgive her for this. Susie forgives me back for other stuff. We both know people do things others disapprove of and hurt each other without wanting to do so.

Al is talking in the hall with his friend the priest who went to seminary with Susie's priest friend. Father Joe will know when Susie arrives that she has been driving over the speed limit. *My fault. Everybody will talk about us. I must be in control.*

Al • 2001

Al was worried. Margie looked pale. Her breathing was punctuated by raspy sounds, and she was coughing blood into a handkerchief. He asked her how she felt. "Not too bad," Margie answered. He did not believe her.

That is the thing about love. You just never want it to end. Margie and Al had been together sixty years since their meeting at the Eagles Club.

Margie sat on the couch staring at, not really watching the TV program. Al got up, kissed her lightly on the forehead and asked if he could get her something. Margie could have asked for the moon and Al would have tried to get her a piece.

Margie ate little at dinner. Al had warmed up leftovers in the microwave. They dined at a favorite restaurant the evening before. Margie had eaten only a few bites of food that night. Al carried the rest home for her and placed it in the refrigerator with other cartons of half-eaten food. This sparse consumption on Margie's part was becoming a pattern over the last year. Margie would agree to go out to meet Al's need to socialize and dine on a variety of foods, but she had no energy to eat an entire meal. Al wanted to treat Margie like the queen she was to him. He realized she was too tired to cook meals. When he saw before him the downhill trajectory of her energy level and health, he became scared.

No one could blame Al. He could not imagine life without Margie. It is a trauma of the aging that loved ones must face watching a beloved's light dim and their strength diminish all while the dying try with courage to protect the feelings of the ones who they will leave behind. Trying to hold onto our loved one when the inevitable end of this life is near is an instinctive reaction to anticipated loss.

Al could see Margie was becoming too skinny. Although Margie was five feet six inches tall, she weighed only seventy-eight pounds. This was her weight the last time Susie came into town to take her mother to the doctor. Al thought Margie could have lost even more weight by now.

Margie told Al she asked Susie to accompany her for her next medical check-up. She said that the doctor did not listen to her at her most recent appointment when she went alone.

Al knew when he went into the bedroom in the evening that Margie and Susie would stay up in the living room talking at length while he slept. He knew that Margie told Susie stuff she did not tell anyone else.

He did not hear Margie when she told Susie she wanted someone to come into the home to help her with bathing. This help would ease her shortness of breath. Not being able to catch her breath was scary. She would get dizzy. Margie worried about falling over. They agreed hospice care was the inevitable next step. She was saddened and afraid to break the news to Al.

Al was not surprised that Margie wanted Susie to go to the doctor with her. He knew it was always difficult for Margie to ask for the things she wanted from others. Al was good at knowing her needs. He understood her reluctance to ask for help. It all went back to the circumstances of Margie's early life being the one responsible to help care for her eight younger siblings. Al watched Margie do so much for others and ask so little for herself. Margie was no different than most of us who drag our childhoods with us.

Margie's medical appointment did not go as planned. The doctor at first did not agree that Margie was ready for hospice care. He smiled at Margie and declared loudly to Susie, "Your mother will live a long time."

He was a doctor who could only deliver good news, Susie thought. He was not listening. Susie spoke up. She told the doctor she had witnessed a change in her mother's spunk, her inability to walk more than ten feet without resting, the anxiety provoked by her mother's air hunger, and an increased rapidness in her mother's breathing pattern. She asked the doctor if he could look at her mother's ankles which were swollen with fluid. She questioned the doctor about her mother's weight loss, which the doctor said he had not realized. A nurse weighed Margie at the start of the appointment.

Susie listened to her mother's statement that she was tired and done trying. In contrast, the doctor talked over Margie's soft voice saying she was so very exhausted she did not want to go on. The doctor replied, with a cheery, "Oh, she is doing fine!"

When the doctor moved away to the computer to enter notes, Margie nudged Susie's arm and whispered she wanted to leave the room. The doctor said he could not recommend hospice but would write a new prescription "to pep you up."

Waiting in the anteroom, Margie's eyes filled with tears. "You understand I am so tired that I cannot keep going on. Why doesn't he help me?" Susie got up and went to talk to the nurse. Serendipitously, the nurse at the desk had read The Final Entrance and knew of Susie's nursing work. Five minutes later, the nurse came out of the doctor's office carrying a prescription for hospice care. With one phone call, a hospice assessment was set up.

Al watched as Margie declined more. Her gait faltered. He saw her place her hands on the walls to try and balance herself going down the hallway. Then the national *9/11* event came. Margie's inner spirit weakened.

Al saw Margie's despondency deepen as she sipped on the watered-down drink that he made for her. He saw her staring blankly out the patio doors. Margie told Al she was worried for the world that the grandchildren would inherit. Al felt her sadness, went into the bedroom, and wept.

Then, one evening, Margie fell. Al tried to pick her up, but he could not. Al did what he always did in emergency situations. He picked up the phone and called Susie who said she would change clothes and drive to Milwaukee.

Ten minutes went by as Susie got ready. As she had her hand on the doorknob to leave, the phone rang again. Al said, "Your mother wants to talk to you, Susie."

Margie's voice was clear. "Do not come this time, Susie. I am in bed. I do not want you to come this time. I can make this decision." Susie remembered her agreement with her Mama that no longer accepting medical therapy was her mother's choice alone.

Al took the phone back and said he thought things looked okay. They agreed to talk the next day.

Susie • September 15, 2001

One evening shortly after 9/11, Dad called to tell me he needed my help with Mama. I quickly changed out of my pajamas. As I grabbed my car keys, the phone rang again. Mama was on the line. "Don't come this time," she said. "This time I am asking you to stay home. I am ready to go."

I listened to Mama. I could tell what she was thinking. For once, I did not go. But the next day I found it impossible to not make the drive to check on things. When I arrived, Mama had just been transported by ambulance to the hospital. Dad slouched back in a recliner. He was exhausted from the upheaval.

I let Dad rest. In the afternoon, we headed for the hospital. Dad turned on the TV in Mama's room. I pulled up a chair to the bedside so I could hear Mama's soft voice over the blaring noise. Mama as always, wanted me to give her news about each grandchild. Nurses came in and out adjusting IV rates.

Dad fell asleep in front of the TV. As evening approached and dusk darkened the sky outside the window, Mama looked over at him and asked me to drive him home. Taking care of each other was a hallmark of their marriage.

As I left the hospital room with Dad by my side, I whispered good-bye and hugged Mama. Along the way of the winding corridor, I stopped and directed Dad to use the bathroom before heading onto the highway. I pointed to the sign outside the men's room. I said, "Meet me here. Do not go anywhere else." Dad nodded in agreement.

I raced back to Mama's hospital room. I couldn't help but cry. I sat on the bed and lifted Mama into my arms. I said, "Mama, I love you so much and forever." Mama hugged me back as tightly as a seventy-eight-pound woman could and said, "I love you. I wish we could have given you more."

I replied, "But Mama, you gave me everything." Our tears overflowed mixing into comingled drops falling down on the two of us. A nurse stood by the bedside rubbing her damp eyes with a tissue. She looked downward trying to not intrude.

Leaving Mama was a hard thing to do. But I knew the best gift I could give her was control over her death. I understood that Mama always thought polio was her fault. I realized Mama never could erase the thought that people looked upon her as a mother who was not clean enough and did not protect her baby from the virus.

I wanted to give Mama the understanding that she was as good a mother as there could be. That is every mother's hope. As I clutched Mama's tiny body, I said, "But Mama, you gave me everything…everything I needed plus more."

I drove Dad home stopping to buy him his favorite take-out meal, a fish dinner with latkes. I baked homemade chocolate chip cookies using Mama's recipe and spices while Dad drank a beer and ate dinner. All was just as Mama wanted. I took over caring for Dad. Mama slipped quietly into death during the night.

I reminded myself that eternity is not something that comes later. We are all in it now. Mama's light and love abide within me.

Al • 2012

Margie always told me Susie was a daddy's girl. She would laugh and improvise the Cole Porter song and sing to me, *"Susie's heart belongs to daddy, Da, da, da, da, da, da, da, da, dad."*

I know Margie sang the song because she wanted me to feel good. I liked that Margie was happy when singing the song to me. She was sad that I was the one who always went to be with Susie at the hospital when she stayed at home with Mike. I told Margie we did our best because we worked together. I would sing her Gershwin's *"I got starlight and I have sweet dreams. Who could ask for anything more?"*

You get the life given you and carry it and learn as you go. My mother and brother dying didn't make me callous to the hurts of life. I became determined. I do believe: *No matter how hard it gets, you will survive. Feel sorrow and let it go. Keep reaching for your goal.*

Margie said I gave Susie her smile. But it was both of us who did. Margie did so many things like teaching Susie to read and sew. I told Margie that Susie loved us both the same.

I told Susie to smile big when I took her pictures. Susie would laugh when she was little and say, "I caught you smiling back!" When she smiled, my face lit up too.

I keep my favorite picture of Susie in my top dresser drawer. All I have to do is walk over to the window and hold it up to the light to remember that day. Susie was sitting on a bench by the shore of Lake Nokomis. Her polio leg was flopping over. She was smiling right at me. I remember that day.

Al

I miss Margie all the time. I kept two of Margie's sweaters. Susie put each in a plastic bag to lock in the scent of Margie. For a long time, I hid them in my lowest dresser drawer. The aroma made me cry. But a happy cry. Margie wore Tabu cologne. I would close each bag after feeling her presence and put the bags back in the drawer. Susie said people who find comfort taking in the familiar scent of their loved one after the person has died are not crazy. She said that I might not want to tell everyone.

Susie and Mike helped me through five heart attacks, a stroke and just being sad because I was missing Margie. I fell, Mike took me to the hospital, and then I got stuck in a nursing home.

Susie lived out-of-state then. I wanted out of the nursing home. I wanted to be by the things of Margie and me: Our TV with a remote I can work, our clock that chimed on-the-hour, and the bed we shared with the pretty blanket she loved. I want to sit where we sat together looking at the migrating geese outside the window.

Mike arranged a conference call between the social workers, nurses, me, and him at the nursing home. He explained that Susie was my Healthcare Power of Attorney. I wanted to go home. Staff told Mike I was better off in the nursing home where I would have less chance of falling. Mike asked Susie to speak up for me.

Susie thanked the staff for getting me through my injury from the fall at home. She said we were all grateful for the physical therapy rehabilitation. I was walking without a walker except for long distances. I was in my right mind.

Susie explained that Mike was able to check every morning and every afternoon on me. He only lived three blocks away from my apartment. Susie told staff she understood that they felt I would be safer at the nursing home. But safer was not what I wanted.

I could hear Susie's voice over the microphone set on the conference room table, "My dad should be able to have what he wants. He is a very smart man. When I was a polio child in the hospital, he took me home against medical advice. Why? He believes that we are all healthier when we keep on moving and are surrounded by love. Yes, there was a risk then just as there is one now. I would have been crippled for life if he did not make that very brave decision. He always told me to get up when I fell down. That is what he wants for himself now. Mike will help him."

Susie ended with "I want my Dad to have the same opportunity for happiness as he gave me." My tears blocked my seeing a bit. Mike handed me his handkerchief. Nobody said nothing. It was dead silent in the room. People looked at me. The staff told Mike to get a home monitor. I left the nursing home that day with Mike's protecting presence.

Al's favorite picture of Susie

When Susie visited, I talked to her about dying. I wanted her help writing something to give everyone at my funeral like she did for Margie. I wished people to know that life is what you make of it. It is how you deal with the circumstances that come your way. Margie and I found happiness despite facing uncertainty, turmoil, and pain.

We looked over the box of letters from her Susie's kids that I have always kept under the bed. When Margie was alive writing to grandchildren in college was a hobby of mine. It took me at least a week to write each letter. I would keep a pad of paper on the hassock by my recliner. Margie helped me spell. I printed them all in block letters. Together we mailed letters at the nearby post office. I was so happy when the kids wrote back. Margie read their letters to me again and again. They were doing what I asked them to do: *Work, Study, Play, Rest.*

Susie • 2012

The presence or the absence of a father affects a daughter dramatically. Dad gave me everything a girl would want in a father. He was a stellar example of goodness.

I find him everywhere especially when I allow the noise of the world to quiet. His spirit drops into my thoughts. I pick up the memory of his kindness to others and pass it around.

His philosophy that positive benefits come to both the giver and receiver when we help one another repeats in my life like the refrain of a cherished song. His worldview that good things can rise out of bad circumstances when we work hard to make it so, gives me hope.

In his last years, he began to talk to Mama as if she sat there beside him. He told me he would see her as he lay down at night to sleep. The more he talked about her the more I knew he was getting closer to meeting her.

It did not surprise me when I got the call Dad was dead. I was sad but also happy for him. His body was worn out by time and use. He longed to be with his beloved, Margie. He was talking on the phone, dropped it, and was gone in a flash. Dad struggled through life but not death.

Dad's life really will never end. I see him in the kindness of my children. Their challenging work, generosity, and winsome smiles that brighten others' days, bear witness of his words to them: *Work, Study, Play, Rest.* They followed his instructions and now, as adults, are giving back to people who happened like their grandfather to face to rock-bottom life circumstances. Dad's words fell on ears open to his wisdom. His legacy is magnificent.

Dad's message distributed at his death:

TO MY CHILDREN, GRANDCHILDREN AND GREAT-GRANDCHILDREN

WE WERE BORN AND RAISED DURING THE POVERTY CYCLE IN THIS COUNTRY.

WE LIVED THROUGH THE 1929 AND 1930 MARKET CRASH AND THE DEPRESSION.

WE SURVIVED. SO, NO MATTER HOW HARD IT GETS, YOU TOO WILL SURVIVE.

IT IS TIME TO BID LIFE GOOD-BYE, BUT DON'T FEEL BAD. IT IS SOMETHING EVERYBODY FACES SOONER OR LATER.

THE FUTURE OF OUR COUNTRY IS IN THE HANDS OF THE YOUNG. LIFE GOES ON.

NO MATTER HOW HARD IT GETS, YOU WILL SURVIVE. FEEL THE SORROW AND LET IT GO. KEEP REACHING FOR YOUR GOAL.

YOUR FATHER, GRANDFATHER AND GREAT-GRANDFATHER

BIG AL

THE MAN WITH THE GOLDEN TAN
THE SILENT SWIMMER

Susie • 2022

Today, Tomorrow, and Forever

I have no regrets.

I am grateful.

My love is by my side.

I have precious memories, a lovely family, and sweet friends.

Happiness brings me moments of tears.

I believe kindness is the highest form of intelligence.

We all have a responsibility to ourselves and others.

Much in life evolves from the dynamics in the family in which we grow up. The goodness and kindness of my parents made my path possible. When people love us even though we are not perfect, we pass on the same consideration.

Wherever I go, there I am, with my parents beside me. Their goodness and kindness shall remain with me all my days.

Grace is a gift people give when they put themselves aside and are thoughtful of the needs of one another. I am grateful for the grace I have received from others.

If I had a wish guaranteed to come true, it would be that every child could grow up with parents who did their best despite uncertain circumstances. The polio virus fated our lives to be scary and challenging. Holding onto each other kept us afloat.

Inner peace makes me smile.

It Only Takes One

Who carried the polio virus to me? We will never know. It takes only one person to infect another with poliomyelitis.

The person who passed the polio virus on to me could have been asymptomatic. Or people might have mistaken their symptoms or those of their child's for just not feeling well with stomach flu and/or fever. Asymptomatic or "light" cases of polio were not always reported.

Childhood cases went under the radar when children grew up not experiencing the most recognizable and publicly known after-effect of polio that of limping due to nerve damage and concomitant leg muscle atrophy. Their illnesses were not known to them until later occurring signs and symptoms became evident. The stigma of polio was based on public opinion that it was primarily a disease of poor hygiene. This reproach kept many cases of polio hidden.

Polio is Making a Comeback: What Can You Do?

On February 12, 2022, Israel reported a three-year-old child was paralyzed by polio virus. The Democratic Republic of Congo revealed thirty-five cases of polio in February 2022. These followed announcements in January 2022 of polio cases in Afghanistan, Nigeria, Somalia, and Madagascar. In late 2021, Ukraine, Niger, Mozambique, Yemen, and Malawi detailed information of new polio cases. (This data current April 5, 2022.) Afghanistan's and Pakistan's reporting systems may not be valid.

Use of the **oral polio vaccine (OPV)** has reduced wild poliovirus cases by 99.9% since 1988. **Oral polio vaccine** has not been used in the U.S. since 2000. The U.S. vaccine does not contain live polio virus. The U.S. vaccine contains **Inactivated Polio Vaccine (IPV)**. IPV cannot cause polio.

When a population is under immunized or unimmunized, vaccine-derived viruses from the use of oral polio drops (not used in U.S.) can circulate, mutate, survive, and spread especially in areas where there is inadequate sanitation and lack of access to clean water.

Oral polio vaccine cases are rare (800 cases in 10 years). In comparison, without OPV vaccination, it is estimated that 6.5 million children would have become infected by wild polio virus during the same time period.

You can track polio cases around the world:
https://polioeradication.org/polio-today/polio-now/;
https://tinyurl.com/48rrrdj4

The Global Polio Eradication Initiative (GPEI) is a public-private partnership led by national partners with the **World Health Organization (WHO), Rotary International**, the **Centers for Disease Control and Prevention (CDC)**, the **United Nations Children's Fund (UNICEF)**, the **Bill & Melinda Gates Foundation** and **Gavi, the Vaccine Alliance**.

You can donate to fight polio:
https://polioeradication.org/financing/donate/;
https://tinyurl.com/2p9d9sfa

Polio is a Global Disease that has to be Fought on our own Shores

The **Centers for Disease Control and Prevention (CDC)** records indicate that no cases of polio have been reported as originating in the United States since 1979.

It takes only one traveler with polio to bring the disease to the United States.

People most at risk are:

- Those who never had polio vaccine.
- Those who have not received all the recommended doses.

The best way to keep the United States polio-free is to maintain high immunity (protection) against polio in the population through vaccination.

The **COVID-19 pandemic** has slackened our immunization of children with childhood polio vaccinations. Health experts warn that interruption in vaccination of children could lead to outbreaks of polio within the United States.

You can combat the mistruths fostering dangerous health futures for children of the world.

Mistrust of vaccination leads to lower rates of vaccination. Friends and grandparents can assist parents to understand the polio vaccination schedule and get kids to appointments.

To educate vaccine-hesitant parents, those of us who have lived through epidemics can speak out about how polio crippled children.

> **Schedule for childhood polio vaccination in the United States:**
>
> First dose at 2 months;
>
> Second dose at 4 months;
>
> Third dose at 6 to 18 months; and
>
> Booster dose at 4 to 6 years.

UNICEF and **WHO** have published warnings that pandemic-related disruptions in vaccination rates—in some areas falling to 50%—leave people vulnerable to new cases of polio and measles. WHO has determined that more children in Africa could die of measles than **COVID-19**, taking us back decades in our fight against childhood illnesses and preventable deaths.

The **Taliban** does not see polio vaccination as a priority. It has at times banned vaccination. **Doctors Without Borders** issued a 2021 survey showing the people of Afghanistan have diminished access to healthcare due to the country's violence and economic instability. Afghan people voice they are fearful of seeking treatment. Security concerns make people not get vaccinations.

India accounts for one-third of all unimmunized children in the world. Seven million children are not fully protected against "old" diseases such as measles, rubella, tetanus, and whooping cough.

With a team of nurse educators and student nurses, I went to India in 2014 to administer vaccinations. In rural communities, we met parents who had tears in their eyes and hands gently folded as steeples. They bowed to thank us for helping to protect the future of their children's health through vaccination.

People waited patiently in long lines formed at dawn and ending at dusk, in over one-hundred-degree temperatures with fidgeting kids in their arms. We held their children, rocked them, and sang songs to calm them as we gave inoculations.

As we traveled on rural roads, groups of men brandishing automatic weapons stopped our vehicles. Fortunately, we were able to continue our mission to immunize.

The Centers for Disease Control and Prevention Global Immunization Division continues immunization work estimating it saves two to three million lives a year. One hundred and thirty million babies are born worldwide each year. Each global citizen can help prevent these children from contracting polio.

People involved in saving children's lives from disease for which there are preventative vaccinations is shrinking. It will take moral leadership, challenging of mistruths, and building well-funded and protected social networks to educate and directly provide healthcare around the world.

***

It only takes one person to infect a child with polio and change their life forever.

***

After the Fact: The Sequelae of Polio, Dealing with the Long-Haul Symptoms

Polio will not just paralyze you. Speeding along your neurological tract chewing up neurons along the way as fast as a ten-year-old eats M&Ms, the virus spreads its destruction throughout the polio victim's body.

The everyday maladies of a polio life are much more extensive than the paralysis alone. The term ***polio sequelae***, used here to describe the symptoms *accompanying* paralytic polio virus damage, captures a more complete picture of polio.

People may not have heard of the sequalae of polio. ***Sequela*** (singular), comes from the Latin word *sequel* which means "that which follows." Polio sequelae are conditions that are born of and follow previous polio infection.

These impairments occur with random scope and intensity. The roadmap of viral damage varied between survivors. Therefore, polio survivors do not share sequelae identical in type and severity.

Age mattered. Infants, children, and adults experienced different changes during acute polio. Age of polio onset plays a factor in skeletal muscle changes due to polio. Scoliosis and limb shortening are associated with polio virus infection before major growth spurt. We know that babies grow an average of ten inches their first year. A child grows about two and one-half inches per year until adolescence. The major growth spurt occurring at age eight to thirteen years for girls and age ten to fifteen years of age for boys leads to the end of growth for most but not all children at around seventeen years of age.

It makes sense that the length of prolonged stress on weakened muscles and skeletal deformities diverge in relationship to age at infection. The extent of early damage by the polio virus is thought to be a factor in predisposing later functional complaints commonly referred to as ***post-polio syndrome.***

The stigma of polio:

Not all children infected with the polio virus displayed symptoms that parents recognized as polio. There were children that incurred "light cases" with symptoms such as fever, tiredness, weakness, headache, gastrointestinal distress, and muscle stiffness. Parents thought the children were sick but not with polio.

The children may have been too young when sick to remember their illnesses. Some people first learned as adults that they "might have had polio" as a child.

Polio Place, a service of **Post-Polio Health International**, has documented many cases wherein children were not told they had polio at the time of their infection or during their childhoods. As adults, some of these people learned that symptoms they now experience are related back in origin to a bout with polio.

Why were children not told they might have polio? One reason is that the stigma of polio led family members to not tell to protect themselves from the shame associated with the disease. Community members often characterized polio survivors and their family members as less sanitary and a danger to those around them. People would defame polio family members saying they had brought the disease into their household through sinful behavior.

In addition, people held a moralizing judgment against those affected by the polio virus and this played out in words like, "It happened to them not me because they are dirty." Some doctors who cared for patients with polio (along with their family members) were shunned.

> *Our mother instructed us we could not play with our neighbor children because their father was a doctor who cared for polio victims. My mother was afraid the doctor would bring the polio virus home to his children, and we would catch it from them.*
>
> Iowa Girl, 1948

Polio survivors at first considered dangerous because of fear of them being infectious, were also later barred from participation in other activities. In the 1940s and 1950s, schools often excluded children with disabilities from full participation in activities. Parents figured that it was best not to tell children they had polio because knowing might lead to questions they could not or did not want to answer.

Polio survivors learned to hide their disability and pain and move onward noncomplaining. Many chose to follow the advice my Mama gave me: *Just smile so others won't feel so badly.* Polio survivors pretended they were okay which led to inconsistent or nonexistent follow-up of sequelae.

The medical community in the 1940s and 1950s had its hands full focusing on acute cases of polio. Only in later years did tracking reveal the long-lasting effects of sub-acute and acute polio.

Polio survivors, now aging, report that the 1980s emergence of the term ***post-polio syndrome*** brought them face-to-face with the repercussions of acute polio. When the medical malady ***post-polio syndrome*** originated, many people had already hidden their defects for decades. Countless doctors attributed their patients' polio sequelae to separate and distinct disease processes. For other polio survivors who complained later in life, physicians chalked up their signs and symptoms as due to their personalities or aging.

You might look at a polio survivor and think pain is their most debilitating sequela of polio. Yes, pain may pervade the everyday life of the polio survivor. But most polio survivors will tell you that *extreme fatigue* is the key symptom that penetrates and paints the landscape of their life. "How much can I push myself today?" is the daily question a survivor of polio asks.

Doctors who might have worked with kids who had polio are long dead. Today there are few polio specialists. A 2009 study indicated, there were only a "handful." If you asked medical school graduates how many polio survivors are alive in the U.S., they might not have an answer and may not be prepared to address polio survivors' questions.

Dynamics of polio virus travel through body: When polio strikes, the virus travels. By following its pathway, the symptoms become understandable. The virus enters the mouth, infecting first the pharynx which is the passageway behind the mouth and nose. The pharynx provides a route to the esophagus and digestive system and, also to the trachea and lungs.

Circular muscles in the wall of the pharynx push food down the esophagus. Longitudinal muscles lift the wall of the pharynx during swallowing. A flap of tissue called the epiglottis covers the passageway to the lungs when food is channeled into the esophagus.

On its way through the gastrointestinal tract, the polio virus attaches to an immunoglobulin-like receptor, the **poliovirus receptor CD 155** on the cell membrane. For about seven days, it replicates. Then, the polio virus spreads to the intestine and deep cervical and mesenteric lymph nodes where it continues to replicate on its way into the bloodstream.

In one percent of infections, poliovirus continues to spread along nerve fiber pathways. It replicates and specifically attacks and destroys motor neurons within the spinal cord and brain stem. Depending on the location of the destruction, a person experiences spinal, **bulbar** or **bulbospinal** paralysis.

Deformity of a limb is the most evident outcome of polio. A more complete picture of the sequelae of polio follows.

Deformity of the leg/hip and spine: Polio may paralyze any muscle of the body but most often halts movement of the legs. Arm muscles are the next most often muscle group affected by the polio virus.

Deformities affect gait (how one walks) and how the joints work together. Each polio survivor is changed in unique ways. There is shortening of muscle fibers. There is muscle wasting. An affected limb (in most cases the leg), becomes thinner than the limb on the opposite side of the body because the bones and muscles in the transformed leg do not develop normally due to poor innervation. The affected limb may be permanently shorter.

My polio leg is shorter than my "good leg." Because of this, my gait is wobbly and my body leans toward the weaker side. My balance is off, so I may compensate by looking down because I do not want to fall over something or not be prepared to go downhill or uphill. I may not look up and smile at you when walking toward you. Not that I do not want to smile and say hello. When I am tired and in pain, it is a struggle to do so.

I drive using both feet. One is for the brake and the other presses the gas pedal. A grandson looked down at my feet when I was carting him to school one day and exclaimed, "Grandma Susie, you drive ambidextrously!"

Muscles are not uniformly affected by invasion of the polio virus. Some muscles may be only partly affected. Others act totally floppy. Using shoulder muscles to make up for weakness in lower limbs and arms, sometimes causes people who have had polio to have rotator cuff problems.

A leg paralyzed by the polio virus cannot be raised straight up. When laying down for extended periods, those with polio may rotate their hip outward for comfort. This can become a fixed deformity. Asymmetric hip musculature may cause curvature of the spine. The spine and hips of children with polio required routine examinations.

The **tibialis anterior muscle** tends to be the *most severely* paralyzed muscle by polio. This muscle runs down the front of the leg. The muscle *most commonly* paralyzed by polio is the **quadriceps femoris** which is a large muscle group that lies over the front and sides of the thigh. This is a big muscle normally and it consists of four muscles which are the rectus femoris, vastus lateralis, vastus medialis, and vastus intermedius.

Foot deformities: Polio can cause muscular weakness and paralysis leading to "**foot drop**" which disrupts normal gait. Muscles of the foot may be partially or completely paralyzed.

Foot drop is a severe muscle weakness which causes the foot to bend forward and downward. The person with polio may still be able to move the foot to the left or right side. Flail foot is a condition in which there is no movement in any direction.

When you see a person having difficulty lifting their foot fully off the floor and instead, sliding their toes across the floor, you are observing foot drop. To compensate for the toes hitting the floor, which may cause tripping, the person often lifts the foot higher and outward to take a step.

Foot drop can be a dangerous condition because tripping may occur especially when coming upon uneven surfaces or objects in one's path. Although as a kid my body somehow learned to fall without injury (I never broke a bone.), I learned early on to watch the ground for people, animals, and downed branches that might be in the way.

In addition to foot drop, ankle contracture may impede walking. This condition places stress on calf muscles. Treatment may be Achilles' tendon release surgery.

An **AFO (ankle-foot-orthotic)** is a brace commonly used to treat foot drop. This device keeps the foot in a normal position. An arthrodesis is a surgical procedure that permanently fixes the foot, so it does not drop down.

Bracing: Polio survivors may use bracing to maintain proper alignment and stabilize movement in the lower extremities. It is important to periodically assess braces for fit and integrity as a polio survivor faces changes in status.

The most commonly used leg brace by post-polio survivors is a short leg brace called the **molded ankle-foot brace (MAFO)**. It is made of plastic that fits inside the shoe to prevent foot drop. This orthotic (artificial support device) also braces weakened calf muscles and helps prevent buckling at the knee.

Some polio survivors use a brace longer than the MAFO. It is called a **knee-ankle-foot orthosis (KAFO)**. It runs the length of the knee, ankle, and foot. It stabilizes joints to assist with safe walking. Made of molded plastic, it runs up the back of the lower leg and is attached behind the thigh. It locks at the knee. Variations in the KAFO address the particular strengths and movement abilities of the polio survivor.

Crutches or canes/poles are used to supplement stability. Folks who use an MAFO may find a cane or pole a good stabilizer. Survivors who wear a KAFO, generally use two forearm crutches. The International Centre for Polio Education advises survivors that overuse of canes and crutches may lead to other upper body maladies such as carpal tunnel syndrome.

Bracing needs vary with characteristics unique to each survivor. Knees, hips, necks, and symptoms of cord compression all may require specialized orthopedic assessment in order to provide appropriate support measures.

Cervical spondylosis, cord compression symptoms and radicular sensory symptoms: Some polio survivors exhibit cervical spondylosis (wear and tear affecting the spinal disks of the neck), cord compression (pain in the neck or lower back, burning pain, numbness and cramping spreading through the arms, hands, buttocks, or legs) and/or radicular sensory symptoms (numbness and tingling). These changes can be addressed by a number of modalities. Physical therapy, corticosteroid injections, and chiropractic treatment are common approaches. There are occasions when surgery is required to relieve pressure on nerves.

Upper Arm Muscle Damage: Paralysis of the arm region affects strength in the arms, shoulders, and hands. Muscle atrophy of the arms from polio virus damage may not be as noticeable as the gait disturbances that occur with leg muscle damage.

The **deltoid muscle** is the most frequently paralyzed. It is located at the top of the arm and is the spot where a person is given their annual flu injection, or a tetanus shot when treated for an injury in the emergency room. When the deltoid muscle is affected, rotator cuff muscles may also be. In addition, muscles around the elbow and hands can be harmed by polio virus infection.

A polio survivor who has weakness in the upper arm may compensate by using both hands to hold a drinking glass up to their mouth. If one arm is affected and not the other, the person may choose to use the stronger arm for lifting and other tasks that require strength. Polio survivors who display upper arm debility are more likely to also have weakness of respiratory muscles.

Electromyography (EMG) may be used to assess upper extremity damage from polio. EMG is a method of measuring the response of a muscle to an electrical nerve stimulation of the muscle during rest and contraction. EMG detects flickers of movements occurring in diseased motor neurons. A neurologist performs the EMG. A technician may assist for portions of the testing.

The EMG procedure can be an outpatient procedure. With the patient lying down, the physician inserts small electrode needles into muscles. Muscle activity is displayed on an oscilloscope (screen).

EMG research reveals that there often (in one study 42% of the time) has been a subclinical involvement of the arms although the patient's polio history during the acute phase did not document any paralysis of the arms. EMG studies may guide polio survivors to treatment of symptoms not apparent during acute polio.

A polio specialist did electromagnetic (EMG) studies on my arms when I reached adulthood. Findings showed I had damage to both arms. I was not told this as a child.

My body's reaction to the polio virus damaging my arm innervation—becoming ambidextrous—came before I knew it would be a smart thing to do. *Bodies do the most amazing things to compensate without us telling them to do so. I am grateful.*

Vagus nerve damage: Although it is the longest nerve in the autonomic nervous system, the vagus nerve is not in everyone's vocabulary. I do not think my parents knew the name, but they had to deal with the repercussions brought on by the polio virus damaging mine. The vagus runs from the brain down through the chest and into the abdomen.

The vagus nerve regulates a lot of things about which people do not give conscious thought. These include the functioning of the heart, smooth muscles, gastrointestinal system, and various glands. It regulates involuntary functions such as breathing, heart rate, blood flow, and digestion.

The vagus sends signals from the brain stem to muscles in the throat, esophagus, stomach, and intestines. In addition, the vagus nerve slows heart rate and damage to the nerve leads to tachycardia (fast heartbeat, over one hundred beats/minute).

Gastroparesis (slow gut): Living with polio means facing daily challenges with gastrointestinal (GI) motility. The symptoms of malfunction due to vagus nerve damage can be embarrassing.

Polio can ruin nerves that keep the digestive tract working. Motility (movement) is slowed down or does not work very well at all. This prevents the stomach from emptying on a regular basis. The colon follows suit as the gastrointestinal tract is the only pathway for digested food and thus, stool to get out.

My parents recalled to me that they were very worried when they brought me home from the hospital because I did not have a bowel movement the next day. My mother was accustomed to my brother having many full diapers.

The doctor made a house call the next evening. He brought over a brown glass bottle of glycerin suppositories. He showed them how to use them. And he also gave them a talk about how the gastrointestinal tract worked.

My parents became obsessed with emptying of my bowel. They kept a daily log. As a kid, I spent hours in the bathroom. If their special notebook did not have a mark in it, I would have to sit in the bathroom. When the stomach does not empty properly, it is painful for a youngster. I counted every bathroom tile a zillion times to distract myself. I listened out the open window to other kids in the yards around our house. They were playing after supper while I was just sitting.

A former polio poster child died in her later years from an intestinal blockage, one of the hidden, but *constant hovering* fears of polio survivors who suffer life-long polio virus damage to the vagus nerve.

Abdominal bloating that is related to slow gastric motility can be painful and embarrassing. When my brother learned about sex, he asked my mother if I could be pregnant (I was ten years old!). My stomach could inflate to an immense size due to gastroparesis.

Every morning as a child, I drank mineral oil along with cod liver oil. Sometimes castor oil was forced down me while I held my nose. I ate prunes. I drank warmed prune juice. My parents enforced the "apple a day" rule. I was allowed only high fiber wheat bread. Bread made with white flour was outlawed for me.

Key to my survival was my parents' diligence at making the slow gut move. Daily exercise was not an option. It was mandatory. When I was able to walk, even if it meant stiffly pulling a braced leg along, my parents expected me to do so to aid my gastrointestinal tract functioning.

My parents took me to a proctologist for regular check-ups. A proctologist is a colorectal specialist. I did not know any other kid who had their own gastrointestinal doctor. Embarrassing!

As Director of Nursing at a skilled care facility, I was called to the room of a newly admitted patient who had polio and was rehabbing after knee replacement. She complained of pain in her back. I watched her walk. Bent over, she held one hand on her stomach and the other at the base of her spine.

I asked her to tell me how she felt. "My pain got worse overnight." she said. "It feels like there is a heavy weight on my spine. I can't straighten up."

Her hospital record indicated she had not had a bowel movement in five days. The doctor prescribed a narcotic post knee transplant. Her medications did not include a bowel stimulant or stool softener.

The nurse on duty called the doctor for an order for a series of enemas and daily over the counter senna and softener products. The dietary manager interviewed the woman about her preferences for foods consistent with a high fiber, high vegetable, and fruit diet.

Staff calculated the patient's fluid needs based on kilogram of body weight. The patient was advised about the amount of water she best drink daily. A senna tea supplement was offered to her every other evening.

After a week of the new regimen, the polio survivor no longer complained of back pain. Her frequency of stools improved. The bonus was she started participating in Tai Chi class. The patient said that before the new treatment regimen, she felt too bloated and restricted by pain to exercise.

Difficulty swallowing and regurgitation: All polio survivors experienced a degree of **bulbar** polio. The vagus nerve innervates brain stem neurons damaged by the polio virus. These neurons are responsible for controlling breathing, heart rate, and swallowing.

Low blood pressure and **elevated heart rate (tachycardia)** along with impaired breathing were leading causes of death for patients with **bulbar** polio. **Cardiologists** are key to assess and treat the polio survivor to put in place measures to alleviate blood pressure and heart rate issues associated with eating and vagus nerve damage.

Polio survivors must eat slowly to avoid **gastric regurgitation**. They have to digest each bite, or eructation, commonly known as burping, occurs. Burping can turn into fits of hiccupping.

Heightened potential for **gastroesophageal reflux disease (GERD)** in polio survivors may be due to deformity of the spine, swallowing problems and generalized weakness. Acid reflux into the larynx can lead to heartburn and hoarseness when stomach acid leaks back up into the esophagus. Some people with GERD describe this backflow symptom as chest pain. It is important that a cardiologist rule out cardiac disease when chest discomfort occurs.

Polio survivors also commonly report **hiatal hernias**. These occur when the stomach pushes through the hiatal opening in the diaphragm where the esophagus passes to connect to the stomach. Hiatal hernias may allow food and acid to back up into the esophagus leading to heartburn, and more burping. Embarrassing!

Polio survivors may experience **fatigue after meals**. This makes sense because when stomachs fill with food, the vagus nerve is over stimulated. This excitement of the vagus nerve triggers a corresponding drop in blood pressure and increase in heart rate. The polio survivor may feel heart palpitations at this time.

Food and medications get caught in the upper esophagus when the vagus nerve damaged by the polio virus does not stimulate muscles in the esophagus to move food efficiently downward. Studies of polio survivors and swallowing have shown that when food gets stuck, the esophagus becomes irritated. These cascading events can trigger an **esophageal spasm** which in turn stimulates the vagus nerve leading to a drop in blood pressure and the heart rate to either speed up or slow down.

Swallowing difficulty is called **dysphagia** (duh·sfay·juh). It may worsen later in the day when the person who has had polio is more fatigued. Polio survivors find timing of medications and cutting pills into pieces are important safety measures. Do not be surprised if your friend or family member who has had polio always keeps water and a bit of food readily available to help with swallowing. Polio survivors may experience worsening dysphagia with aging.

Drinking **alcohol** excessively and using **recreational drugs** with their unpredictable, uncertain outcomes and difficulty swallowing do not go together. Additionally, emergency rooms now face elderly patients who have ingested **edible cannabis products** in amounts that make their heads spin and send them falling down with injury. The consequences can be deadly.

Swallowing in a reclined dentist chair can be troublesome for the polio survivor because fluids may not readily go down the throat while lying down. Patients who have had polio should alert their dentist before routine exams and treatment. Lying back in a dentist chair when dental staff, without warning, squirt fluid into the polio survivor's mouth may cause the person to aspirate (inhale liquid into the lungs). It is important for the polio survivor to have the time, space, and supportive surfaces on which to brace themselves to sit up from a reclining position in the dental chair.

Polio survivors have found positive ways of dealing with vagus nerve damage. Not reclining right after a meal is one. Another is eating at least three to four hours before going to bed. Both reduce reflux. Eating smaller meals more frequently and taking smaller bites of food while washing the food down with fluid between bites are also helpful maneuvers.

Avoiding smoking and the foods that trigger a person's reflux are also important. Polio survivors are urged to keep a log of foods that are bothersome and avoid these. Medications taken before meals to relax muscles have been shown also to help prevent muscle spasms of the esophagus.

Other digestive issues: Damage to vagus innervation of the gastrointestinal tract causes survivors of polio have more episodic **diarrhea, colitis, constipation,** and **gastric ulcers** than the general population.

Polio survivors should be aware that **nonsteroidal anti-inflammatory drugs (NSAIDs)**, which may be recommended for pain relief, inhibit platelet aggregation, and consequently prolong bleeding time. NSAID use may lead to gastric ulcers.

Since **polio survivors are six times more likely to develop ulcers than the average person**, use of NSAIDs is fraught with danger. People who have a polio history must weigh the potential for harm in considering nonsteroidal anti-inflammatory drug use.

NSAIDs Commonly Used in the United States

Aspirin (acetylsalicylic acid)
Celebrex (celecoxib)
Voltaren-XR, Cambia, Cataflam, Zipsor, Zorvolex (diclofenac)
Motrin, Advil (ibuprofen)
Indocin (indomethacin)
Ketoprofen (ketoprofen)
Aleve, Anaprox, Naprelan, Naprosyn (naproxen)
Daypro (oxaprozin)
Feldene (piroxicam)

A silver lining the polio survivor gut:

In 2018, **Steven Lehrer** and **Peter H. Rheinstein**, used **The Cancer Genome Atlas (TCGA)** to study the relationship of the polio virus cellular receptor (PVR) to **colon cancer**. Their discovery illuminates a bright spot for polio survivors.

When the incidence of colon cancer in polio survivors was examined and compared to people never infected by the polio virus, polio survivors were found to have less colon cancer. Infection with the polio virus as a child or adult may induce resistance to colon cancer later in life.

Tachycardia: Tachycardia means the heart is beating over one hundred beats per minute. It is meant to beat below one hundred beats per minute. Too fast a heart rate interferes with the chambers of the heart passing blood forward and around the body.

Polio survivors are well-served by consultation with a cardiologist to evaluate and monitor cardiac status. A **cardiologist** can evaluate chest pain symptoms that may be related to GERD or cardiac dysfunction.

Polio survivors should know how personal exercise routines may raise their heart rate and/or cause changes in breathing rate and/or pattern. Using a small monitor around the chest and making recordings, a person can send readings to a computer link and printer. This enables the polio survivor to share with their healthcare team how exercise affects their heart rate and breathing.

Breathing and Sleep Issues: Polio researcher **David Bodian** (1910-1992), medical scientist and polio researcher at the John Hopkins School of Hygiene and Public Health, was first to note that every polio survivor had damage to neurons in the brain stem, the center in the brain responsible for breathing. Bodian's research in the 1940s demonstrated that the poliovirus multiplied within both the brain and the spinal cord.

His work showed that even when breathing deficits were not demonstrable clinically, the polio virus damaged motor neurons in the brain. When Bodian inspected the autopsied brains of poliomyelitis victims, he found that most had brain changes due to polio virus damage.

When patients demonstrated breathing difficulties, doctors diagnosed patients with "**bulbar polio**." An iron lung machine was required to support breathing. Changes in the brain affecting breathing went undiscovered for some polio survivors until later in their lives.

Both structural and muscle changes due to polio reduce effective breathing. Chest wall conditions related to **scoliosis** or **kyphosis** restrict getting air in and out of the lungs. Scoliosis and kyphosis reinforce hypoventilation.

Functional deterioration of muscles controlling breathing is common for polio survivors. **Reduced chest muscle strength** leads to decreased maximum inspiratory and expiratory pressures which are measurements of maximal efforts of respiratory muscles. The intercostal and diaphragm muscles of polio survivors are weakened reducing the effectiveness of breathing. The dynamics involved in polio survivors worsening breathing may also be explained as at least in part due to a decrease in respiratory strength related to aging. Differentiating between changes related to sequelae of poliomyelitis and getting older can be challenging.

Taking a full breath while lying down may become increasingly difficult for the polio survivor. Breathing in a lying position requires a diaphragm already damaged by the polio virus to work harder to pull air in and move air out. The diaphragm must work to push aside the intestines and other abdominal organs which is not the case when a person is upright when gravity accomplishes this maneuver. Obesity hampers healthy breathing. The polio survivor may find **weight loss** hard to achieve due to limited mobility.

Periodic measurement of oxygen and carbon dioxide levels along with respiratory muscle strength and functioning is recommended to assess the polio survivor's need for a device to assist with breathing or coughing. Findings may surprise polio survivors who never thought they experienced respiratory involvement. Evaluation of breathing and subsequent interventions may improve the quality and length of a polio survivor's life.

Sleep disturbances are reported by about 80% of polio survivors. Sleep disorders are more common in polio survivors than in the general population. Polysomnographic sleep studies show the polio survivor spends less time in deeper sleep called rapid eye movement (REM), than superficial sleep. This holds true more so for those having **bulbar** involvement early on in life. Sleep disturbances also can be related to pain due to muscle overuse leading to spasms and to postural abnormalities such as curvature of the spine. Other factors are related to vagus nerve damage causing stomach regurgitation and decreased respiratory excursion (ability) when the polio survivor assumes a lying down position.

Sleep-related disordered breathing (SRDB) is due to damage to brain stem nerves, decreased strength and tone of the upper airway, and higher rates of obesity in polio survivors. Polio survivors, with their varying degrees of brain and breathing disorders, may develop **obstructive sleep apnea (OSA)** and/or **central sleep apnea (CSA).** Hypoventilation wherein the survivor does too little breathing may lead to an imbalance in gas exchange: carbon dioxide builds up and oxygen goes down. Breathing may be periodically interrupted, leading to **daytime tiredness** and **sleepiness**. Use of **continuous positive airway pressure devices (CPAP)** or **bilevel positive airway pressure (BiPap)** improves oxygenation of the blood.

Other factors disturbing the polio survivor's sleep are related to vagus nerve damage causing stomach regurgitation and decreased respiratory excursion (ability) when the polio survivor assumes a lying down position. **Heat intolerance** may cause periodic awakenings.

Sleep impairment may spin into a cycle of nighttime awakenings, inadequate rest, daytime fatigue, morning headache, and inability to think clearly. A polio survivor may find compensatory ways to make their sleep less fragmented. If not, they may spend years on this gerbil wheel of unrest.

Healthcare providers should observe for low volume of voice projection and use of accessory muscles to breathe as these are signs of under-ventilation during sleep. In addition, a polio survivor may have difficulty speaking for more than a brief time. A **pulmonologist** can devise an appropriate treatment plan.

It is important for polio survivors who present with sleep disturbances to inform healthcare professionals of a history of polio. Polio survivors with a history of being in an iron lung during the acute phase should make their healthcare professionals aware and relate their age when in the iron lung. A personal healthcare chart history of asthma may be a facade covering over a history of childhood polio with unrecognized **bulbar**. involvement.

Aging is associated with increased prevalence of sleep disturbance. Poliomyelitis sequelae add onto aging another layer of mechanisms for prevalence of sleep disorders. Healthcare professionals should screen for sleep disorders in polio survivors. Presentation of sleep disorders by polio survivors may be confusing as one sifts out the natural effect of aging. However, lack of attention to sleep disorders can worsen a patient's pain and fatigue, increase risk for cardiovascular disease, and affect the polio survivor's mood and quality of life.

Note to Prescribers and Pharmacists

Muscle, joint and spine pain are common among polio survivors. Ninety-one percent of polios survivors report experiencing pain significantly more severe than that of the general population. Thirty-five percent reported mild pain, 35% reported moderate pain and 30% severe pain.

Muscle pain is described as a deep ache in muscles that will not go away. Fasciculations (simultaneous involuntary contraction of groups of muscle fibers) cause twitching and pain.

Pain is worse after overuse of affected muscles. Many polio survivors push through daytime activities accumulating fatigue due to the stress of unrelenting pain. Once pain has set hold for hours, it is difficult to back it down to a level that allows restful sleep.

Although muscle spasms, and pain due to orthopedic abnormalities and fasciculations are a recognized side effects of damaged nerves and muscles due to poliomyelitis, there remains a belief among some healthcare practitioners that polio survivors have a painless disease because of lack of sensory nerve involvement.

Nighttime is a particularly troublesome time for this population to have unrelenting pain due to muscle spasms. Polio survivors voice that pain interferes with sleep more than any other activity of daily life.

Lack of sleep may lead to falls due to tiredness with accompanying injury or worse. It is time for healthcare professionals to not turn a blind eye to pain being a persistent problem in the post-polio population of the United States which is estimated to be over 300,000 persons.

The opioid crisis has brought more scrutiny over prescription of scheduled medications. **Prescribers** need to write prescriptions that meet indication for use guidelines.

> **Pharmacists** have a role to support the quality of life for polio survivors. They are gatekeepers ensuring prescriptions are not withheld or postponed due to lack of documentation of the reason for use and/or uncertainties about prescribing long-term.

Fainting: Fainting has been reported to be more common in patients who have had polio, but this finding is controversial. A 1995 Post-Polio Survey found that fainting was not more prevalent among polio survivors than in the general population.

Polio survivors who fainted at least once reported significantly more daily fatigue than those who had never fainted. This finding suggests that the extent of damage to the brain's blood pressure control system neurons may show a link between the extent of brain stem damage and low blood pressure.

One third of polio survivors report that a feeling of faintness occurs when in a hot environment such as a hot shower or sauna which may cause blood pressure to fall. Warmth such as in warm tub baths causes arteries and veins to relax. Blood moves toward the skin. Because blood that has pooled in the legs lowers their blood pressure, polio survivors may report feeling dizzy or faint when they stand after a warm bath necessitating grab bars for safety.

Like persons suffering from **chronic fatigue syndrome (CSF)**, polio survivors may report amassing of blood in their legs leading to "blue feet" and low blood pressure.

Decreased tolerance of cold temperatures: In the acute stage, the polio virus marched on through the body damaging the hypothalamus which controls body temperature. In addition, spinal cord nerves that tell the brain to constrict capillaries (small blood vessels) in the skin when a person is in a cold environment were killed off. Damage was unique to each polio survivor.

Destruction of these two systems has left many polio survivors unable to keep warm blood from coming to the surface of their skin. Limbs become cold. Blood may become trapped in capillaries making the feet look bluish.

Ambient cold temperatures bathing the motor nerves slows their conduction, making them inefficient for muscle contracting. Colder tendons and ligaments become more rigid and impair muscle movement.

Fifty percent of polio survivors report intolerance to cold. They say their pain increases as the temperature around them decreases. Sixty-two percent of polio survivors report that cold precipitates muscle weakness. Thirty-nine percent describe increasing fatigue in cold environments.

Polio survivors report that they compensate by dressing for an environmental temperature twenty degrees cooler (Fahrenheit) than the ambient temperature. They say that wearing layers and insulating garments improves their comfort. **Electromyography (EMG)** testing has to be done in an environment at least 75 degrees Fahrenheit to obtain valid results.

Heat intolerance: While much attention has been given to cold intolerance, researchers are now exploring the relationship between surface arteries not opening and heat intolerance reported by polio survivors. This phenomenon is related to damaged nerves that control body temperature.

What do polio survivors who have heat intolerance report? Some say they feel uncomfortably warm. This feeling of discomfort is accompanied by a varied extent or absence of sweating. They say they have hot flashes. Hot flashes are described as a sudden warmth in the upper body, especially around the face, neck, and chest. Skin in these parts may become reddened and the phenomenon is likened to blushing. Night sweating may affect sleep.

Heat intolerant polio survivors find the most comfortable ambient temperature in the range of 61 degrees to 72 degrees Fahrenheit.

They report other symptoms accompanying heat intolerance as nausea, faintness, dizziness, itchy skin, and anxiousness.

Muscle fasciculations/spasms/cramps: Muscles damaged by the polio virus twitch. These involuntary movements are labeled **fasciculations**. Occurring spontaneously from fine muscle fibers, fasciculation occurs in **seventy percent** of polio survivors who have experienced lower limb paralysis.

Normal muscles do not produce electrical signals during rest. Damaged muscles of the polio survivor keep twitching. The EMG reading of a patient with fasciculations demonstrates increased jitter and blocking. The twitching is due to chronic denervation and muscle atrophy accompanying neuron damage.

Muscle spasms bring on an extremely painful feeling. The area of spasm may feel lumpy and hard. The polio survivor may describe the spasm as a knot. A spasm can be small or cover a longer area such as the length of a calf or thigh muscle. Polio survivors also report spasms in the neck and back. Stretching and the use of an electronic stimulation device such as a **transcutaneous electrical nerve stimulation (TENS)** unit may ease the pain.

A **muscle cramp** is defined in polio literature as a short-lived, painful, involuntary contraction of part of an entire muscle, most often in the leg. When we observe this in athletes in the sports arena, they stop and stretch. When polios survivors feel calf muscle cramps, they may find their lower leg muscle painful, and their toes forced downward. The polio survivor may awaken and get out of bed to stretch to relieve the cramp.

A Nerve Conduction Study (NCS) measures an electrical impulse's speed and strength of conduction through a nerve. This test may be done in conjunction with an EMG. Like the EMG, the NCS documents the intensity and location of damage in nerves and muscles.

Fasciculations can disturb sleep. A way to stop fasciculations, other than rest and stretching, is the use of **muscle relaxants** (antispastic and antispasmodic medications) to calm the twitching. Muscle relaxants have potentially harmful side effects especially for the elderly. Common side include dizziness, drowsiness, and lowering of blood pressure. These increase a person's risk for falls. Users must be diligent in following safety measures.

The Post-Polio Institute studied polio survivors who used **alprazolam (Xanax)** or **diazepam (Valium)** to calm damaged nerves to allow nighttime sleep. The organization reports no cases of addiction in over thirty years of review of polio survivor cases.

Polio survivors may use a variety of topical anesthetic agents to reduce feeling the pain of spasming during sleep. Creams, lotions, gels, or patches containing Capsaicin or special pharmacy-formulated lidocaine cream may lessen pain but should be discussed with a physician to ensure understanding the side effects.

Planned exercise can build muscles which may relieve fatigue, weakness, discomfort, and prevent injury. Swimming in warm not chilly water is known to reduce pain and increase mobility.

It is essential that trainers understand the polio survivor requires regular rest periods amidst exercising. Studies of polio survivors show that excessive exercise of denervated muscles leads to increased weakness. The polio survivor walks a fine line between doing strengthening exercises which might exacerbate weakness and keeping muscles and bones healthy.

It is key for the polio survivor to take short walks, not long hikes which are likely to bring on excessive fatigue, weakness, and increased potential for falls. Polio survivors must each evaluate what a short walk versus a long walk means for them keeping in mind the polio virus varied its pattern of destruction.

During a **Magnetic Resonance Imaging (MRI)**, the technician kept saying to me, "Please stop moving your right leg." I explained that I was not moving my leg. The calf muscle twitched on its own. The MRI was picking up chronic fasciculations.

Joint disease: Joints wear out due to misalignment and damaged muscles related to polio and aging.

Hip: In the United States, more than 450,000 people **undergo total hip replacements (total hip arthroplasty)** each year. Osteoarthritis is the most common underlying reason for hip replacement.

Osteoarthritis is a "wear and tear" age-related type of arthritis that occurs in adults aged fifty years and older. Cartilage that cushions the bones of the hip joint diminishes. Osteoarthritis may also be caused and/or accelerated by subtle irregularities in how the hip developed in childhood.

Polio survivors are at higher risk than the general population for hip degeneration due to muscle imbalance between abductors and adductor muscles of the hip. This disparity causes tension in the joint leading to changes and degeneration of the joint. In addition, discrepancy in leg length exacerbates degenerative disease. Surgeons note that post-polio patients should understand that leg length discrepancy persists after hip surgery.

Polio patients that have hip replacements in the United States on either their affected polio leg or unaffected leg have similar complications and outcomes as those reported in the general population having hip replacement for osteoarthritis.

Knee: Knees ache and weaken. About one-half of all adult Americans will develop knee osteoarthritis, In the United States, there are one million **total knee replacement s (TKRs)** per year.

This number is expected to rise exponentially due to the aging population. By 2030, the projected number of procedures for total knee surgery in the United States will increase by to around 3.5 million. Sixty percent of all knee replacements are done for women.

Due to pain and instability in walking, polio survivors may consult with an **orthopedic surgeon** about elective TKR on the unaffected or minimally affected leg. Polio survivors are not only aging in place. They experience added burdens. The polio virus negatively affects quadriceps muscle functioning. Abnormal alignment and ligament laxity (looseness) may amplify osteoarthritic damage to the joint.

Orthopedic surgeons preoperatively evaluate the uniqueness of each polio survivor's knees. Surgeons select the knee implant that has design attributes best suited to the needs of the patient.

Surgeons assess the strength of the **quadriceps** prior to TKR. Quadriceps weakness may lead to acquired compensatory hyperextension of the knee. In some polio patients, there may be instability of the knee due to extensive extension of the leg. Surgical options such as a **rotating hinge prosthesis** may be used for patients with knee osteoarthritis and loss of quadriceps strength.

Use of specialized recoil braces to support joint alignment is a technique that may be employed to provide stability for patients with less anti-gravity quadriceps strength. Anti-gravity strength is the strength of muscles to oppose gravity and keep a person upright. Antigravity muscles include the calf, quadriceps and muscles of the back and knee.

Polio survivors generally report good pain relief and significant improvement in knee function post-surgery. Knee replacements last fifteen to twenty years. However, the surgical revision rate (seven percent on average at just over six years) post TKR is higher among polio versus non-polio patients. This outcome may be due in part to quadriceps functioning. The strength of quadricep muscle is a prognosticator for positive functional outcomes. Patients may need to strength this muscle prior to surgery.

Decreased bone density: Poliomyelitis is a risk factor for osteoporosis. Up to 96% of polio survivors have osteoporosis.

Bone mineral density is lower than their age and gender matched groups. The femoral neck (hip), or atrophic polio affected limb are the most common sites.

Osteoporosis literally means "porous bones." Porous bones are brittle and break easier than healthy bones. With normal aging, bones lose their thickness and strength. These changes are referred to as decreased mineral density.

Bone in the polio affected leg usually has significantly lower bone density than that of the other leg. This decrease in mineral density is due to flaccid paralysis, muscle disuse, less weight-bearing, and limited growth of the limb.

Polio survivors have four times the rate of falls as the general population. Fractures mostly involve the femoral neck (hip), or atrophic polio affected limb.

Factors increasing the polio survivor's fracture risk include aging, lack of physical exercise regimens to strengthen muscles and bones, and reduced sunlight exposure leading to Vitamin D deficiency. Walks outdoors are recommended for polio survivors.

DEXA-scan may be used to measure bone strength and track loss. Therapies with calcium and Vitamin D along with anti-osteoporotic therapies such as intravenous solutions, injections or oral medications may be administered to address bone changes.

Extensive fatigue: A comparison study of reported fatigue concluded that 67.9% of polio survivors voiced "substantial fatigue" versus 22% of subjects without a polio history. A survey of patients with neuromuscular disorders revealed that the fatigue of polio survivors was higher than that reported by people with multiple sclerosis, spinal cord injury, or muscular dystrophy.

Polio fatigue has been categorized into three types: **Physical (neuromuscular), general, and mental fatigue**. Physical which comes from the limited endurance of muscles affected by polio is characterized by aching pain and weakness. General fatigue is described as a feeling of total body exhaustion. Mental fatigue refers to diminished ability to concentrate, remember, and lack of motivation to participate in activities of daily living.

Multiple polio sequelae are swallowed up and overshadowed in the broader sequela of extensive fatigue. Polio survivors may not remember a time when exhaustion was not beyond their control.

The general population defines fatigue as tiredness due to something they did or encountered. Physical exertion, or emotional stress such as job loss, a relationship break-up, or a tragedy are typical events that send a person into an exhausted state.

Knowing what brought about one's tiredness gives people clues as to how to remedy the situation. Most folks can change their lifestyle in ways that rid themselves of fatigue. People know their tiredness may affect not only their physical state but also their mental and emotional well-being interfering with their ability to listen to others, to concentrate, to process information, and/or take part in a conversation.

When faced with fatigue, it is common for most people to pause. Some folks self-isolate when they feel tired, binging with screen time, reading, gaming, trying out new recipes, treating themselves to spa time, exercising, recreating outdoors and/or spending downtime with valued friends and family. All are pathways to recovery.

Polio survivors in contrast cannot throw off their fatigue as easily as other folks do. Polio survivors suffer fatigue in a degree related to the amount of damage to their brain stem, and the destruction the virus caused throughout cardiovascular, respiratory, gastrointestinal, and musculoskeletal systems. The virus that snuck in and muddled up their bodies remains in control of their daily life.

Hitting the polio wall is the polio survivor's way of describing an exhaustion that cannot be relieved by just resting, games, change in scenery, distraction, or entertainment. The polio survivor who *hits the polio wall* has to admit defeat and say, "I cannot go on." Conceding is not easy for polio survivors who have honed overcoming challenges their entire lives.

Resting cannot alone cure polio fatigue. The polio virus continues in control from the time of acute infection onward through life-long exhaustive states.

Polio fatigue is not equated with **myalgic encephalomyelitis/chronic fatigue syndrome (ME/CFS)** although researchers debate if ME/CFS is due to a damage from a virus that entered the brain. Comparing polio and ME/CFS, polio patients' lives are impacted to a greater extent by the muscle-related symptoms of weakness, twitches and spasms, joint pain, and gait instability than by fatigue. The lives of patients with ME/CSF are walloped by fatigue without the polio elements.

Most medical schools do not have course of study in their physician training related to polio or myalgic encephalomyelitis/chronic fatigue syndrome (ME/CFS). Therefore, symptoms, when reported, may be misunderstood. Like polio survivors, the estimated 836,000 to 2.5 million Americans who report ME/CFS symptoms may not find a diagnosis or appropriate treatment.

Anesthesia considerations for the polio survivor: It is important that the polio survivor relay their particular symptoms related to altered breathing and swallowing. Knowing a patient's history establishes baseline values and gives operative staff a look at positioning issues that may arise.

From physical assistance for positioning to proportioning of anesthesia and nerve blocks, the healthcare team's familiarity with differences the polio survivor presents when undergoing surgery is essential.

Attention should be paid not only to the biological changes inherent within the polio survivor but also the childhood experiences of being ripped away from their families and spending months to years in a hospital where they may have experienced psychological, physical, and sexual abuse by hospital staff. Polio survivors facing surgery bring their feelings to the table with them and need reassurance that their safety is of upmost importance during this time period when they have no control.

Preoperatively, staff should take measurements for **anti-embolic (compression)** stockings keeping in mind that polio survivors' legs may differ in shape and length. Two sizes (sets) of stockings may be required.

Polio survivors are more likely to awaken from anesthetic shivering because their hypothalamus has been damaged by the polio virus. Warm blankets to address the polio survivor's cold intolerance should be at hand.

Postoperative staff understanding how the polio virus damaged the reticular activating system (RAS) and vagal nuclei can proactively address pain, choking, standing, walking, and fainting issues that require careful intervention in ways specific to polio survivors.

Physicians should consider the patient's neuromuscular symptoms in choosing to use general or regional anesthesia. Before administering a **neuromuscular blockade**, baseline twitch response should be determined. For polio survivors this response may be smaller than normal in some muscles.

To address **hypoventilation**, nurses should encourage deep breathing and coughing in the post operative recovery unit. Teaching use of incentive spirometry prior to surgery is an appropriate, proactive measure to address hypoventilation related to the polio survivor's respiratory dysfunction.

Polio survivors are more likely to **vomit post op**. **Fainting** may occur with vomiting. Clearing secretions such as vomit may be addressed by placing the polio patient on their side post op and monitoring secretions.

A common side effect of general anesthetic is **slowing of the gut and urinary system**. Polio survivors report inability to urinate after surgery. This is due to damage the polio virus inflicted on bladder nerves. In addition, they may require medication to prevent constipation which could lead to gastroparesis.

To improve patient safety during the peri-operative period, hospitals attention to staffing is imperative. Research has shown that 37-52% of adverse outcomes are preventable. Special considerations for polio survivors undergoing surgery should be part of an organization's systematic plan for improvement of surgical outcomes. This translates into education for surgeons, anesthesiologists and healthcare workers caring for the polio survivor.

Polio survivor personality: The personality characteristics of children with polio have been scrutinized since the 1940s. As polio survivors matured, they melded their intrapersonal and interpersonal knowledge, experiences, and emotions into their personality.

The varied extent of polio virus damage, hospitalization, type of treatments received along the way, family dynamics, social and school life would suggest that the personalities of people who had polio are shaped by life experiences. A polio survivor's approach to the circumstances tossed at them is deep-seated in the characteristics of their personality.

There are traits that innumerable survivors of polio share. These include being cheerful, good, and obedient, over-achieving, leading a life helpful to others, and performing to please others.

This is not to say that every polio survivor behaves in these ways. *There are ornery, self-centered polio survivors.* People may be more affected by life circumstances aside from polio which induce them to cope and behave differently.

The cheerful, good, and obedient child: The horrors of the polio virus pandemic reverberated in the developing personality of the children isolated in hospitals. Polio children felt their parents' shame. Wanting to lessen the burden of parents who loved and sacrificed to care for them, they displayed behaviors they thought were part of the persona of the child of their mother's and father's dreams.

Children who are polio survivors became the absent sound of their parents' grief. They chose behaviors meant not to anger. Children grew up learning to soothe and protect the feelings of others.

Torn away from parents and dependent on hospital staff to have their needs met, polio survivors hospitalized as children learned that they had to be good. Warm packs were not always comfortable, and splints and braces limited movement and escalated pain, but children in polio wards had no choice but to accept whatever was done to them. They were alone among many others who could not object. Staff stretching their legs and arms was agonizing and for a child in a polio ward, unavoidable.

Crying was not acceptable at the isolation hospital. Even if in severe pain and feeling unable to participate in more therapy which exacerbated discomfort, children hospitalized with polio forged on. They knew that staff had to be appeased. Adults who were hospitalized as children with polio report some staff punished them for noncompliance. This could be verbal admonishment to stop their crying or isolation from others in the ward.

One young polio survivor recalled a nurse scolding her to stop crying or she would never see her parents. Another child reported a nurse reprimanded him to get over asking for his favorite stuffed animal because it had been already incinerated. A nurse tersely lectured the child saying, "Do you want someone else to touch it and get polio?"

Polio survivors report not only psychological, emotional, and physical trauma but also sexual abuse. Staff had the authority to put their hands anywhere they wanted. Some healthcare workers might have been curious to see if their poking might bring a physiological response.

Polio children were silent during staff abuse because they wanted to please, their limbs were immobilized by braces, they were confined to bed, and they felt exhausted. One child hospitalized for polio recalled that she did not want to make staff angrier, so she smiled through staff misconduct.

In the 1940s and 1950s, nurses were advised to not spoil the hospitalized child. If a child kept ringing the call device to get a nurse's attention, polio survivors remember that the bell was taken away. At the time, healthcare workers believed that children would "get over" any distress.

Polio survivors report memories of time in an iron lung—even if placed in one at an early age. Some polio survivors tell vivid details. Others have found that like muscle memory, a picture (visual memory) of being in the lung haunts them. Polio survivors remember being afraid in the iron lung.

The polio ward's constant glaring lighting—staring up at it often day in and day out—is frequently reported as a characteristic of the environment of the child hospitalized with polio. Newspapers published sepia pictures of paralyzed children lined up in rows and young people in iron lungs looking upward toward the ceilings.

A 1995 National Survey revealed that more emotional (34%) and physical (94%) abuse was reported in the polio survivor group in than the general population. This self-report included feelings of having to hide their own feelings to appease others and not escalate abuse.

In addition, polio survivors revealed that this abuse led them to fear criticism throughout their lives. They refrained from telling people who hurt them to stop.

Healthcare staff were overburdened and demoralized by the unpredictability of transmission of the polio virus, long shifts, and heart-breaking, demanding work. Nurses, now in their nineties, tell anecdotal stories of fatigue and fear but, also, a sense of purpose—a calling.

A nurse's recollection of her first day on a polio ward.

"I did not want to be working on the polio ward. The head operating room (OR) nurse brought together the nurses who staffed the OR. She told us that all surgeries were postponed due to the polio virus. The operating room theaters had been cleared. The head nurse instructed us to report immediately to the iron lung unit.

I wanted to call my mother. She would not want me to take a chance of getting polio. I did not contact her. Instead, I kept walking slowly down the corridor with the other nurses to enter the polio ward. I knew sickness was what I pledged to deal with as a nurse.

The first baby I took care of looked so small in the iron lung. I put my finger inside her hand, but she pulled her fist into the iron lung. She was screaming, her face a bit bluish. An older nurse shouted for her to stop crying, but that did no good.

I checked the gauges on the iron lung repeatedly. I was so scared. I was trained in a hurry when I arrived on the isolation ward to pump the bellows if the electricity went off. I was taught to pump two iron lungs at a time.

I prayed the little girl would get better. I hoped I would forget her face when I went home. I still picture me standing there frightened beside her."

Posted on one hospital ward for polio children was a sign listing this advice:

> **LISTEN TO THE DOCTORS**
> **OBEY THE NURSES**
> **DO NOT FIGHT**
> **DO NOT BE BAD**
> **BE GOOD IN SCHOOL**
> **DO YOUR HOMEWORK**
> **DO NOT TALK AT DINNER or IN SCHOOL**
> **LITTLE FOLKS SHOULD BE SEEN AND NOT HEARD**

Polio taught me and others to hide the truth and to pretend to be fine for the good of those around me. *You can hurt me. I will not tell. I won't cry.* I learned this mantra as a way of survival through childhood polio and carried it into young adulthood.

Trying to bury real emotions and disability, polio survivors described how they never talked with others about their physical pain. It is no wonder that the sequalae of polio were not discussed openly until decades later…*after the fact.*

Children who had polio often concealed their symptoms so others would not judge them diminished in comparison. They did not ask for help. Fearful of criticism, children of polio did not complain.

The over-achievers: All parents want their children to fit in. One way of making it seem that you do is by excelling. When the polio child performed over and above expectations, parents were relieved.

Parents' guilt at allowing the child to get polio, was assuaged when the child was viewed as a bright star. The child recognized this early on and toiled hard to achieve success.

Working despite pain and weakness, polio children moved into adulthood with a sense of purpose, a drive to be like others and even more. They dispelled any notion they did not have what it took to achieve remarkable things. Polio survivors describe pushing themselves to the point of exhaustion until they reached an age when symptoms finally forced them to face reality and stop doing so much.

The history books are full of polio survivors who made a name for themselves in a variety of fields. Readers can check *Wikipedia* for a listing which includes **Frida Kahlo** (1907-1954), **Itzhak Perlman** (1945-), **Wilma Rudolph** (1940-1994), **Fred Whipple** (1906-2004), and **Daniel J. Wilson** (1945-2021).

One of the most well-remembered polio survivors who reached the pinnacle of her field was **Dorothea Lang** (1895-1965), an American photojournalist who contracted polio at age seven. Her right leg remained weakened, and she walked with a limp. This did not stop her from walking and talking with those suffering in the Great Depression. Her photography brought to everyday people the faces of men standing in food lines and at soup kitchens, and women staring out with despair with fear blanketing their eyes. Her photos revealed the truth of the times. One of her most famous images is that of a mother with her children. It is titled *Migrant Mother*.

Lang indicated polio was the master of her fate saying, "It was perhaps the most important thing that happened to me. It formed me, guided, instructed me, helped me, and humiliated me. All those things at once. I've never gotten over it and am aware of the force and power of it."

National polio organizations gathered and reviewed the education and achievements of survivors of polio. When compared to other people with similarly severe disability, polio survivors were more educated and had risen to higher positions in their chosen fields.

Despite disappointment in physical strength due to polio virus damage, the determination of polio survivors to succeed in personal and professional arenas using teamwork and leadership led most often to positive, humanitarian contributions.

Type A Personality: Categorizing of personality traits is a tricky dilemma. Being an achiever does not necessarily mean that polio survivors are all Type A Personality. This classification of personality characterizes people not only as ambitious, always on the move, hardworking and successful, but also aggressive, impatient, and quick to judge and show anger.

One thought as to why data regarding polio survivors as Type A personalities may be skewed is that Type A polio survivors may be more willing to participate in research studies and groups related to polio survivors. A preponderance of Type A participants may make it seem that this type of personality is more prevalent when it is not.

While some polio survivors may be Type A, others may be type B, which is a personality type associated with a more relaxed, accepting way of being in the world. Less intent on winning than but wanting to play the game very well, these people enjoy life. Type B people are described as more creative and patient than average, and team-players. Polio survivors though busy, ambitious, and successful may not show the anger and hostility characteristic of Type A personality traits.

An important history lesson: Type A and B personality type categorization grew out of 1950s analyses of men between the ages of 35 and 59 who were at risk for heart attacks. The study asked questions like "Do you do daily tasks like eating and chores fast? Do you feel guilty if you do not work but take time to relax?"

Researchers hypothesized that persons whose answers defined them as rigid, organized, concerned about what others think about them, anxious, and holding lofty expectations for themselves, could be grouped as Type A personality. Called "workaholics," while these people were very productive, they had twice as many heart attacks.

Research connected the dots between people with Type A personality and those that suffered cardiac disease and cancer. Studies were funded by the tobacco industry. Convenient connections deflected the conversation away from the real association between heart attack, cancer, and smoking.

Philip Morris supplied the capital for an institute named in part for the man who made up the label "**Type A Behavior Personality (TABP).**" Mistruth as a business strategy and a health hazard was operating even then. History repeats itself.

In 2012, criticism of the development of Type A and Type B personality types emerged when it was discovered that the tobacco industry financially supported this research to lessen the hot magnifying glass on the real connection between smoking, heart disease and cancer. Review of the findings of Friedman and Rosenman substantiated there was no strong or consistent finding to associate TABP with heart disease.

Tobacco Industry Money Deflects Smoking Relationship to Cancer and Heart Disease

Type A Behavior Personality (TABP) was first described in the 1950s by cardiologists **Meyer Friedman** and **Ray Rosenman**. Their research declared that TABP was a risk factor for coronary heart disease in White middle-class men. Authors declared that TABP was the chief cause of heart disease pushing aside other causes such as smoking, diet, lack of exercise or obesity.

Friedman labeled study of the aforementioned factors as "extremely expensive epidemiological studies." Instead, Friedman proposed that TABP was one of the most important factors in coronary artery disease. He encouraged doctors to advise patients to change their personality behavior in advance of experiencing a heart attack.

Despite lack of evidence, TABP was popularized in books fueling the notion that personality not smoking caused heart disease. Quasi scientific circles described an aggressive and time-conscious personality as the scapegoat for coronary heart disease thus dimming the beam of light focus off smoking.

The tobacco industry also sought Friedman to provide research discrediting smoking as a cause of cancer. Philip Morris Vice President, Jetson Lincoln called the funding of Friedman's projects, "a really large potential for shifting the blame away from smoking." A Lincoln interoffice memo under the heading of "Friedman Advocacy" stated, "Success for the Friedman project will have a strong tendency to discredit the major prospective mortality studies that indict smoking."

The direct link between personality and heart disease and cancer promoted by the tobacco industry is now considered questionable. We know now that smoking kills. In 2020, an estimated 500,000 Americans died of smoking-related illnesses.

Joseph Goebbels

Polio survivors who have displayed cutthroat tactics have been memorialized in history and political science books.

Joseph Goebbels (1897-1945) was minister of propaganda for the German Third Reich under **Adolph Hitler** and Germany's Chancellor (in 1945). He suffered from polio which he incurred as a young child and left him with a deformed, painful right foot and leg along with a two-inch discrepancy in leg length. Due to his disability, Goebbels was rejected from military service during World War I.

Joseph Goebbels grew up in a family of devout German Catholics. His father worked as supervisor in a factory. His mother was a blacksmith's daughter. He became estranged from his parents who did not approve of his alliance with Nazism.

It may have not been political philosophy that drew Goebbels to serve Hitler. As a child, he was schooled with Jews, had Jewish friends, and was once engaged to a half-Jewish girl. Ironically, even during the height of Nazism, Goebbels availed himself of healthcare provided by Catholic nuns who were nurses rather than be cared for by "Brown Sisters" * of the Nazi regime.

He received a Ph.D. from Heidelberg studying history, German, art, and literature. Goebbels professed wanting to be a writer. But his first novel as well as two plays were unsuccessful ventures. He failed to get a job as a newspaper reporter. And then, quite by accident, he heard Hitler speak in Munich in 1922.

Goebbels joined a group of national socialists. He developed skills as a convincing speaker. Hitler found in Goebbels a young man with a gift for speaking and inspiring audiences. In 1929, Goebbels became Reich Propaganda Leader of the Nazi party.

Goebbels was quite willing to admit that his speeches and writings were usually on the "primitive" side. "Our propaganda is primitive," the Associated Press reported him as saying, "because the people think primitively. We speak the language the people understand." Goebbels wrote: "Masses are uninformed stuff. Only in the hands of the political artists do the masses become a people and the people a nation."

Goebbels' diaries reflect that he unscrupulously used his vast powers to foster anti-Semitism by fabricating stories about atrocities allegedly committed by the Jews and by instructing reporters to not report on Nazi destruction of Jewish holy sites and businesses. Goebbels's personal notes also recount his gossiping with men who could inform him of the weaknesses of rivals in order that he keep power in his own hands. He encouraged Hitler to dismiss without a hearing anyone who did not please him. Goebbels' diaries also describe situations wherein, in response to flattery, he would reverse his position about a person.

Goebbels' diaries reveal that his goal was extermination not only of Jews, but he also planned to destroy all Christian churches. He did not have enough time to accomplish this goal before his death.

Goebbels and his wife poisoned their six children with cyanide before taking their own lives. It was well-known that Goebbel's wife, Magda sought to divorce Joseph for his philandering, but Hitler intervened not wanting a public scandal.

Goebbel's legacy will never be forgotten. Nazi efforts to create an Aryan master race, in 1933, called for sterilization of all persons with a physical deformity saying they were unworthy of life and a burden on society. In 1939, Adolf Hitler ordered the killing (via poison gas), which he labeled as "mercy death," of 70,000 German and Austrian people with disabilities. Hitler's forces murdered an estimated 275,000 people with disabilities.

* Membership (*formal or informal*) in the "National Socialist Sisterhood" was a requirement to work as a nurse in Nazi Germany.

Most polio survivors developed positive personalities over their lifetimes. By listening to their personal stories of determination and strength, family, friends, and healthcare providers will come to know people who dealt with all the havoc the polio virus brought to their everyday lives and responded not in revenge for what was taken away from them but with kindness for the graces given them.

Everyone wants to be treated as the unique individuals they are. Listening to the stories of individual polio survivors is the first step in knowing them.

The helpers: Polio survivors do care for others. This can be a life-affirming characteristic and a factor in choosing a career. Childhood polio survivors know others look at them as damaged, so they seek to do things for people to be liked by them.

They smile and often give more than they get from others. When kindness is given them, they will show gratefulness, and many times when it is withheld, polio survivors will still be polite.

Polio survivors work hard not to fail at helping others. This trait may lead to resentment if family members ask the polio survivor to do more than their fair share.

They say they "must help others out." Polio survivors cannot say "no" when asked. Those who have survived polio comprise more than their share of professionals in occupations that provide health and education services serving as teachers, nurses, and doctors.

Polio survivors did not stop working because of their polio. Because of it, they became the most caring and hardest working employees.

Polio survivors have long been the caregivers. Now, others must step up to assist them. For people in the end-stage of living with polio sequelae, a healthcare system needs to be composed of medical personnel educated about the long-term effects of polio. This holds true for other diagnoses wherein understanding, compassion, and empathy are lacking due to knowledge deficits and educational gaps in training.

The performers: Children with polio felt like they had to do what healthcare staff in hospitals demanded them to do even if the therapy hurt terribly and their energy was depleted. Kids learned that performance might bring praise.

Parents pushed their children when released from the hospital to be like other children. Polio survivors picked up skills to perform as if they were without disability. When they were young, children with polio were encouraged to exercise in order to build up their weakened selves. Parents told them to go outside, breathe fresh air, and play.

Many polio survivors cast off their crutches and braces and learned to walk independently despite doctors' forewarnings of being crippled for life. Hiding one's polio deformities and denying the pain and suffering was commonplace.

Walking out of the hospital was symbolic of surviving polio. Parents would take a deep breath of gratefulness if their child could get up on their legs and move forward on their own. Children demonstrated the myth that they were no longer unwell— their polio "cured"— when they walked even if aided by braces and crutches. Parents, feeling shame and embarrassment due to the stigma of having a child with polio, could believe their child was not disabled anymore and would be readily accepted into society.

Children had to deal with the reality that people were often repulsed by their physical deformities. Those polio survivors who could not walk were often viewed as failures and endured less acceptance by the public from their seated position. At the time of polio, societal standards marked instantly the person confined in a wheelchair as handicapped.

Part of the polio survivor's performance kit is the ability to deal with the stares and unthoughtful comments of people make about their disability. Some people are well-meaning and simply curious.

Statements of pity or disdain fall quickly off other people's tongues. There are those who put up a brick wall between themselves and polio survivors saying, "My parents had me vaccinated." (The vaccine was not available until 1955.) Mimicking, mocking, labeling, and disregarding persons with disabilities reveals much about the person doing so.

When I was a young child, my mother would take me shopping. Tired shoppers would rest on benches with their heavily laden bags at their feet. When we would walk by, these folks would look up and stare at me as I limped by.

My mother would lean over and coach me, *Smile, Susie, so they will not feel so badly.* I would do as my mother said because I was an obedient, good child. *You can hurt me. I will not tell. I won't cry.* Most would look down when I smiled. I realized people were uncomfortable with my disability when I saw they could not look me in the eye. Now I understand each person I meet deals with my wobbly walk in their own way with a manner which reflects their personality and life experiences.

Polio Seen Through the Eyes of Children

A neighbor was walking with her children and me when her youngest blurted out, "Why do you walk so funny?" My friend firmly grabbed her child's arm, wagged an outstretched finger in the child's face while saying, "Don't talk like that." I looked at them and said, "It is all right. She is just saying what she is seeing." It is a fact my walking can be described by a child as "funny" looking because in a child's vocabulary this just means it is something out of the ordinary that she has not seen before.

A grade schoolteacher asked me to visit her classroom because the kids were making fun of a fellow student with a disability. She wanted me to show the class my polio leg and talk about all I did even though one leg was smaller.

The class sat on the floor, and I walked around them and through the circle they formed. I rolled up my pant legs so they could all see the differences in size and shape. Encouraging them to scan the bigger one next to the smaller one, I mentioned that it was a natural reaction to look at and compare things that are different.

I said I was a nurse who cared for people who had all sorts of differences. Some patients had hearts that did not work. Many people could not walk. Others had arms that would not move the way they wanted. Numerous people could not speak.

I said I was fortunate that I could swim forty-five minutes of laps every other day. I told them I loved to read and write. I mentioned I loved playing basketball. I told the children that playing with friends and family was my favorite thing to do just like them.

During the question-and-answer period that followed my presentation, I sat down on the floor among the kids.

The first question the children asked was: Can I touch your hair?

The second question was: Can I touch your hair?

I was the only blonde person among the children and teacher. My hair color not my disability stood out to them.

We all have our differences.

What our differences are depends on who is looking.

What I best remember about this time, was seeing a whole lot of outstretched little kid hands as they reached out to help me get up off that classroom floor.

Pool Ladies

A recent incident reminds me of how adults may become less able to trouble themselves to help a disabled person than the children who offered their hands.

I walked into the pool area. People in and around the deck of the pool had covered all surfaces of all the benches and one lone chair with their gym bags and shoes.

Because polio has left me without the ability to stand and take off my shoes, I asked a woman if she could please move her bag so I might sit down and take off my shoes. I explained I had a knee replacement a month before and that, coupled with polio prevented me from standing to take off my shoes.

The woman said, "No, my bag will get wet if I put it on the floor." I asked another woman and got the same reply, "I do not want my bag or towel wet."

When I returned home from the pool shortly after having left the house to go there, my husband asked me why I was home so soon. I told him that I could not get into the pool.

In our conversation, he expressed wonder that I did not yell at the women at the pool. I said that experience has shown me that people who do not care about others, also generally do not listen. This is the nature of people of privilege who may have not experienced loss. We all eventually incur loss as we age. The time will come when they need a little help.

Instead of taking a morning lap swim, I sat at my computer and crafted a letter to a person on the board that governs pool use. I explained the issue. I suggested that the board provide more chairs and hooks for bags and towels.

Management personnel wrote back, "Thank you not just for alerting us, but also for giving great suggestions what to do to correct the situation."

The next week there were additional chairs poolside. There were new hooks to hang bags and towels.

Polio survivors say to themselves, *You can hurt me. I will not tell. I won't cry.* And then, as over-achievers, they say, "We will take steps necessary to get things done."

Franklin Delano Roosevelt played it his way by claiming: "I'll walk without crutches. I'll walk into a room without scaring everybody half to death. I'll stand easily enough in front of people so they will forget I'm a cripple."

Because he had wealth, daily personal, side-by-side assistance, and access to Warm Springs Resort (which was beyond what the common American had at their disposal), he could hide the sequalae of polio from the public. Only the people closest to FDR saw him in a wheelchair.

Some polio survivors became actors. They enfolded their personalities into those of the characters they played. They were successful at hiding their personal history with polio. Other actors had their acting careers halted because directors felt polio symptoms were not compatible with the appearances of the characters they needed to play.

- **Alan Alda** (1936-): His parents used the therapies of Australian bush nurse, Sister Kenny's treatment at home. They applied hot compresses along with stretching exercises instead of casts to polio affected limbs to reduce muscle spasms.

- **Mia Farrow** (1945-): At age eight, during an outbreak in Los Angeles County, she contracted polio. Farrow spent time in an iron lung during hospitalization on an isolation ward.

- **Ida Lupino** (1918-1995): Although her polio symptoms in 1934 lasted only a few days, her physical abilities were changed. When her Hollywood contract as an actor was broken, she became a producer and director. Her 1949 film, *Never Fear* captured her polio experience. Lupino shared that she realized she needed to focus on her brains, not just her good looks.

- **Joni Mitchell** (1943-): A Canadian singer and songwriter, she contracted polio when she was nine years old. She played ukulele and guitar. Since her left hand was weakened by polio, she compensated by developing alternative instrument tunings and ways of composing songs. Mitchell was honored at the Kennedy Center for the Arts in 2021. In an interview that day, she said, "*I think the polio was a rehearsal for the rest of my life. I've had to come back several times from things. And this last* *one was a real whopper. I'm hobbling along. I'm doing all right."*

- **Donald Sutherland** (1935-): He spent five years in a hospital after contracting polio when he was seven years old. During this time, he recounted that he developed a fierce love of reading.

- **Johnny (Johann) Weissmuller** (1904-1984): The Olympic five medal winner in swimming and actor (Tarzan film series), experienced a case of polio at age nine. His doctor encouraged him to exercise to gain strength. He started swimming competitively first at his local YMCA.

- **Neil Young** (1945-): Canadian American singer (dual citizenship 2020), musician, songwriter, and inductee of the Rock and Roll Hall of Fame contracted polio at age six before vaccine development. During an outbreak in the summer of 1951, he became partially paralyzed on his left side. He traveled to Florida with his family because they believed the warm Florida weather more conducive to recovery. When the polio vaccine became available, Young was vaccinated. In February 2022, Young removed his music from Spotify, an audio streaming service, to protest a podcast that spread **COVID-19** misinformation. Other musicians such as Joni Mitchell followed. Director-General Tedros Adhanom Ghebreyesus (1965-), Former Minister of Foreign Affairs of Ethiopia of the **World Health Organization** praised musicians for their actions.

Resilience: Resilience consists of positive traits and behaviors that help people deal with changes in life. People with resilience survive and thrive even when life circumstances are tough. They adapt.

Polio survivors pushed disability down under a veneer of cheerfulness, obedience, kindness, helpfulness, and overachieving to become resilient. They did not "recover" but adapted to their individual situations using personal strengths and the support of strong relationships (family and community) to modulate weaknesses.

Resilience has been identified as a strength of the majority of polio survivors. There are three main factors feeding into the development of resilience: psychological and natural tendencies, support from others, and external support systems. A recent study reported that scores of polio survivors on the Resilience Scale for Adults (RSA) were comparable with young healthy adults. RSA data revealed that polio survivors rated family cohesion higher than the norm benchmark.

Despite physical ailments including further decline in their later years, aging polio survivors describe their psychological health as good. Studies show their mental health to be less affected by physical debility than that of the general population.

Having adapted to disability, the inevitable declines with aging do not render polio survivors feeling powerless. They have learned to plan, and balance work and rest. Energy conservation, which they have long used, is a helpful aptitude when facing the effects of aging. These skills are the foundation for resilience.

Research confirms that life-long challenges have led polio survivors to be resilient. Their work participation, whether paid or voluntary is associated with better mental health.

People who cope well with age-related changes are more satisfied with life. Self-reliance, optimism, and ongoing feelings of hope within polio survivors may ameliorate depression.

While polio survivors show a willingness to adapt to declining physical health, they voice that healthcare professionals are often dismissive when they seek help to deal with their post-polio and aging mix of symptoms. Polio survivors describe having negative experiences with health professionals who admit they know nothing about polio.

Is there an ethical responsibility for society, community policy and program planners, and healthcare professionals to make certain that knowledge and practices keep up with the realities polio survivors face? Polio survivors are the pioneers in developing resilience despite the sequelae of viral infection wreaked damage throughout their bodies. Can healthcare professionals better serve the survivors of polio and other people facing long-haul symptoms of viral infections?

Separation anxiety: Sick with fever, stressed with breathing difficulty, and weakened by paralysis, kids with childhood polio were wrested from their parents' arms and suddenly deposited in a place that was filled with strange sights, smells, noises, and unfamiliar people. A child brought into an isolation hospital ward with polio might not see their parents for weeks.

Hospitalized children were surrounded with staff members who were worried because they knew the gravity of the polio epidemic meant not only disability or death for the patients but possibly also for themselves, due to their heightened risk for contact with the virus. In this jarring environment, scars formed, permeated, and changed the fabric of families.

Some parents stood for hours behind a small square of glass cut into a door on the polio ward to catch a glimpse of their child. Others would cluster by first floor hospital windows hoping their child might be wheeled into view.

There were parents who brought ladders and climbed up to see into hospital windows. Medical staff were often too busy to talk to anxious parents. Frantic parents camped in their cars waiting for news. No rooming houses or what were called "auto courts" would take them in. The government rallied and stepped in providing accommodations through State welfare departments and the Salvation Army.

Many parents had no choice but to return home, leaving their child behind. Women were responsible to take care of other children and family. Men returned to their jobs. Parents balked at isolation restrictions but doing what was best for the health and well-being of the community was viewed as a patriotic duty.

Children hospitalized for polio recall the anxiety caused by separation from their parents often at young ages. Staff did not encourage sharing their feelings about missing their parents and family members.

Overworked, tired, and stressed health workers mistakenly used language to distance themselves from the children. They placed barriers blocking out the sadness of children's faces everywhere in front of them. "Be brave," was a commonly reported staff directive.

Interviews conducted with polio survivors report the common pressure on polio survivors to minimize how suddenly being all alone in the hospital affected them. When polled, 84% of polio survivors studied reported anxiety related to their polio related hospitalization. They described their childhood experience as filled with feelings of helplessness and lack of control over their lives.

Debunking the myth that children in the long term were not upset with hospitalization, polio survivors shared detailed memories of separation from their parents in an environment where children were continually sad and crying. They said these memories have not gone away. Their polio hospitalization had not been put behind them.

When children returned home, talking about their polio experience was often verboten. Altogether shut out of conversations, children had no help to process their experiences.

Family members told polio survivors to not complain because people do not like spending time with whiners. Parents did not talk about their child's weaknesses. Once children were home, parent's conversations centered on rehabilitation and recovery not the terrible times of the past.

One cannot blame the parents. It is the circumstances the family experienced that molded each family member's role around the polio survivor. People all around world were enamored with FDR's well-publicized strength and endurance, along with the myth of his ability to completely overcome polio. "You can do it, too," the nation and parents mimicked to their children.

One concludes that not all parents treated their child disabled by polio in a supportive manner. Survivors tell of rejection by one or both parents with fathers being the more likely to be the parent unable to accept a crippled child.

Separation anxiety has an official medical diagnosis code. **Separation Anxiety is an anxiety disorder** consisting of persistent and excessive anxiety beyond that expected for a child's developmental level related to separation or impending separation from the attachment figure as evidenced by at least three of the following criteria from the **Diagnostic and Statistical Manual of Mental Disorders (DSM-5)**:

- Recurrent excessive distress when anticipating or experiencing separation from home or from major attachment figures;

- Persistent and excessive worry about losing major attachment figures or about possible harm to them, such as illness, injury, disasters, or death;

- Persistent and excessive worry about experiencing an untoward event (for example, getting lost, being kidnapped, having an accident, becoming ill) that causes separation from a major attachment figure;

- Persistent reluctance or refusal to go out, away from home, to school, to work, or elsewhere because of fear of separation;

- Persistent and excessive fear of or reluctance about being alone or without major attachment figures at home or in other settings;

- Persistent reluctance or refusal to sleep away from home or to go to sleep without being near a major attachment figure;

- Repeated complaints of physical symptoms (for example, headaches, stomachaches, nausea, vomiting) when separation from major attachment figures occurs or is anticipated; and/or

- Repeated nightmares involving the theme of separation.

Polio survivors are known for their optimistic thinking, ability to manage in tough situations and trying to meet the expectations of others. Growing up in a hospital environment helped me use these strengths to shape the future for other hospitalized people.

Working as a critical care nurse in a pediatric intensive care unit that allowed parents to visit only for five minutes at a time only heightened my lived awareness that the medical community could do better to reinforce family bonds. One of my first pieces of research looked at the interface of patients and family in ICU. The findings are presented in "Visitation Needs Reported by Patients with Cardiac Disease and Their Families," (*Heart & Lung: The Journal of Critical Care*). This work was a little payback for all the kind staff who showed love for children and cared for me.

Survivor guilt: Although the parents of children who had polio are no longer alive, our understanding of the trauma they went through is important to discuss. Mothers and fathers gave up their children to care in isolation hospitals, witnessed their babies and children in iron lungs and braces, considered and authorized experimental treatments, and participated for their entire lives watching what the polio virus carved out for their child's health, social acceptance, career, and happiness.

The campaign to eradicate polio included posters warning parents to vaccinate their children or face the consequence of having a disabled child. Disability represented a parent's failure to prevent disease. Pictures of children with braces, using crutches, and in wheelchairs evoked fear, shame, and guilt as part of the public health campaign for vaccination.

The term "**survivorship guilt**" was coined in the 1960s. This type of guilt evolves in people who have survived a life-threatening situation. Self-blame is at its core. Parents rebuked themselves for not doing the right thing or enough. They asked, "Why my child, not me?" "What could I have done to prevent my child from getting polio?"

Reliving what they may have failed to do or how what they did brought the virus to invade their child was a theme that haunted their days and nights. Parents replayed in their minds the events leading up to the polio diagnosis for their child, asking themselves if they had done something they should not have, if they had missed an early cue that would have spared worsening of the disease in their child, and if they did something morally wrong to deserve this misfortune.

Such rumination of the facts leading up to their child's polio could have led to false beliefs such as the disease was due totally to their irresponsibility. Some parents overestimated their ability to keep their child safe from the sweeping epidemic of polio virus.

Parents of children with polio who replayed the sad and scary events of the epidemic often harbored feelings of fear of the unknown, helplessness, irritability, and anger. They displayed mood swings and problems sleeping. For these parents, headaches and stomachaches also accompanied their shame and self-blaming. Some self-medicated with alcohol.

While trying to face down their own demons, parents of polio kids were many times ostracized openly and labeled by people who judged them lacking in parenting skills. Young parents of children with polio were at times abandoned by their own parents who feared transmission of the virus to themselves. Parents were many times deprived of needed understanding, hands-on help, guidance, and encouragement.

Survivor guilts falls under the category of **posttraumatic stress disorder (PTSD)** in the current **Diagnostic and Statistical Manual of Mental Disorders (DSM–5)**. Shame and guilt are important dimensions of PTSD. Shame and guilt may occur during acute traumatic experiences and be prolonged past the time when the immediate crisis has resolved. In other words, parents of polio children may have carried the burden of survivorship guilt to their graves.

Looking Forward

Polio survivors are an aging population whose symptoms have become more recognized and substantial over time due to age-related weakening of systems previously damaged by the polio virus. Understanding that the polio virus destroyed much more than was first evident can improve the care offered survivors. Acknowledging the "long haul" symptoms of polio is a beginning to clearer recognition of the depth and breadth of viral infection.

Polio sequelae do not go away. The Director of the **International Center for Polio Education** advises people with post-polio symptoms to take the helm to address their unique symptoms so they can get off "the post-polio roller-coaster." Talking with a knowledgeable healthcare professional is a start.

TOOLBOX

For
Healthcare Providers, Polio Survivors, Friends, and Family Members

Dealing with Long-Haul Symptoms of Polio Virus Damage

My experiences with polio have taught me about *long-haul* (prolonged) symptoms following a viral infection. This lived education has given me insight into helping people as a nurse.

Even the best of frontline healthcare professionals may not have received education about polio or cared for a patient with a history of polio.

A nurse recently said to me, "This stuff isn't in textbooks. I never learned about it in school."

A physician treating a polio survivor preoperatively stated, *"You must be one of the last ones left."*

A polio survivor declared, "I told my doctor I had swallowing problems that might be related to childhood polio. My parents did not talk about my polio with me but, at a recent family reunion, a cousin told me I had a mild case. I have trouble swallowing especially late in the evening. I am hoping for some guidance."

Multiple polio survivors when interviewed about their quality of life made statements about the futility of talking with healthcare personnel. A spokesperson for a group of polio survivors stated:

"We do not go to doctors anymore because they have no knowledge about post-polio symptoms."

"Most anesthetists wouldn't know what to do if we turned up at the hospital for emergency surgery."

"Polio is considered a dead disease by health-care professionals."

The best advice I can give to all healthcare professionals, friends, and family members is *listen carefully to the voices* of polio survivors. Polio children were brought up to not complain. They tend to function as nondisabled as possible. Survivors have endured difficulties during their lifetimes and been told, "It's in your head." or "You are just getting older."

Note that there are just a handful of polio *specialists* in the United States. Doctors, Physician Assistants, Nurse Practitioners, nurses, physical and occupational therapists, chiropractors, speech pathologists, pharmacists, social workers, and psychologists are called to fill the information and treatment gap for polio survivors. It takes only one professional to learn about polio and improve the health of a polio survivor.

I encourage you to pull up an armchair and have a conversation with the polio survivor. Ask the person to tell their story. You might start with, "How do you feel having survived polio?" *Everyone has a gift to give. Yours may be to listen, to inform, and to guide.*

Polio taught me to look each patient in the eye and not dwell on abnormalities or disabilities until I first got to know the person as an individual. The statement, *"Tell me about you."* will demonstrate to the polio survivor that you are ready to hear their story.

Patients are not a disease. Each is a person experiencing a disease process. It follows that healthcare should be person-centered. Learning a patient's story enables the provider of care to align medical interventions with the person's goals, lifestyle, treatment options, and means of support.

Talking with the individual about what is going on in their life will bring understanding of the person's capabilities as well as deficits in functioning which may underlie safety issues. You might ask: "Are there moments when you feel uncomfortable because of assumptions people make about you having polio? Are there times you are grateful for surviving polio?"

Together, the healthcare professional and polio survivor can come up with support systems to make activities the polio survivor most values safe. They can address long-haul symptoms proactively to improve quality of life.

You might consider this dialogue: What is your day like? What activities fill your morning, afternoon, and evening? What is the thing about polio that prevents you most from doing what you want to do in the day? In the evening? During the night? What bothers you most about living with the never-ending, long-haul symptoms of polio?

You may want to continue conversation by presenting a list of the commonly experienced, prolonged effects of polio. Asking the polio survivor to identify areas that annoy them most may focus further discussion.

A *Polio Survivor Checklist* can define the polio survivor's unique symptoms and concerns. The patient can tick off concerns in the waiting room and this may quicken up office visit time.

Polio Survivor Checklist

Place a number one, two, three or N/A for not applicable in the box to the left of each of the following issues polio survivors may face.

1 = issue bothers me **daily**
2 = issue bothers me **weekly**

3 = issue bothers me at least **every month**

N/A = **not applicable to me**

- ☐ How I look to other people
- ☐ What other people expect of me
- ☐ Walking
- ☐ Tripping
- ☐ Falling
- ☐ Leg cramps/spasms
- ☐ Pain
- ☐ Increased pain with cold
- ☐ Heat intolerance
- ☐ Increased pain with activity
- ☐ Increased pain with stress
- ☐ New joint pain: knee/hip/neck
- ☐ Fatigue
- ☐ Swallowing difficulty
- ☐ Stomachache
- ☐ Arm weakness, shoulder soreness/lifting problems
- ☐ Fast beating heart, feeling the beat in chest (palpitations)
- ☐ Breathing difficulty
- ☐ Sleeping difficulty
- ☐ Fainting
- ☐ Decreased bone density
- ☐ Separation anxiety
- ☐ Feeling isolated

The healthcare provider can look into the eyes of the polio survivor using salient questioning to get to the truth. Patients complain they feel overlooked when healthcare providers focus on entering data using a computer keyboard instead of giving them eye contact.

A brief overview of sequelae of polio and *conversation starters* may allow the interviewer to give full attention to the patient, building empathy and trust, while scanning key points.

Mobility

People with leg/hip/spine and foot deformities are more likely to fall due to:

☐ cognitive decline

☐ balance and tripping issues

☐ weakness and tiredness toward the middle or end of a day

☐ unstable footwear

☐ assistive devices not set up properly or with worn-out parts

☐ rugs, cords, and other clutter in path of walking

☐ unlit areas especially for walking in darkened hallways into bathrooms at night and to and from outdoors. Lights with motion sensors are recommended. Small plug-in versions can be packed in luggage for travel.

☐ flooring products not likely to give a little with falls

☐ beds too low for ease in rising

☐ chairs with wheels

☐ chairs without arms

☐ chairs/couches/exam tables too low or too high for ease of sitting and rising

☐ lack of sturdy countertops/furniture to grab onto when getting up and down. People often brace their arms on countertops, furniture, and against walls to help balance. Polio may affect the deltoid arm muscle. Asking about arm and shoulder stability and pain can uncover mechanical deficits.

☐ Poor accessibility of grab bars and shower heads/on-off switches in bathrooms/tubs/showers

Physical therapy: Evaluations and treatment are best scheduled periodically not only in response to a fall with injury. Braces should periodically be examined for fit and integrity. **Primary care providers** and family members are in key positions to ensure periodic assessments occur.

Occupational therapy: Home visits to suggest safety measures may prevent injuries. An occupational therapist's ideas for ways to expend less energy can improve quality of life. An evaluation of the polio survivor's moving into and out of vehicles should be included. Observation of how bulky items are carried may lead to new ways that support safer walking.

Orthotics: Making walking comfortable and safe is a priority. An **orthotic specialist** can design footwear inserts that help with balance and comfort. Any shoe, boot, or slipper can be fit with cushioning that is molded to the specific abnormalities of the polio survivor's foot.

Conversation starters:

Have you tripped in the past month, past year? If so, where, wearing what type of footwear, time of day, degree of tiredness and pain along with intervening variables such as clutter, light, or distractions.

Have you fallen in the past month, past year?

Have you fallen with injury in the past year?

When you are tired, do you rest?

When did you last have your eye glass prescription checked?

How do you rise out of bed in the morning?

Do you get up out of bed during the night?

> What lights your path going to the bathroom at night?

Pain

The polio survivor you meet may have endured pain for decades. More than one issue may be causing the pain.

Ask the person to describe their pain. *Do not just request a number because no one's number stays the same all day and night.* A number will not tell you if the pain is achy, dull, heavy, or deep-down excruciating, radiating, or cramping? Words tell the healthcare worker far more than a number.

Continue questioning: When, where, what aggravates the pain? What relieves the pain? What have you tried (medicines, topicals, warm baths, positioning, rest) that brings comfort? What have you tried that does not help the pain?

Conversation starters:

Tell me about any aches and pains you have.

When does your pain come and go during a typical day?

Tell me which areas hurt and describe how the pain feels.

What aggravates your pain? (Cold, stress, extensive activity)

What have you tried in prescription, over-the-counter medications? Include topical (*rub-in*) products.

Do you incorporate warm baths/blankets, positioning, pacing, distraction, hypnosis, and/or rest into your pain management plan?

What have you tried for pain control that does not work?

OLDCART: Collecting data through use of this tool, the polio survivor and healthcare provider can get a good picture of pain over time.

O = ONSET

L = LOCATION

D = DURATION

C = CHARACTERISTICS

A = AGGRAVATING FACTORS

R = RELIEVING FACTORS

T = TREATMENTS THAT WORK/DON'T WORK

Muscle Spasms/Cramps/Fasciculations

Involuntary muscle spasms, cramps and fasciculations are annoyances that often lead to pain. Fasciculations can often come at bedtime and disturb sleep. Stretching and use of an electronic device like a **transcutaneous electrical nerve stimulation (TENS)** unit may help relieve the discomfort.

Some polio survivors take muscle relaxant medication. Polio survivors need to be aware that these drugs may interfere in digestion, gastrointestinal movement, and urination. Muscle relaxants may cause dizziness and drowsiness.

Conversation starters:

Do you experience muscles spasms after activity?

Describe how your muscles feel when you hurt.

What do you do to reduce muscle pain?

Do you take medication?

Do you use over the counter (OTC) products? Have you applied warm packs?

Have you used warm baths to soothe muscle pain?

When you lay down to rest or sleep, do you feel jitteriness in your leg muscles? What makes it go away so you can rest/sleep?

Temperature Extremes

Many survivors of polio report that to be comfortable, they dress for temperatures 20 degrees Fahrenheit cooler than what the weather report predicts. For them, the environmental temperature feels colder than it does for others.

Cold causes polio weakened muscles to fatigue. With cooler temperatures, polio survivors report more pain.

The elevated temperatures in hot tubs and very warm baths also cause problems. Polio survivors often feel dizzy and faint in the heat of saunas.

Heat intolerance is an annoyance for some patients who report being comfortable when the ambient temperature is in the range of 61 degrees to 72 degrees Fahrenheit.

Conversation starters:

How do you prepare for being in cold environments such as air-conditioned airports, and planes, theaters, and restaurants?

Do you layer clothing?

Do you choose fabrics with more thermal value (wool, silk, fleece, flannel, down and hemp) for socks, hats, gloves, sweaters, and scarves?

Are you aware to avoid immersion in very warm water such as in hot tubs or warm air such as saunas?

How do you feel in warm rooms/air over 72 degrees?

Fatigue

Fatigue can be isolating. The inability to concentrate on a task is often embarrassing. Polio survivors may not reveal this condition or may confuse their weary brain fog with dementia.

Using **rest periods** to regenerate one's body and mind before fatigue develops can be empowering for the polio survivor. Taking breaks may allow for more engagement with others and enjoyment of life.

Sight of a good armchair and ottoman, a favorite blanket, soft music, a sound machine…all can open the door to rest. Polio survivors benefit from support and understanding that they should take moments to rest.

Consultation with an occupational therapist regarding home devices that will reduce the amount of energy spent on daily tasks is recommended. Fatigue is associated with increased risk for falls. An **occupational therapist** can assess living spaces and suggest safety measures to prevent falls.

Appropriate exercise plays a vital role in post-polio management. A **physical therapist** can guide the post-polio patient in a person-specific routine that will not lead to overuse of damaged muscles.

Conversation starters:

How do you organize your day?

Do you schedule household tasks spreading them out over multiple days of the week rather than clustering them on one or two days?

Can you switch to sitting down while doing some tasks rather than standing? Example, ironing with a small iron at a table rather than using a heavy iron while standing at an ironing board.

Do you tell yourself to stop activity and rest when you have warning signs that you are tiring?

Does it seem appropriate to give up certain types of housework?

Are you aware of how an occupational therapist might help you devise ways to lessen your fatigue?

Are there family or friends who are willing to give you support with more challenging physical activities?

Does fatigue set in at a certain time in your day?

Do you take naps?

Does anything keep you from sleeping at night?

Do you have a sleep routine that is working to provide you with a good night's sleep?

Swallowing & Regurgitation

Every polio survivor should be alert to their heightened potential to choke and their higher risk for esophageal reflux.

- o Eating with drinking alcohol or consuming other sedating substances increases the risk of choking and aspiration of food into the lungs.

- o Taking smaller bites may lessen food getting caught on its way down the esophagus.

- o Drinking fluids between bites helps move food downward.

- o Avoiding foods that trigger gastroesophageal reflux will help reduce belching food back into the throat.

- o Staying upright after meals and eating smaller meals reduces backflow.

- o Eating smaller meals reduces reflux.

- o Staying at a normal weight will lessen the stomach pushing up acid into the stomach.

- o Sleeping with the head of the bed raised can reduce food pressing upward.

- o Smoking is correlated with gastroesophageal reflux.

Dental Precautions

Polio survivors should alert dentists that they may need time and space to sit up when water is squirted in their mouth. A dental chair with firm arms gives the polio survivor a surface on which to brace when rising.

Conversation starters:

How do you space your meals/snacks throughout the day?

Does your stomach get upset?

Do you hiccup a lot?

Is it hard to swallow medications or food?

Do you take NSAIDs?

Do you have a pill cutter to split medications as needed?

Do you feel burning in your throat after meals?

Have you informed your dental hygienist and dentist that you may have swallowing problems?

Tachycardia

Since most healthcare providers working today did not live through the polio epidemic, they may not recognize underlying vagus nerve damage leading to tachycardia.

Distribution of blood within the heart and body is best achieved when the heart rate is below one hundred. With tachycardia, the polio survivor may present with palpitations, weakness, or faintness.

A **cardiovascular consult** including laboratory work, electrocardiography, CT scan and Doppler carotid studies may be done.

Conversation Starters:

Have you felt light-headed in the past year?

Have you fainted in the past year?

Do you ever feel your heart beating fast?

Have you had a cardiovascular work-up in the past year?

Do you have a family history that includes heart attack, stroke, pulmonary embolism, or vascular disease?

Do you monitor your cardiac status during workouts?

> Are you aware to notify surgeons and anesthesiologists that you have had polio?

Breathing and Sleep Issues

Breathing and sleep disorders are more common in polio survivors than the general population. Therefore, review of symptoms and periodic assessments are warranted.

Although most polio survivors did not experience time in an iron lung, research found that every polio survivor had some damage to the brain stem even if no demonstrable deficits showed at the time. Although the brain stem is a small part (2.6% of the weight) of the total brain, it contains neurons that control breathing.

Polio led to weakened breathing muscles. The strength of these damaged muscles (intercostal and diaphragm) of polio survivors declines with age.

Polio survivors report increased difficulty breathing when lying down. Taking a full breath when reclined becomes harder. The intercostal muscles and diaphragm may become less efficient at moving air in and out because gravity, which when a person is upright, moves the intestines and other abdominal organs down and out of the way of respiratory muscles, is no longer operative when lying down.

Obstructive sleep apnea (OSA) and/or **central sleep apnea (CSA)** may require use of **continuous positive airway pressure devices (CPAP)** or **bilevel positive airway pressure (BiPap)** to improve oxygenation of the blood.

Abnormal sleep movements (AMS) have been reported by 52% of polio survivors. AMS have been described as brief contractions or movements of hands, arm, leg, shoulder and/or pectoral muscles. Management of these foreseeable movements which alter the sleep cycle may be addressed by prescription medications. Sixty-three percent of polio survivors say their muscles routinely twitched as they fell asleep and muscle twitching disturbed sleep. Sleep studies have confirmed AMS in polio survivors.

Conversation starters:

Do you feel short of breath during regular daily activities?

Are there times when you have difficulty breathing deep enough to fully expand your lungs?

When you lay down, is it harder to catch a full breath?

Is it difficult to cough strongly enough to clear mucus from your lungs?

When you exercise, do you find yourself short of breath and/or pursing your lips?

Do you have insomnia?

Do you awaken in the night?

Do you move around while you sleep?

Do you sleep during the daytime?

Do you experience restless legs (urge to move legs especially when falling asleep)?

Do your muscles twitch as you fall asleep?

Are you awakened by muscle twitching or moving?

Does your bed partner report you have random movements during sleep?

Were you in an iron lung during the acute phase of polio? How old were you when you were in an iron lung?

Do you smoke?

Because of neuromuscular damage by the polio virus, survivors are encouraged to have routine pulmonary evaluations including muscle strength and functioning along with oxygen and carbon dioxide levels. Periodic pulmonary function tests are used to determine change over time. Evaluation may include an overnight sleep study.

Slow Gut

Diligence at making the bowel function is essential. Slow gut not only directly affects the GI tract but also may increase pain.

Advising patients regarding pharmaceutical, food, fluid, and exercise resources for good gut health and transit of food may solve more than one problem. Sometimes figuring out the connection between food, medicine and pain makes the gut work more effectively.

Conversation starters:

Do you monitor frequency of your bowel movements?

Do you check the form of your bowel movements?

Is constipation an issue for you?

Do you use any form of laxative?

Are you aware of the uses of stimulants, stool softeners and suppositories?

Have you tried a senna tea when you feel constipated?

How many glasses of fluid (8 ounces) do you drink every day?

How many servings of vegetables and fruits do you eat every day?

Do you eat high fiber grain products?

Do you exercise?

NSAIDS & The Gut

It is important healthcare providers educate polio survivors to avoid non-steroidal anti-inflammatory medications. Polio survivors are six times as likely as the general population to develop gastric ulcers. Use of NSAIDs may increase this risk.

Conversation starters:

Are you currently taking a non-steroidal anti-inflammatory drug?

Does your stomach ever hurt?

If so, do you monitor for blood in stools?

Have you tried other drugs as options to address your medical need?

Stigma of Disease

Living with the stigma of polio taught me the best way to provide care tailored to the patient was by getting to know a person before asking questions about their disability. Treating a patient as a disease leaves out key information.

As my parents learned with polio, people may often quickly judge the origins of disease and apply blame. Polio epidemics frightened people. Not knowing how the virus was contracted led to isolation and fear.

I have often been asked how people responded to polio in the 1940s and 1950s. People overwhelmingly rallied to the cause of preventing transmission and finding a cure Everyone wanted to protect themselves, their loved ones, and others.

Americans joined together to donate what they could to the March of Dimes. People donated according to their means to support vaccine research.

No one wanted to be the one who infected a child leading to crippling and possible death. There was a sense of responsibility toward the community.

People voiced gratefulness to the scientists involved in the development of the polio vaccine. Jonas Salk, the man who in 1955 invented the polio vaccine told people the vaccine belonged to them. It was the people's vaccine.

Social barriers, however, prevented some polio survivors from fully entering society. Their deformed limbs were disturbing to others. Mobility devices were less sophisticated, bulky, heavy, and more obvious than many of today's streamline, smooth-moving assistive devices.

There will always be people who stay away from those who do not look like them physically. For them, the inclusion of someone who looks different tarnishes their self-image. Let's face it some people openly and unabashedly make fun of the disabled.

There will always be people who make presumptions about people who limp. I was turned away at the Eiffel Tower by a guard who said my wobbly gait made me ineligible to travel via elevator to the top. He quickly waved me away not asking questions or entertaining more information from me.

I had climbed up 528 steps in St. Paul's Cathedral in London (with a grandson's encouragement and help) and the 1700 steps to Positano on the Amalfi coast in Italy. But, oh well, the Eiffel Tower official had a point, and I was tired, so I had a delicious ice-cream while the others in my party went up to the top.

I visited the Sky Tower in New Zealand. It is the tallest building in Auckland at 1076 feet. The space was very crowded with tourists. Seeing my grandson and I packed tightly and being nudged in a crowd awaiting an elevator to go down after our sightseeing, a guide tapped me on the elbow and whispered a kind offer to a ride down on a "special elevator" away from the maddening crowd.

I stood in a line to climb down a thirty-foot-high brick wall to get into a boat to travel to the Aran Islands in Galway Bay, Ireland. Two boat crew came up to me and said, "If you would like some support, we are here for you." I took them up on their offer, climbing down the wall with a strong man on each side of me.

I am grateful for well-meaning courtesies. These more than make up for the presumptions of others. My grandchildren have given me their arms and pulled me along in a lot of places of the world.

Conversation starters:

Tell me how you feel the people around you view you.

Are there moments when you feel uncomfortable because of assumptions people make about you having polio?

Isolation

Technologies that reduce isolation such as telemedicine, shopping online, communicating via the internet and staying in touch with news via broadcasting can bring friends, family, and the world to a polio survivor's door.

Healthcare personnel can evaluate a patient's means to employ diverse methods to meet their needs and desires.

Conversation starters:

Tell me how you feel about using technology such as computers and phone apps.

Have you taken advantage of telemedicine options?

Do you look online at new accommodation equipment that might ease your daily expenditure of energy?

Who is your best support person? Can you talk openly to this person about your changing needs? Does this person respond in ways that will help you?

Who is your designated advocate for healthcare? Where is your **HCPOA** located? Is your **HCPOA** paperwork accessible for medics in case of emergency?

Do you have means to access home help and meal service as needed?

Are there daily activities such as cleaning, cooking, house repairs, and car maintenance you would like to hand over to another person?

Where do you see yourself housed in two years, four years, six years?

Separation Anxiety

Interviews of children hospitalized with polio reveal the kids remember procedures done to them and the ward milieu. As adults, they describe anxiety related to their helplessness and lack of control.

When polio children went home, they often were blocked from having conversations about their experiences. Many polio survivors have not had anyone to talk to about their feelings.

Conversation starters:

Have you talked with anyone about your childhood hospital polio experiences?

Do you live alone? If so, are you comfortable with this arrangement?

Do you feel anxious when going away, e.g., overnight or on vacation, from home and/or people you love?

Do you worry excessively about loved ones getting hurt?

Do you have fears of yourself being hurt in an accident or tragedy?

When you do travel away from home or loved ones, are you bothered with headaches or stomachaches?

Are you troubled by dreams or awakenings to memories of separation from family/loved ones?

If awakened during the night, what rituals do you have bedside to help you fall back asleep?

What does the future look like for you? Are you more comfortable living with people or living alone?

Joint Disease-Decreased Bone Density

Studies reveal that up to 96% of polio survivors have osteoporosis. This decrease in bone increases risk for fracture.

Wear and tear on joints happen to everyone over 50 years old. The polio survivor is at risk for degeneration of the hip due to muscle and tendon imbalance and leg length discrepancy.

Polio also affects muscle functioning and structural alignment around the knee. Polio survivors find significant improvement in functioning after total knee replacements.

Conversation starters:

Do you have pain, stiffness, or weakness of the knee joint? Hip joint?

Is an orthopedic healthcare provider part of your medical team?

Do you have regular bone density examinations with treatment as needed?

Are you receiving treatment for decreased bone density?

The joy of creating your own toolbox comes from connecting with a patient as a person who is experiencing an illness with long-haul symptoms. At the end of a conversation, the healthcare provider and patient may feel secure that they are providing care appropriate for the polio survivor they have come to know and understand.

OLDCART

Name:

Date/time	Onset (Time pain begins)	Location/s (Where it hurts)	Duration (How long the pain)	Characteristics (Dull, gnawing, Burning, Aching)	Aggravating Factors (What makes it worse, e.g., movement, awakening)	Relieving Factors (What makes it better…elevation, icing, rest, electrical stimulation, distraction, acetaminophen)	Treatments (What have you tried that works to stop the pain: and what does not work)

General Index

A

abortive poliomyelitis 32
arm muscle damage 290

B

blood pressure 34, 294, 305
bone density 307, 308, 341, 359
braces 76, 77, 343
bracing 289
breathing 34, 291, 294, 297, 298, 299, 351, 352, 353
bulbar polio 33, 34, 39, 294, 298, 300
bulbospinal polio 34

C

Centers for Disease Control and Prevention (CDC) 138, 209, 278, 281
cervical spondylosis 289
chest muscle strength 298
chiropractic 70, 71, 184, 290
Clinical Immunization Safety Assessment (CISA) 150
cold intolerance 302, 303, 311
cord compression 289
COVID-19 138, 152, 209, 279, 280, 330
Cutter Incident 149, 150, 151

D

deformity 287, 288, 289, 321, 323
dental precautions 295, 349
digestive issues 291, 292, 296

Dow Chemical Company 192
dysphagia 295

E

Eagles Club 15, 23, 263
Emerson Respirator 48
esophageal spasm 295

F

fainting 302, 304, 311, 341
fatigue 32, 301, 302, 303, 308, 309, 310, 341, 346, 347, 348
Food and Drug Administration (FDA) 122, 172
footdrop 131, 288, 289

G

gastric regurgitation 294
gastric ulcers 296, 353
gastroesophageal reflux disease (GERD) 294
gastroparesis 291, 292, 312
Gates Foundation 278
Gavi, the Vaccine Alliance 278
Global Polio Eradication Initiative (GPEI) 278

H

heart rate 34, 291, 294, 295, 297, 350, 351
heat intolerance 299, 303, 340, 346, 347
HeLa cells 151, 152, 153
hiatal hernias 294
hip arthroplasty 306

Hit Parader 99, 182
Hitting the polio wall 124, 309, 310
hydrotherapy 136

I

inactivated polio vaccine (IPV) 145, 278
iron lung 47, 48, 49, 50, 298, 300, 314, 316, 329, 335, 351

J

Jim Crow laws 134
John Hopkins University 153

K

Kenny Method 61, 62
knee replacement 306, 307
knee-ankle-foot orthosis (KAFO) 289
kyphosis 298

L

left-handedness 10, 11
long-haul symptoms 283, 338, 340, 359
low blood pressure 302
lumbar puncture 37, 45, 46

M

March of Dimes 133, 134, 136, 137, 138, 144, 355
March of Dimes Birth Defects Foundation 138
March of Dimes Poster Child 125, 126, 127, 128, 134, 137
measles 207, 209, 248, 249, 250, 280
Milwaukee Journal, the 118, 175, 181, 224, 226
Milwaukee Road, the 16, 30, 65, 157, 226
molded ankle-foot brace (MAFO) 289
Muscle fasciculations/spasms/cramps 301, 304

N

National Association for the Advancement of Colored People (NAACP) 135
National Foundation for Infantile Paralysis (NFIP) 49, 152
Nobel Prize 145

O

oral polio vaccine (OPV) 145, 146, 278
osteoporosis 308, 359
out-of-body experience/s (OBE) 46, 74, 104, 105, 247

P

Polio Place 284
Polio Vaccine Assistance Act 149
Porch Light Nights 133
President's Emergency Fund 155

Q

quarantines 66, 67, 122, 124

R

radicular sensory symptoms 289
recoil braces 307
Rotary International 278

S

scoliosis 283, 298
separation anxiety 332, 333, 334, 341, 358
sleep disturbances 299, 300, 351, 352, 353
spinal polio 34, 47
stigma of polio 277, 284, 354, 355, 356
swallowing 34, 286, 294, 295, 296, 338, 341, 348, 349, 350

T

Taliban 146, 280
transmission of polio 35, 144, 315
Tuskegee Infantile Paralysis Center 135, 151, 152

U

United Nations Children's Fund (UNICEF) 278

Use it or lose it 71, 126

V

vaccination 138, 144, 145, 146, 147, 148, 149, 150, 151, 248, 249, 250, 277, 278, 279, 280, 281
Vaccine Adverse Event Reporting System (VAERS) 150
Vaccine Safety Datalink (VSD) 150
vagus nerve 291, 292, 294, 295, 299, 350

W

Warm Springs Foundation 130, 131
World Health Organization (WHO) 146, 149, 209, 278, 330

Name Index

A

Alda, Alan 329
Allen, David 240
Anderson, Marian 135

B

Bettelheim, Bruno 194, 239
Bilek, Charlie 181
Bodian, David 297, 298
Bricklin, Dan 234
Brown, Russell W. 152
Bynum, Charles 137

C

Cantor, Eddie 132
Capone, Al 9
Chenault, John 152
Churchill, Winston 151

D

Darwin, Charles 233
Demand, Ms. 91, 92, 96
Dewey, John 206, 240
Diekelmann, Nancy 240
Drinker, Philip 48
DuRose, Margaret 240

E

Eisenhower, Dwight D. 149, 154, 155, 239
Emerson, John Haven 48
Enders, John 145

F

Farrow, Mia 329
Frankl, Viktor 101, 239
Friedman, Meyer 320, 321

G

Gaillard, Norma 152
Gardner, Howard 239
Gershwin, Ira 147
Gessner, Barbara 240
Gey, George 151
Ghebreyesus, Tedros Adhanom 330
Goebbels, Joseph 321, 322, 323

H

Harlow, Harry 194
Henderson, James H.M. 152
Hintz, Max 69, 70, 71, 140
Hitler, Adolf 321, 322, 323
Hoover, J. Edgar 136

K

Kahlo, Frida 318
Kalb, Bernard 147
Kenny, Elizabeth 61, 62, 329
King, Martin Luther, Jr. 135, 136
Klarner, Joyce 179
Koprowski, Hilary 146

L

Lacks, Henrietta 151, 153

Name Index

Landsteiner, Karl 144
Lang, Dorothea 318
Lehrer, Steven 297
Levin, Virginia 179
Lupino, Ida 329

M

Maslow, Abraham 147, 194, 239
Mitchell, Joni 329
Morse, Ralph 147
Moynihan, Patrick 147

N

Nightingale, Florence 71
Nixon, E.D. 135

O

O'Connor, Basil 134, 152

P

Parks, Rosa 135
Paul, Les 15, 21, 22, 24
Perlman, Itzhak 318
Popper, Erwin 144
Pridham, Karen 240

R

Reed, Rita 134
Rheinstein, Peter H. 297
Robbins, Frederick 145

Roosevelt, Eleanor 135, 136
Roosevelt, Franklin Delano (FDR) 130, 131, 134, 328, 329
Rosenman, Ray 320
Rudolph, Wilma 318

S

Sabin, Albert 133, 145, 146, 148
Salk, Jonas 133, 145, 147, 148, 149, 151, 154, 355
Stiglitz, Alfred 147
Sutherland, Donald 330

T

Thomas, Francis 148

W

Weissmuller, Johnny 330
Weller, Thomas 145
Whipple, Fred 318
Williams, Margaret 240
Wilson, Daniel J. 134, 318

Y

Young, Neil 330

Z

Zevon, Warren 108

Family Tree

SCHOENBECK	
William (1897-1980) Paternal Grandfather	Elizabeth Lehrer (1889-1925) Paternal Grandmother
Alvin Howard -Father (Al/Dad) (1919 -2011)	

KNUTH	
Emil (1888-1971) Maternal Grandfather (Pa) (Grandpa)	Elizabeth Draeger (1904-2004) Maternal Grandmother (Ma) (Grandma)
Marjorie Clare – Mother (Margie/Mama) (1922-2001)	

Alvin Howard Schoenbeck (1919-2011) (Al/Dad)	Marjorie Clare Knuth Schoenbeck (1922-2001) (Margie/Mama)
Mike (Brother) 1942-	Susie 1945-

Bibliography

Acute Polio

Breaking the Back of Polio: Yale Medicine Magazine, 2005 – Autumn; https://medicine.yale.edu/news-article/breaking-the-back-of-polio/; https://tinyurl.com/yvnvfhyd; Last accessed 3 9 2022

Bulbar Polio vs Damage to the "Bulb" of the Brain: Polio Survivors Serving Each Other, The Pennsylvania (PA) Polio Survivor's Network, July, 2021; https://www.papolionetwork.org/uploads/9/9/7/0/99704804/july_2021_news_update.pdf; https://tinyurl.com/ytt3v9jc; Last accessed 3 9 2022

Families and Individuals Whatever Happened to Polio?; https://amhistory.si.edu/polio/americanepi/families.htm; https://tinyurl.com/2u6w6huw; Last accessed 3 9 2022

Polio Cleveland Clinic: Polio; https://my.clevelandclinic.org/health/diseases/15655-polio; https://tinyurl.com/bdd99y8d; Last accessed 3 9 2022

Polio: Drugs.com Polio; https://www.drugs.com/health-guide/polio.html; https://tinyurl.com/3y8a7x56; Last accessed 3 9 2022

Polio Interaction Map: European Centre for Disease Prevention and Control: Polio Interactive Map 2021; https://www.ecdc.europa.eu/en/search?s=polio; https://tinyurl.com/2e279n35; Last accessed 3 9 2022

Polio Mayo Clinic: Polio; https://www.mayoclinic.org/diseases-conditions/polio/symptoms-causes/syc-20376512; https://tinyurl.com/bdf7suwh; Last accessed 3 9 2022

Poliomyelitis Medscape: Poliomyelitis; https://emedicine.medscape.com/article/1259213-overview; https://tinyurl.com/y4kk9hd5; Last accessed 3 9 2022

Poliomyelitis Musculoskeletal Key: Poliomyelitis; https://musculoskeletalkey.com/poliomyelitis/; https://tinyurl.com/yckvms38; Last accessed 3 9 2022

Poliomyelitis The National Center for Biotechnology Information (NCBI) Poliomyelitis; https://www.ncbi.nlm.nih.gov/books/NBK558944/; https://tinyurl.com/y2yx975e; Last accessed 3 9 2022

Bibliography

Poliomyelitis University of Michigan Health Looking back on another virus battle: U-M's role in polio history, May 14, 2020; https://www.uofmhealth.org/news/archive/202005/looking-back-another-virus-battle-u-m%E2%80%99s-role-polio-history; https://tinyurl.com/muk7yrfe; Last accessed 3 9 2022

Poliomyelitis World Health Organization (WHO) Poliomyelitis (polio) (Overview);https://www.who.int/health-topics/poliomyelitis#tab=tab_1; https://tinyurl.com/2p8w5p7y; Last accessed 3 9 2022

Poliomyelitis WHO Poliomyelitis, July 19, 2019; https://www.who.int/news-room/fact-sheets/detail/poliomyelitis; https://tinyurl.com/2at5trx9; Last accessed 3 9 2022

Sister Kenny Institute revolutionized treatment of polio patients MINNPOST Sister Kenny Institute revolutionized treatment of polio patient; https://www.minnpost.com/mnopedia/2012/11/sister-kenny-institute-revolutionized-treatment-polio-patients/#:~:text=The%20Elizabeth%20Kenny%20Clinic%20opened,many%20more%20patients%20than%20that; https://tinyurl.com/y82tuwcd; Last accessed 3 9 2022

Spinal poliomyelitis Science Direct Spinal Poliomyelitis; https://www.sciencedirect.com/topics/medicine-and-dentistry/spinal-poliomyelitis; https://tinyurl.com/mrxtd8j8; Last accessed 3 9 2022

Stigma of polio Dirt and Disease: Polio before FDR; https://books.google.com/books?hl=en&lr=&id=dWQ9QZl7xKkC&oi=fnd&pg=PP11&dq=polio+and+stigma&ots=Kthgf3LiOY&sig=oC-mFsXfMdW-iGFr3eMKJpW4chc#v=onepage&q=polio%20and%20stigma&f=false; https://tinyurl.com/5edpjmbm; Last accessed 3 9 2022

What is Polio? Centers for Disease Control and Prevention (CDC) Global Immunization; https://www.cdc.gov/polio/what-is-polio/index.htm#:~:text=Polio%2C%20or%20poliomyelitis%2C%20is%20a,move%20parts%20of%20the%20body); https://tinyurl.com/3s58p5bs; Last accessed 3 9 2022

Blacks and Polio

African-Americans, Polio and Racial Segregation Putting Together the Pieces of Polio History; Polio Survivors Serving Each Other, The PA Polio Survivor's Network; https://www.papolionetwork.org/uploads/9/9/7/0/99704804/african-americans_polio_and_racial_segregation.pdf; https://tinyurl.com/2p9d87f4; Last accessed 3 9 2022

Black Americans Were Slower to Get the Polio Vaccine, Too. RETROREPORT, March 16, 2021; https://www.retroreport.org/articles/black-americans-were-slower-to-get-the-polio-vaccine-too/; https://tinyurl.com/crnv3n8r; Last accessed 3 9 2022

Dancing on Eggs: Charles H. Bynum, Racial Politics, and the National Foundation for Infantile Paralysis, 1938–1954 Bulletin of the History of Medicine, Summer 2010, John Hopkins University Press; https://core.ac.uk/reader/35280989?utm_source=linkout; https://tinyurl.com/38hnrsbf; Last accessed 3 9 2022

Development of the Polio Vaccine: A Historical Perspective of Tuskegee University's Role in Mass Production and Distribution of HeLa Cells Journal of Health Care for the Poor and Underserved November, 2012; https://www.ncbi.nlm.nih.gov/pmc/articles/PMC4458465/; https://tinyurl.com/2p82rws6; Last accessed 3 9 2022

HeLa Cells 1951 British Society for Immunology, 1951; https://www.immunology.org/hela-cells-1951; https://tinyurl.com/2p8fjp3s; Last accessed 3 9 2022

Hidden Black Scientists Proved the Polio Vaccine Worked Scientific American, June 17, 2021; https://www.scientificamerican.com/article/hidden-black-scientists-proved-the-polio-vaccine-worked/; https://tinyurl.com/mssve79z; Last accessed 3 9 2022

Race and the Politics of Polio Am J Public Health. 2007 May; https://www.ncbi.nlm.nih.gov/pmc/articles/PMC1854857/; https://tinyurl.com/49cuwa5e; Last accessed 3 9 2022

Racial Health Disparities Didn't Start with COVID: The Overlooked History of Polio RETROREPORT, March 19, 2021; https://medium.com/retro-report/player-embedded-a03680d17245; https://tinyurl.com/2p9b7erb; Last accessed 3 9 2022

Rita Reed from Blue Island, Ill, the first African American March of Dimes poster child,1947 American Journal Public Health. May,2007; https://tinyurl.com/59cf36ut; Last accessed 3 9 2022

Segregated Treatment and Research Georgia State University Library; https://exhibits.library.gsu.edu/current/exhibits/show/health-is-a-human-right/healthcare-for-all/segregated-treatment-and-resea; https://tinyurl.com/76rzfyjb; Last accessed 3 9 2022

Bibliography

The Legacy of Henrietta Lacks John Hopkins Medicine; https://www.hopkinsmedicine.org/henriettalacks/importance-of-hela-cells.html; https://tinyurl.com/2p9yvsrk; Last accessed 3 9 2022

Bullying

How to Stop People from Mocking WikiHow; https://www.wikihow.com/Stop-People-from-Mocking; https://tinyurl.com/yckt3ks4; Last accessed 3 9 2022

Mockery Wikipedia; https://en.wikipedia.org/wiki/Mockery; https://tinyurl.com/txac7kum; Last accessed 3 9 2022

The Right and Wrong of Ridicule Psychology Today, October 8, 2018; https://www.psychologytoday.com/us/blog/ambigamy/201810/the-right-and-wrong-ridicule; https://tinyurl.com/3dc5u4sb; Last accessed 3 9 2022

Why do people mock others who don't conform to their ways of living life? Why can't they accept the fact that different people have different lives and thus different ways? Quora; https://www.quora.com/Why-do-people-mock-others-who-dont-conform-to-their-ways-of-living-life-Why-cant-they-accept-the-fact-that-different-people-have-different-lives-and-thus-different-ways; https://tinyurl.com/yak74u8u; Last accessed 3 9 2022

Deformities

Foot drop Mayo Clinic: Foot Drop; https://www.mayoclinic.org/diseases-conditions/foot-drop/symptoms-causes/syc-20372628; https://tinyurl.com/ycfc62k2; Last accessed 3 9 2022

Joint Deformities Post-Polio Health International (PHI), 2011; https://www.polioplace.org/living-with-polio/joint-deformities; https://tinyurl.com/5eeajeby; Last accessed 3 9 2022

Knee flexion Deformity from Poliomyelitis Treated by Supracondylar Femoral Extension Osteotomy International Orthopaedics, December 29, 2005; https://www.ncbi.nlm.nih.gov/pmc/articles/PMC2231572/; https://tinyurl.com/yc2f2en2; Last accessed 3 9 2022

Lower Limb Deformities in Poliomyelitis Sequelae Lower Limb Deformities (Springer, 2020); https://link.springer.com/chapter/10.1007/978-981-13-9604-5_5; https://tinyurl.com/v7f4d2kj; Last accessed 3 9 2022

Polio and the Late Effects of Polio Better Health Channel; https://www.betterhealth.vic.gov.au/health/conditionsandtreatments/polio-and-post-polio-syndrome; https://tinyurl.com/4w8upamx; Last accessed 3 9 2022

Polio Lower Limb Deformity SlideShare, September 16, 2015; https://www.slideshare.net/NaveedJumani/polio-lower-limb-deformity#:~:text=Causes%20of%20deformity%20in%20Polio,e.g.%20Sitting%20with%20knee%20flexed.&text=7.&text=In%20time%20the%20affected%20limb,contractures'%2C%20of%20certain%20muscles; https://tinyurl.com/2p8nbc5a; Last accessed 3 9 2022

Poliomyelitis and the postpolio syndrome British Medical Journal June 4, 2005; https://www.ncbi.nlm.nih.gov/pmc/articles/PMC558211/; https://tinyurl.com/2b93ftur; Last accessed 3 9 2022

Residual Deformities after Polio and Their Treatment Bone and Spine; https://boneandspine.com/residual-deformities-after-polio/; https://tinyurl.com/4fwb2fey; Last accessed 3 9 2022

Residual Poliomyelitis of Lower Limb-Pattern and Deformities Indian Journal Pediatrics, March-April 1991; https://pubmed.ncbi.nlm.nih.gov/1879904/; https://tinyurl.com/3befd2zr; Last accessed 3 9 2022

Spinal Poliomyelitis Science Direct; https://www.sciencedirect.com/topics/pharmacology-toxicology-and-pharmaceutical-science/spinal-poliomyelitis; https://tinyurl.com/yckmycar; Last accessed 3 9 2022

The Iliotibial band: Its Role in Producing Deformity in Poliomyelitis The Journal of Bone and Joint Surgery, January 31, 1949; https://pubmed.ncbi.nlm.nih.gov/18106756/; https://tinyurl.com/bdj3j7xm; Last accessed 3 9 2022

What is Foot Drop? Spine Health 10/15/2019; https://www.spine-health.com/conditions/leg-pain/what-foot-drop; https://tinyurl.com/2p8mjpad; Last accessed 3 9 2022

Eleanor Roosevelt & Civil Rights

Dedication of the Eleanor Roosevelt Schoolhouse The Little Whitehouse NEWSLETTER; https://gastateparks.org/sites/default/files/parks/pdf/littlewhitehouse/LittleWhiteHouse_NewsletterWinter2019.pdf; https://tinyurl.com/2p8zj6x6; Last accessed 3 10 22

Eleanor Roosevelt HISTORY Eleanor Roosevelt Updated April 3, 2020; https://www.history.com/topics/first-ladies/eleanor-roosevelt; https://tinyurl.com/2p8ud3vv; Last accessed 3 10 22

Bibliography

Eleanor Roosevelt's "My Day": Household The White House Historical Association; https://www.whitehousehistory.org/staff-at-the-roosevelt-household; https://tinyurl.com/9ac3fajr; Last accessed 3 10 22

Roosevelt, (Anna) Eleanor Stanford University Research and Education Institute; https://kinginstitute.stanford.edu/encyclopedia/roosevelt-anna-eleanor; https://tinyurl.com/5n7zaaby; Last accessed 3 10 22

Segregated Treatment and Research Georgia State University Library; https://exhibits.library.gsu.edu/current/exhibits/show/health-is-a-human-right/healthcare-for-all/segregated-treatment-and-resea; https://tinyurl.com/76rzfyjb; Last accessed 3 10 22.

The Infantile Paralysis Fight at Tuskegee Post-Polio Health International (PHI), 2011; http://www.polioplace.org/sites/default/files/files/InfParFightTuskegee.pdf; https://tinyurl.com/2p9ev26y; Last accessed 3 10 22

Timeline of Eleanor Roosevelt's Life PBS: American Experience http://www.shoppbs.pbs.org/wgbh/amex/eleanor/timeline/index_3.html; https://tinyurl.com/yn4p7z3k; Last accessed 3 10 22

Tuskegee Airmen and WWII C. Alfred "Chief" Anderson with Eleanor Roosevelt, March 1941 The First Lady's flight The Little Whitehouse NEWSLETTER; https://gastateparks.org/sites/default/files/parks/pdf/littlewhitehouse/LittleWhiteHouse_NewsletterWinter2019.pdf; https://tinyurl.com/2p8zj6x6; Last accessed 3 10 22

Chiropractic

Chiropractic Origins, Controversies and Contributions Journal of the American Medical Association, JAMA Internal Medicine November 9, 1998; https://jamanetwork.com/journals/jamainternalmedicine/fullarticle/210354; https://tinyurl.com/yc6pd7pk; Last accessed 3 10 22

Chiropractic *Science Direct*; https://www.sciencedirect.com/topics/medicine-and-dentistry/chiropractic; https://tinyurl.com/yckshpdh; Last accessed 3 10 22

Chiropractic: In Depth National Institute of Health National Center for Complimentary and Integrative Health; https://www.nccih.nih.gov/health/chiropractic-in-depth; https://tinyurl.com/4ew6m8by; Last accessed 3 10 22

History of Chiropractic and Polio David D. Palmer Health Sciences Library; https://blogs.palmer.edu/library/2015/11/12/history-of-chiropractic-and-polio/; https://tinyurl.com/22nxu3z3; Last accessed 3 10 22

The Role of Chiropractic Care in the Treatment of Post-Polio Syndrome The PA Polio Survivors Network; https://www.papolionetwork.org/uploads/2/7/7/2/27726699/vickys_article.pdf; https://tinyurl.com/2p8nf9w9; Last accessed 3 10 22

Electromyography (EMG)

Electromyography (EMG) John Hopkins Medicine Health Electromyography(EMG); https://www.hopkinsmedicine.org/health/treatment-tests-and-therapies/electromyography-emg#:~:text=Electromyography%20(EMG)%20measures%20muscle%20response,the%20skin%20into%20the%20muscle; https://tinyurl.com/vhvwsrh9; Last accessed 3 10 22

Electromyography (EMG) Mayo Clinic Electromyography (EMG); https://www.mayoclinic.org/tests-procedures/emg/about/pac-20393913; https://tinyurl.com/ycxmsx97; Last accessed 3 10 22

Franklin Delano Roosevelt (FDR)

A Crippling Fear: Experiencing Polio in the Era of FDR Bulletin of the History of Medicine, Fall 1998; https://www.jstor.org/stable/44445077; https://tinyurl.com/2rfanm3h; Last accessed 3 10 22

FDR and Polio National Archives Franklin D. Roosevelt Presidential Library and Museum; https://www.fdrlibrary.org/polio; https://tinyurl.com/7ap7sv9w; Last accessed 3 10 22

FDR's Cover-Up: The Extent of His Handicap The Washington Post January 24, 1982;https://www.washingtonpost.com/archive/opinions/1982/01/24/fdrs-cover-up-the-extent-of-his-handicap/9e3f26df-c0a4-4cb6-9852-754fd54d3cae/; https://tinyurl.com/34m5mjk4; Last accessed 3 10 22

Franklin D. Roosevelt Wikipedia https://en.wikipedia.org/wiki/Franklin_D._Roosevelt; https://tinyurl.com/8k9rp6ct; Last accessed 3 10 22

Polio Chronicles: Warm Springs and Disability Politics in the 1930s Asciepio, 2009; https://pubmed.ncbi.nlm.nih.gov/19753689/; https://tinyurl.com/2p9fzw9w; Last accessed 3/16/22

Bibliography

Segregated treatment and Research Georgia State University Library; https://exhibits.library.gsu.edu/current/exhibits/show/health-is-a-human-right/healthcare-for-all/segregated-treatment-and-resea; https://tinyurl.com/76rzfyjb Last accessed 3 10 22

Sons of the Commander in Chief: The Roosevelt Boys In World War II National Archives Franklin D. Roosevelt Presidential Library and Museum; https://fdr.blogs.archives.gov/2018/01/31/sons-of-the-commander-in-chief-the-roosevelt-boys-in-world-war-ii/; https://tinyurl.com/ybpfbbfz; Last accessed 3 10 22

Goebbels

Brown Sisters of Nazi Regime Experiencing History: Holocaust. Sources in Context; https://perspectives.ushmm.org/item/request-to-replace-nurse-anna-hoelzer#:~:text=This%20nurses'%20association%20was%20designed,of%20allegiance%20to%20Adolf%20Hitler;https://tinyurl.com/2p9xmkv6; Last accessed 3 10 22

Joseph Goebbels German propagandist Britannica; https://www.britannica.com/biography/Joseph-Goebbels; https://tinyurl.com/yvz9cefa; Last accessed 3 10 22

People with Disabilities United States Holocaust Memorial Museum; https://www.ushmm.org/collections/bibliography/people-with-disabilities; https://tinyurl.com/4at6xnwa; Last accessed 3 10 22

The Deformity of Evil GayCityNews; https://www.gaycitynews.com/the-deformity-of-evil/; https://tinyurl.com/y3ysfypk; Last accessed 3 10 22

The Goebbels Diaries HAMISH HAMILTON LONDON, 1948; https://dspace.gipe.ac.in/xmlui/bitstream/handle/10973/34067/GIPE-024088-Contents.pdf?sequence=2&isAllowed=y; https://tinyurl.com/yc4nd9hr; Last accessed 3 10 22

The Goebbels Diaries The Historical Journal, The Goebbels Diaries, 1989; https://www.jstor.org/stable/2639546; https://tinyurl.com/4myk6jym; Last accessed 3 10 22

The Man Behind Hitler Joseph Goebbels PBS The Man Behind Hitler, Joseph Goebbels (1897-1945). https://www.pbs.org/wgbh/americanexperience/features/goebbels-biography/; https://tinyurl.com/ua59njs8; Last accessed 3 10 22

HeLa Cells

HeLa Wikipedia; https://en.wikipedia.org/wiki/HeLa; https://tinyurl.com/2p8w3uw4; Last accessed 3 10 22

HeLa Cells 1951 British Society for Immunology; https://www.immunology.org/hela-cells-1951; https://tinyurl.com/2p8fjp3s; Last accessed 3 10 22

Hit Parader

Hit Parader Wikipedia; https://en.wikipedia.org/wiki/Hit_Parader; https://tinyurl.com/3j88vapj; Last accessed 3 10 22

Hit Parader Magazine Early Years POPBOPROCKTILUDROP https://kimsloans.wordpress.com/hit-parader-magazine/; https://tinyurl.com/2p8vm3ss; Last accessed 3 10 22

Hope

Hope in Health Care: A Synthesis of Review Studies Historical and Multidisciplinary Perspectives on Hope, July 21, 2020; https://link.springer.com/chapter/10.1007/978-3-030-46489-9_11; https://tinyurl.com/yh6678cm; Last accessed 3 10 22

How Hope can Keep you Healthier and Happier The Conversation https://theconversation.com/how-hope-can-keep-you-healthier-and-happier-132507; https://tinyurl.com/bde89p68; Last accessed 3 10 22

Psychological Resilience and Depressive Symptoms in Older Adults Diagnosed with Post-polio Syndrome Rehabilitation Nursing July-August 2010; https://www.ncbi.nlm.nih.gov/pmc/articles/PMC3432643/; https://tinyurl.com/bdw7d4kv; Last accessed 3 10 22

The Role of Hope in Subsequent Health and Well-being for Older Adults: An Outcome-wide Longitudinal Approach Global Epidemiology November 2020; https://www.sciencedirect.com/science/article/pii/S259011332030002X; https://tinyurl.com/2p94d4er; Last accessed 3 10 22

Iron lung

A Practical Mechanical Respirator, 1929: The "Iron Lung" The Society of Thoracic Surgeons, 1990; https://www.annalsthoracicsurgery.org/article/0003-4975(90)90508-4/pdf; https://tinyurl.com/3e4y2387; Last accessed 3 10 22

Bibliography

Emerson Respirator or Iron Lung The OHIO STATE UNIVERSITY Health Sciences Library; https://hsl.osu.edu/dept/medical-heritage-center/emerson-respirator-or-iron-lung; https://tinyurl.com/3ewcvmxs; Last accessed 3 10 22

Flashback: Iron Lung Pfizer; https://www.pfizer.com/news/articles/flashback_iron_lung#:~:text=The%20iron%20lung%20was%20born,motor%20with%20two%20vacuum%20cleaners; https://tinyurl.com/4ywky753; Last accessed 3 10 22

Iron lung (c. 1933) Library of Congress; https://www.loc.gov/resource/highsm.05216/; https://tinyurl.com/mrxysmju; Last accessed 3 10 22

Iron Lung Wikipedia; https://www.loc.gov/resource/highsm.05216; https://tinyurl.com/56bae4td; Last accessed 3 10 22

Iron Lung Wood Library Museum of Anesthesiology; https://www.woodlibrarymuseum.org/museum/iron-lung/; https://tinyurl.com/4kujhmad; Last accessed 3 10 22

Iron lungs for polio victims, 1930s-1950s Rare Historical Photos; https://rarehistoricalphotos.com/iron-lungs-polio-1930s-1950s/; https://tinyurl.com/5726nwk7; Last accessed 3 10 22

The Iron Lung Science Museum; https://www.sciencemuseum.org.uk/objects-and-stories/medicine/iron-lung; https://tinyurl.com/bdzjaa5b; Last accessed 3 10 22

The Long View: The Iron Lung Gavi: The Vaccine Alliance; https://www.gavi.org/vaccineswork/long-view-iron-lung; https://tinyurl.com/bdfpyw9y; Last accessed 3 10 22

What America Looked Like: Polio Children Paralyzed in Iron Lungs The Atlantic January 10, 2012; https://www.theatlantic.com/national/archive/2012/01/what-america-looked-like-polio-children-paralyzed-in-iron-lungs/251098/; https://tinyurl.com/yckwj6j6; Last accessed 3 10 22

Kindness/Positive Demeanor

Effectiveness of Positive Thinking Training Program on Nurses' Quality of Work Life through Smartphone Applications International Scholarly Research Notices, May 14, 2017; https://www.ncbi.nlm.nih.gov/pmc/articles/PMC5446857/; https://tinyurl.com/97z8uv8m; Last accessed 3 10 22

The Compassionate Connection: The Healing Power of Empathy and Mindful Listening Family Medicine Book and Media Reviews 2019; https://journals.stfm.org/familymedicine/2019/july-august/br-julyaug19-billington; https://tinyurl.com/yjt4v7bb; Last accessed 3 10 22

The Cultural Implications of Silence Around the World Culture Wizard; https://www.rw-3.com/blog/cultural-implications-of-silence; https://tinyurl.com/ykrvb4ew; Last accessed 3 10 22

The Descent of Man, and Selection in Relation to Sex Wikipedia; https://en.wikipedia.org/wiki/The_Descent_of_Man,_and_Selection_in_Relation_to_Sex; https://tinyurl.com/4pa3rpdk; Last accessed 3 10 22

The Healing Power of Kindness Dignity Health; https://www.dignityhealth.org/hello-humankindness/power-of-compassion/the-healing-power-of-kindness#:~:text=Science%20shows%20that%20delivering%20health,about%20how%20kindness%20affects%20patients; https://tinyurl.com/2p9c4suf; Last accessed 3 10 22

Left-handedness Bias

15 Famous Left-Handed Musicians you Should Know Hello Music Theory, January 24, 2022; https://hellomusictheory.com/learn/famous-left-handed-musicians/; https://tinyurl.com/bddcjjpr; Last accessed 3 10 22

Are left-handed people smarter? Live Science Newsletter, September 20, 2021; https://www.livescience.com/are-left-handed-people-smarter; https://tinyurl.com/2s377fef; Last accessed 3 10 22

Best Left-Handed Athletes of All Time Stadium Talk, January 8, 2020; https://www.stadiumtalk.com/s/best-left-handed-athletes-49fb6ddc95a043c3; https://tinyurl.com/yvfstt5t; Last accessed 3 10 22

From Barack Obama to Julius Caesar, here are 12 world leaders who were left-handed Inside, August 13, 2021; https://www.businessinsider.com/left-handed-world-leaders-list-barack-obama-winston-churchill-2019-8; https://tinyurl.com/yc8msfye; Last accessed 3 10 22

Left-Handedness: Genes or Chance? MyHeritage Blog, January 13, 2019; https://blog.myheritage.com/2019/01/left-handedness-genes-or-chance/; https://tinyurl.com/yckvvdb4; Last accessed 3 10 22

Bibliography

Left-handed surgeons: are they left out? Current Surgery Nov-Dec 2004; https://www.researchgate.net/publication/8138060_Left-handed_surgeons_Are_they_left_out; https://tinyurl.com/mwr6x246; Last accessed 3 10 22

Left-Handers Once Experienced Severe Stigmatization And Discrimination History of Yesterday, September 20, 2021; https://historyofyesterday.com/left-handers-once-experienced-severe-stigmatization-and-discrimination-f172c2fde6ef; https://tinyurl.com/ycknbdd2; Last accessed 3 10 22

List of musicians who play left-handed Wikipedia; https://en.wikipedia.org/wiki/List_of_musicians_who_play_left-handed; https://tinyurl.com/yrux4xkm; Last accessed 3 10 22

The history and geography of human handedness Language Lateralization and Psychosis, 2009; http://www.medicine.mcgill.ca/epidemiology/hanley/bios601/CandHchapter06/HistoryGeographyHumanHandedness.pdf; https://tinyurl.com/yjpdeh7e; Last accessed 3 10 22

The Left Hand of (Supposed Darkness) Miriam Webster; https://www.merriam-webster.com/words-at-play/sinister-left-dexter-right-history#:~:text=Sinister%2C%20today%20meaning%20evil%20or,and%20images%20depicting%20Eve%20on; https://tinyurl.com/ycx6nxvk; Last accessed 3 10 22

The 38 Most Famous Left-Handed Celebrities in History Best Life, January 26, 2021; https://bestlifeonline.com/famous-left-handers/; https://tinyurl.com/5n6r9hx2; Last accessed 3 10 22

Lumbar puncture/spinal tap

Acute Poliomyelitis Workup Medscape; https://emedicine.medscape.com/article/306440-workup; https://tinyurl.com/599cfbbh; Last accessed 3 11 22

Artifacts: Laboratory Bill for Spinal Tap Post-Polio Health International (PHI); https://www.polioplace.org/history/artifacts/laboratory-bill-spinal-tap; https://tinyurl.com/mr49vejj; Last accessed 3 11 22

Diagnostic Methods CDC Search; https://www.cdc.gov/polio/what-is-polio/lab-testing/diagnostic.htmlSpinal Tap images; https://tinyurl.com/nhcywyt7; Last accessed 3 11 22

Spinal Tap Smithsonian National Museum of American History; https://amhistory.si.edu/polio/americanepi/medical2.htm; https://tinyurl.com/5xpps22y; Last accessed 3 11 22

Testing & Diagnosis for Poliomyelitis in Children Boston Children's Hospital; https://www.childrenshospital.org/conditions-and-treatments/conditions/p/poliomyelitis/testing-and-diagnosis; https://tinyurl.com/ytmhwdka; Last accessed 3 11 22

What happens during a lumbar puncture (spinal tap)? National Center for Biotechnology Information; https://www.ncbi.nlm.nih.gov/books/NBK367574/; https://tinyurl.com/2p9yprkm; Last accessed 3 11 22

March of Dimes

Bynum, Charles H. Social Networks and Archival Context (SNAC); https://snaccooperative.org/view/6066978; https://tinyurl.com/zddv7v3r; Last accessed 3 11 22

Charles Hudson Bynum Post-Polio Health International (PHI); https://www.polioplace.org/people/charles-hudson-bynum; https://tinyurl.com/mr3kz8d6; Last accessed 3 11 22

March of Dimes March of Dimes; https://www.marchofdimes.org/mission/eddie-cantor-and-the-origin-of-the-march-of-dimes.aspx; https://tinyurl.com/ycykymms; Last accessed 3 11 22

March of Dimes Encyclopedia.com; https://www.encyclopedia.com/sports-and-everyday-life/social-organizations/private-organizations/march-dimes; https://tinyurl.com/2p8xn2bd; Last accessed 3 11 22

March of Dimes: Faces of the March of Dimes Mission March of Dimes; https://www.marchofdimes.org/mission-stories/faces-of-the-march-of-dimes-mission.aspx; https://tinyurl.com/fkw49w4d; Last accessed 3 11 22

March of Dimes: WHO WE ARE March of Dimes; https://www.marchofdimes.org/mission/who-we-are.aspx; https://tinyurl.com/46r63u65; Last accessed 3 11 22

The Inspiring Depression-Era Story of How the 'March of Dimes' Got Its Name Time, January 3, 2018; https://time.com/5062520/march-of-dimes-history/; https://tinyurl.com/495e5j75; Last accessed 3 11 22

Whatever Happened to Polio? Smithsonian National Museum of American History; https://amhistory.si.edu/polio/howpolio/march.htm; https://tinyurl.com/3dhx5y75; Last accessed 3 11 22

Bibliography

Milwaukee in the 1930s, 1940s, 1950s

Al Capone Wikipedia; https://en.wikipedia.org/wiki/Milwaukee; https://tinyurl.com/2p8smzz2; Last accessed 3 11 22

Great Depression Encyclopedia of Milwaukee; https://emke.uwm.edu/entry/great-depression/; https://tinyurl.com/yckux36f; Last accessed 3 11 22

Les Paul Encyclopedia of Milwaukee; https://emke.uwm.edu/entry/les-paul/; https://tinyurl.com/jcvd7hdd; Last accessed 3 11 22

The Historic Eagles Club The Rave: https://www.therave.com/historic_eagles_club.asp; https://tinyurl.com/nbkebbxe; Last accessed 3 11 22

The Milwaukee Road Magazine The Milwaukee Road Magazine, May-June, 1965; https://milwaukeeroadarchives.com/MilwaukeeRoadMagazine/1965MayJune.pdf; https://tinyurl.com/mveaf4zn; Last accessed 3 11 22

Unpacking The History Of Milwaukee's Eagles Club WUWM, Milwaukee's NPR; https://www.wuwm.com/regional/2018-07-20/unpacking-the-history-of-milwaukees-eagles-club; https://tinyurl.com/2vvxyr6s; Last accessed 3 11 22

Near-Death Experiences

Greyson NDE Scale International Association for Near-Death Studies; https://iands.org/research/nde-research/important-research-articles/698-greyson-nde-scale.html; https://tinyurl.com/2h3dvt24; Last accessed 3 11 22

Near-Death Experiences Getting Comfortable With Near Death Experiences: An Overview of Near-Death Experiences, Missouri Medicine; https://www.ncbi.nlm.nih.gov/pmc/articles/PMC6179792/; https://tinyurl.com/2py5z59t; Last accessed 3 11 22

Near-Death Experiences in Patients Undergoing Cardiopulmonary Resuscitation Journal of Near-Death Studies, Summer 1991; https://digital.library.unt.edu/ark:/67531/metadc799322/; https://tinyurl.com/4s7dnb4h; Last accessed 3 11 22

Near-Death Experiences (NDEs) University of Virginia Division of Perceptual Studies; https://med.virginia.edu/perceptual-studies/our-research/near-death-experiences-ndes/; https://tinyurl.com/5saaky7z; Last accessed 3 11 22

What do near-death experiences mean, and why do they fascinate us? The Guardian, March 7, 2021; https://www.theguardian.com/society/2021/mar/07/the-space-between-life-and-death; https://tinyurl.com/2p96tktb; Last accessed 3 11 22

What Near-Death Experiences Reveal about the Brain Scientific American June 1, 2020; https://www.scientificamerican.com/article/what-near-death-experiences-reveal-about-the-brain/; https://tinyurl.com/mtz9pbhw; Last accessed 3 11 22

Nursing During Epidemics/Pandemics

A Nurse Is Not Just a Nurse: The Challenges of Nursing During a Pandemic and Beyond New England Journal of Medicine, March 17, 2021; https://catalyst.nejm.org/doi/full/10.1056/CAT.21.0053; https://tinyurl.com/2p8sa6f2; Last accessed 3 11 22

Epidemics and Pandemics American Nursing History; https://www.americannursinghistory.org/epidemics-and-pandemics; https://tinyurl.com/ye2av6cb; Last accessed 3 11 22

Expanding nursing's role in responding to global pandemics Nursing Outlook, July-August 2018; https://www.ncbi.nlm.nih.gov/pmc/articles/PMC7118451/; https://tinyurl.com/yckw26cs; Last accessed 3 11 22

Inactive Nurses Asked to Join Polio Fight The Journal Times (Racine, WI), September 9, 1945; https://www.newspapers.com/clip/54973826/the-journal-times-racine-wi-9-sep/; https://tinyurl.com/mudz2f; Last accessed 3 11 22

Nurses Are Playing a Crucial Role in this Pandemic—as Always Scientific American May 4, 2020; https://blogs.scientificamerican.com/observations/nurses-are-playing-a-crucial-role-in-this-pandemic-mdash-as-always/; https://tinyurl.com/3ufdmfmx; Last accessed 3 11 22

Poliomyelitis: Focus on the Epidemic in the United States American Nursing History; https://www.americannursinghistory.org/poliomyelitis; https://tinyurl.com/yka8bxtt; Last accessed 3 11 22

The Physiological Challenges of the 1952 Copenhagen Poliomyelitis Epidemic and a Renaissance in Clinical Respiratory Physiology Journal of Applied Physiology, August 2005; https://www.ncbi.nlm.nih.gov/pmc/articles/PMC1351016/; https://tinyurl.com/y2tumbe6; Last accessed 3 11 22

Polio Personality

A personality profile of patients diagnosed with post-polio syndrome Neurology, October, 1994; https://pubmed.ncbi.nlm.nih.gov/7936226/; https://tinyurl.com/2p9y57xh; Last accessed 3 11 22

How Surviving Polio has Impacted My Personality Skin Stories: Association for Progressive Communications, December 18, 2017; https://medium.com/skin-stories/how-surviving-polio-has-impacted-my-personality-405d1690b98f; https://tinyurl.com/2p88m8zk; Last accessed 3 11 22

List of Polio Survivors Wikipedia; https://en.wikipedia.org/wiki/List_of_polio_survivors; https://tinyurl.com/3ev5sabj; Last accessed 3 11 22

Personality Traits and Chronic Disease: Implications for Adult Personality Development The Journals of Gerontology. Series B, Psychological Sciences and Social Sciences, November 2013;https://www.ncbi.nlm.nih.gov/pmc/articles/PMC3805287/; https://tinyurl.com/2p93mfv2; Last accessed 3 11 22

Posttraumatic stress disorder Diagnostic and Statistical Manual of Mental Disorders, DSM-5; https://www.ncbi.nlm.nih.gov/books/NBK207191/box/part1_ch3.box16/; https://tinyurl.com/yckw6azj; Last accessed 3 29 22

Separation Anxiety Diagnostic and Statistical Manual of Mental Disorders, DSM-5; https://www.ncbi.nlm.nih.gov/books/NBK519712/table/ch3.t11/; https://tinyurl.com/tat2x4rs; Last accessed 3 29 22

The Polio Personality: DOES IT EXIST? Central Virginia Polio Support Group; https://www.cvppsg.org/wp-content/uploads/2012/02/thepoliopersonality.pdf; https://tinyurl.com/2p9y6upw; Last accessed 3 11 22

The Psychology of Polio as Prelude to Post-Polio Sequelae: Behavior Modification and Psychotherapy PA Polio Network (Orthopedics, 1991); https://www.papolionetwork.org/uploads/9/9/7/0/99704804/psychology_of_polio_as_prelude_to_post-polio_sequelae.pdf; https://tinyurl.com/2p8zthwt; Last accessed 3 11 22

The strange and somewhat icky reason we call people 'Type A' personalities goes back to the tobacco industry Insider, August 5, 2016; https://www.businessinsider.com/type-a-personality-traits-smoking-marketing-2016-8#; https://tinyurl.com/yckp9kpd; Last accessed 3 11 22

Type A and Type B Personality Theory Wikipedia; https://en.wikipedia.org/wiki/Type_A_and_Type_B_personality_theory; https://tinyurl.com/2p9283tj; Last accessed 3 11 22

The "Type A" Polio Survivor The PA Polio Survivors Network; https://www.papolionetwork.org/uploads/9/9/7/0/99704804/type_a_polio_survivors.pdf; https://tinyurl.com/4s462v9m; Last accessed 3 11 22

Type A Behavior Pattern and Coronary Heart Disease: Philip Morris's "Crown Jewel" American Journal of Public Health, November 2012; https://www.ncbi.nlm.nih.gov/pmc/articles/PMC3477961/; https://tinyurl.com/2p9f2cyk; Last accessed 3 11 22

Polio Survivors in United States/World

After Effects of Polio can Harm Survivors 40 Years Later March of Dimes; https://www.marchofdimes.org/news/after-effects-of-polio-can-harm-survivors-40-years-later.aspx; https://tinyurl.com/4fxyz4mp; Last accessed 3 11 22

Decades after polio, Martha is among the last to still rely on an iron lung to breathe NPR October 25, 2021; https://www.npr.org/2021/10/25/1047691984/decades-after-polio-martha-is-among-the-last-to-still-rely-on-an-iron-lung-to-br; https://tinyurl.com/mr34yesf; Last accessed 3 11 22

Facts about Post-Polio Syndrome Christopher & Dana Reeve Foundation; https://www.christopherreeve.org/living-with-paralysis/health/causes-of-paralysis/post-polio-syndrome-poliomyelitis; https://tinyurl.com/2p9avwz7; Last accessed 3 11 22

Polio Survivors in the U.S., 1915-2000 Age Distribution Data Post-Polio Health International (PHI) October 2006; https://post-polio.org/wp-content/uploads/2021/04/PolioSurvivorsInTheUS1915-2000.pdf; https://tinyurl.com/4jkvmfwm; Last accessed 3 11 22

Rare Disease Data base Post Polio Syndrome National Organization for Rare Disorders; https://rarediseases.org/rare-diseases/post-polio-syndrome/; https://tinyurl.com/3985jy6x; Last accessed 3 11 22

10 Oldest Living Polio Survivors in the World Oldest.org;(Updated 2021); https://www.oldest.org/people/polio-survivors/; https://tinyurl.com/2p8axvup; Last accessed 3 11 22

Bibliography

Polio and Other Pandemics

What polio in post-WWII America can teach us about living in a pandemic PBS NOVA, July 28, 2020; https://www.pbs.org/wgbh/nova/article/polio-pandemic-coronavirus-vaccine/; https://tinyurl.com/my3d2fwx; Last accessed 3 11 22

Prohibition

Historical Essay Prohibition Wisconsin Historical Society; https://www.wisconsinhistory.org/Records/Article/CS1962; https://tinyurl.com/msfkjb72; Last accessed 3 13 22

Prohibition Encyclopedia of Milwaukee; https://emke.uwm.edu/entry/prohibition; https://tinyurl.com/ypftr4aa; Last accessed 3 13 22

Quarantines

Clear waters and a green gas: a history of chlorine as a swimming pool sanitizer in the united states Bulletin for the History of Chemistry, 2007; http://www.scs.illinois.edu/~mainzv/HIST/bulletin_open_access/v32-2/v32-2%20p129-140.pdf; https://tinyurl.com/47y9hyde; Last accessed 3 13 22

Inactivation of Poliomyelitis Virus by "Free" Chlorine American Journal of Public Health, June 1946; https://ajph.aphapublications.org/doi/pdf/10.2105/AJPH.36.6.639; https://tinyurl.com/yckcn56u; Last accessed 3 13 22

Mechanisms of inactivation of poliovirus by chlorine dioxide and iodine Applied and Environmental Microbiology, November, 1982; https://www.ncbi.nlm.nih.gov/pmc/articles/PMC242149/; https://tinyurl.com/5rmkvrtz; Last accessed 3 13 22

Observe Polio Quarantine, Mothers-to-be Warned Milwaukee Sentinel, September 3, 1948; https://www.marquette.edu/cgi-bin/cuap/db.cgi?uid=default&ID=4467&view=Search&mh=1; https://tinyurl.com/h276c33y; Last accessed 3 13 22

Polio and Swimming Pools: Historical Connections The College of Physicians of Philadelphia, June 28, 2012; https://www.historyofvaccines.org/content/blog/polio-and-swimming-pools-historical-connections; https://tinyurl.com/2vhhcfuj; Last accessed 3 13 22

Polio Elimination in the United States CDC; https://www.cdc.gov/polio/what-is-polio/polio-us.html; https://tinyurl.com/2p8zhawz; Last accessed 3 13 22

Poliomyelitis Quarantine British Medical Journal, December 25, 1954; https://www.ncbi.nlm.nih.gov/pmc/articles/PMC2080165/; https://tinyurl.com/2p9xvhs2; Last accessed 3 13 22

Preventing Polio Smithsonian; https://www.si.edu/spotlight/antibody-initiative/polio; Last accessed 3 13 22

Recycling in 1950s

Homefront: Milwaukee Children during the Second World War Children in Urban America; https://www.marquette.edu/cgi-bin/cuap/db.cgi?uid=default&ID=3591&view=Search&mh=1 https://tinyurl.com/2p8wycut; Last accessed 3 13 22

Lost memory: the paper drives of World War II The Australian Library Journal, 1998; https://www.tandfonline.com/doi/pdf/10.1080/00049670.1998.1075585; https://tinyurl.com/2p99hukj; Last accessed 3 13 22

Paper Preservation Self-Assessment Program, University of Illinois at Urbana-Champaign; https://psap.library.illinois.edu/collection-id-guide/paper#ragpaper; https://tinyurl.com/4axkx78e; Last accessed 3 13 22

Recycling – A Way Of Life In The 1950s And 1960s Historic UK: The History and Heritage Accommodation Guide; https://www.historic-uk.com/CultureUK/Recycling-1950-1960s/; https://tinyurl.com/yc7254r9; Last accessed 3 13 22

Scrap for Victory! Library of Congress, January 15, 2015; https://blogs.loc.gov/now-see-hear/2015/01/scrap-for-victory/#:~:text=During%20World%20War%20II%20scrap,needed%20to%20fight%20the%20war; https://tinyurl.com/2m4fku3h; Last accessed 3 13 22

Scrap Drives OHIO History Central; https://ohiohistorycentral.org/w/Scrap_Drives; https://tinyurl.com/bd8sp37z; Last accessed 3 13 22

Waste Paper for War La Crosse Tribune, February 14,1945; https://www.lacrosselibrary.org/sites/default/files/u117/07-waste_paper_for_war.pdf; https://tinyurl.com/2p8khpz2; Last accessed 3 13 22

Bibliography

Resources for Polio Survivors

A Polio Survivor's Guide: Funding Resources for Medical & Adaptive Equipment Post-Polio Health International (PHI)); https://post-polio.org/wp-content/uploads/2021/08/PHIFundsDirectory2020.pdf; https://tinyurl.com/uw2ycu4a; Last accessed 3 13 22

Bruno Bytes PA Polio Survivors Network; https://www.papolionetwork.org/bruno-bytes.html; https://tinyurl.com/5hf6yhft; Last accessed 3 13 22

Informative Polio Resources, Polio Survivors in the 21st Century, Updated August 5, 2021; https://survivorsofpolio.com/; https://tinyurl.com/5cm8jrvf; Last accessed 3 13 22

Polio Doctors Post-Polio Health International (PHI), 2011; http://www.polioplace.org/living-with-polio/polio-doctors; https://tinyurl.com/5n7yyza3; Last accessed 3 13 22

Polio Place Post-Polio Health International (PHI) 2011; http://www.polioplace.org/living-with-polio/support-groups; https://tinyurl.com/yc7daaas; Last accessed 3 13 22

Post-Polio Directory 2021 Post-Polio Health International (PHI) https://post-polio.org/wp-content/uploads/2021/06/PDIR-2021C.pdf; https://tinyurl.com/5cu9z3sw; Last accessed 3 13 22

Post-Polio Health International (PHI) Post-Polio Health International (PHI) (Formerly International Polio Network -- including International Ventilator Users Network [IVUN]); https://post-polio.org/; https://tinyurl.com/4jeh2bfc; Last accessed 3 13 22

Post-Polio Resource Locator Post-Polio Health International (PHI); https://post-polio.org/networking/directory/; https://tinyurl.com/2p8v23kw; Last accessed 3 13 22

Post-polio syndrome (PPS) Christopher and Dana Reeve Foundation; https://www.christopherreeve.org/living-with-paralysis/health/causes-of-paralysis/post-polio-syndrome-poliomyelitis; https://tinyurl.com/tmwza3dy; Last accessed 3 13 22

Post-Polio Syndrome Central Post Polio Syndrome Central; http://skally.net/ppsc/; https://tinyurl.com/2p8sfvuk; Last accessed 3 13 22

Post Polio a voice for people with polio; Victoria, Inc.; https://www.postpoliovictoria.org.au/resources-2/; https://tinyurl.com/y62zvm22; Last accessed 3 13 22

RareAction Network NORD (National Organization for Rare Diseases); https://rarediseases.org/advocate/take-action-locally/join-rare-action-network/; https://tinyurl.com/mpnpvpeb; Last accessed 3 13 22

Resources for Polio Survivors and Health Professionals Australian Polo Register; https://www.polionsw.org.au/resources; https://tinyurl.com/4vmpuzp8; Last accessed 3 13 22

The Lincolnshire Post-Polio Network MossRehab Einstein Healthcare Network; https://www.mossrehab.com/?id=191&sid=2; https://tinyurl.com/bdebvuxw; Last accessed 3 13 22

The PA Polio Survivor's Network PA Polio Survivors Network https://www.papolionetwork.org/uploads/9/9/7/0/99704804/july_2021_news_up date.pdf; https://tinyurl.com/2p8avwwd; Last accessed 3 13 22

Resurgence of Polio

Circulating vaccine-derived poliovirus; Polio Global Eradication Initiative; March 9, 2021; https://polioeradication.org/polio-today/polio-now/this-week/circulating-vaccine-derived-poliovirus/#:~:text=If%20the%20vaccine%2Dvirus%20is,the%20longer%20the se%20viruses%20survive; https://tinyurl.com/4wsjm6hm; Last accessed 3 15 22

Circulating vaccine-derived poliovirus confirmed in Israel and the occupied Palestinian territory Polio Global Eradication Initiative; https://polioeradication.org/news-post/circulating-vaccine-derived-poliovirus-confirmed-in-israel-and-occupied-palestinian-territory/; https://tinyurl.com/53zbn5ck; Last accessed 3 11 22

Could the World See a Resurgence of Polio? Experts Fear a Cautionary Tale in Measles STAT August 19, 2019; https://www.statnews.com/2019/08/19/could-the-world-see-a-resurgence-of-polio-experts-fear-a-cautionary-tale-in-measles/; https://tinyurl.com/2p8bp5uz; Last accessed 3 11 22

Doctors warn of polio 'outbreak' threat as 2 new preliminary positive cases found The Times of Israel, March 11, 2022; https://www.timesofisrael.com/doctors-warn-of-polio-outbreak-threat-as-2-new-preliminary-positive-cases-found/; https://tinyurl.com/4f86d7bp; Last accessed 3 16 22

Bibliography

Epidemiology and Prevention of Vaccine-Preventable Diseases CDC; https://www.cdc.gov/vaccines/pubs/pinkbook/polio.html; https://tinyurl.com/2p96juk8; Last accessed 3 16 22

Expert warns polio's return could shatter Israel's public health image, hurt tourism, The Times of Israel, 3/13/22: https://www.timesofisrael.com/expert-warns-polios-return-could-shatter-israels-public-health-image-hurt-tourism/; https://tinyurl.com/2s47aw2r; Last accessed 3 16 22

Global Immunization CDC Updated 10/22/21; https://www.cdc.gov/polio/index.htm; https://tinyurl.com/mt39axn7; Last accessed 3 11 22

Israel Detects First Polio Case Since 1989 WebMD, March 8, 2022; https://www.webmd.com/children/news/20220308/israel-detects-first-polio-case-since-1989#:~:text=March%208%2C%202022%20%2D%2D%20Israel,in%20Israel%2C%20the%20ministry%20said; https://tinyurl.com/y84hf7x7; Last accessed 3 11 22

Israel finds first case of polio in over 30 years in three year old girl who was NOT vaccinated against the virus, Daily Mail, March 8, 2022; https://www.dailymail.co.uk/health/article-10591567/Israel-finds-case-polio-30-years-four-year-old-girl.html; https://tinyurl.com/57kjyfhm; Last accessed 3 16 22

Malawi declared polio outbreak WHO, February 17, 2022; https://www.afro.who.int/news/malawi-declares-polio-outbreak; https://tinyurl.com/2p83cxrn; Last accessed 3 16 22

Our Progress Against Polio CDC; https://www.cdc.gov/polio/progress/index.htm; https://tinyurl.com/mrxy5r6d; Last accessed 3 11 22

Patients in Afghanistan Face Growing Obstacles to Care Global Health July 20, 2021; https://jamanetwork.com/journals/jama/fullarticle/2782174; https://tinyurl.com/mr3hx33z; Last accessed 3 11 22

Polio Elimination in the U.S. CDC; https://www.cdc.gov/polio/what-is-polio/polio-us.html; https://tinyurl.com/2d8n64ef; Last accessed 3 16 22

Polio revisited: reviving knowledge and skills to meet the challenge of resurgence Journal of Children's Orthopedics, October 2015; https://www.ncbi.nlm.nih.gov/pmc/articles/PMC4619376/; https://tinyurl.com/2p9af5nh; Last accessed 3 11 22

Polio this week as of 09 March 2022 Polio Global Eradication Initiative; https://polioeradication.org/polio-today/polio-now/this-week/; https://tinyurl.com/2p97656z; Last accessed 3 11 22

Progress Toward Polio Eradication — Worldwide, January 2019–June 2021, CDC, August 27, 2021; https://www.cdc.gov/mmwr/volumes/70/wr/mm7034a1.htm; https://tinyurl.com/yc2np4dr; Last accessed 3 15 22

Polio Vaccination: What Everyone Should Know CDC; https://www.cdc.gov/vaccines/vpd/polio/public/index.html; https://tinyurl.com/2ssu8kw6; Last accessed 3 11 22

Poliomyelitis WHO July 22, 2019; https://www.who.int/news-room/fact-sheets/detail/poliomyelitis; https://tinyurl.com/2at5trx9; Last accessed 3 11 22

Strengthening Capacity: Keeping it Simple and Real in India CDC; https://www.cdc.gov/globalhealth/immunization/stories/keeping-it-simple-and-realistic-in-india.htm; https://tinyurl.com/4z6rkwtt; Last accessed 3 11 22

The Campaign To Wipe Out Polio Was Going Really Well ... Until It Wasn't NPR October 30, 2020; https://www.npr.org/sections/goatsandsoda/2020/10/30/929080692/the-campaign-to-wipe-out-polio-was-going-really-well-until-it-wasnt; https://tinyurl.com/2p85v5n6; Last accessed 3 11 22

The Pandemic Tanked Rates of Childhood Vaccination—for Everything Wired, March 2, 2022; https://www.wired.com/story/the-pandemic-tanked-rates-of-childhood-vaccination-for-everything/; https://tinyurl.com/5appxhbx; Last accessed 3 11 22

Update on Vaccine-Derived Polio Outbreaks Worldwide, January 2020-June 2021, CDC December 2021; https://www.cdc.gov/mmwr/volumes/70/wr/mm7049a1.htm; https://tinyurl.com/3jj9r8tx; Last accessed 3 16 22

Urgent Action Needed to Prevent Measles, Polio Resurgence WIRED March 2, 2022: https://jamanetwork.com/journals/jama/article-abstract/2774063; https://tinyurl.com/2zhfydu4; Last accessed 3 11 22

Sequelae of Polio: The Long-Haul Effects

Note post-polio is spelled in various ways. At times using one word. Other times using two. Sometimes with a hyphen. Other times, italicized.

Bibliography

A benign motor neuron disorder: Delayed cramps and fasciculation after poliomyelitis or myelitis Annals of Neurology 1982; https://onlinelibrary.wiley.com/doi/abs/10.1002/ana.410110418; https://tinyurl.com/27jp89jp; Last accessed 3 11 22

A brief history of postpolio syndrome in the United States. Archives of Physical Medicine and Rehabilitation August 2011; https://pubmed.ncbi.nlm.nih.gov/21658679/; https://tinyurl.com/y8bzrn56; Last accessed 3 11 22

Ability and Perceived Difficulty in Daily Activities in People with Poliomyelitis Sequelae Journal of Rehabilitative Medicine, January 2001; https://pubmed.ncbi.nlm.nih.gov/11480469/; https://tinyurl.com/2p8cd87t; Last accessed 3 11 22

Abnormal Movements in Sleep as Post-Polio Sequelae PA Polio Network, 2018; https://www.papolionetwork.org/uploads/9/9/7/0/99704804/abnormal_movements_in_sleep.pdf; https://tinyurl.com/27zhtwex; Last accessed 3 11 22

Achalasia. A Possible Late Cause of Post-Polio Dysphagia Digestive Diseases and Sciences, March 1996; https://pubmed.ncbi.nlm.nih.gov/8617125/; https://tinyurl.com/2p85sezu; Last accessed 3 11 22

Achalasia: A Vagal Disease Scandinavian Journal of Gastroenterology, June, 2004; https://pubmed.ncbi.nlm.nih.gov/15223675/; https://tinyurl.com/mvf7d7hh; Last accessed 3 11 22

Achalasia Occurring Years after Acute Poliomyelitis Arquivos de Gastroenterologia April-September 1993; https://pubmed.ncbi.nlm.nih.gov/8147735/; https://tinyurl.com/yrmcm7zt; Last accessed 3 11 22

After Effects of Polio can Harm Survivors 40 Years Later: Few Doctors Recognize Little-Known Condition March of Dimes; https://www.marchofdimes.org/news/after-effects-of-polio-can-harm-survivors-40-years-later.aspx; https://tinyurl.com/4fxyz4mp; Last accessed 3 11 22

Aging Well with Post-Polio Syndrome: Don't Take Fatigue Lying Down Post-Polio Health Summer 2011; https://agerrtc.washington.edu/sites/agerrtc/files/files/PPH27-Fatigue-3su11p10.pdf; https://tinyurl.com/5e9eakbs; Last accessed 3 11 22

And They Shall Walk: Ideal Versus Reality in Polio Rehabilitation in the United States Asclepio, 2009; https://pubmed.ncbi.nlm.nih.gov/19753691/; https://tinyurl.com/34372scm; Last accessed 3 11 22

Anesthesia Warning Card PA Polio Network, March 2022; https://www.papolionetwork.org/uploads/9/9/7/0/99704804/march_2022_news_update.pdf; https://tinyurl.com/8myyn5a9; Last accessed 3 18 22

Anaesthetists (sic) need to be wary of postpolio syndrome Post Polio A Voice for People with Polio, Victoria, Inc. ANZA Bulletin, September, 2015; https://www.poliohealth.org.au/wp-content/uploads/201509-ANZCA-Bulletin-PPV-Article.pdf; https://tinyurl.com/y9vmdkbv; Last accessed 3 16 22

Arthritis By The Numbers Arthritis Foundation, 2019; https://www.arthritis.org/getmedia/e1256607-fa87-4593-aa8a-8db4f291072a/2019-abtn-final-march-2019.pdf; https://tinyurl.com/5n6tf2xr; Last accessed 3 11 22

Asymmetrical bone loss in a patient with poliomyelitis: an indication for anti-osteoporotic therapy Clinical Cases in Mineral and Bone Metabolism, January-April 2016; https://www.ncbi.nlm.nih.gov/pmc/articles/PMC4869960/; https://tinyurl.com/22s8kzhs; Last accessed 3 11 22

Bone Mineral Density Among Individuals With Residual Lower Limb Weakness After Polio American Academy of Physical Medicine and Rehabilitation, September 6, 2018; http://media.mycrowdwisdom.com.s3.amazonaws.com/aapmr/courses/SAE-P/SAEP1902/2-Bone_Mineral_Density_Among_Ind.pdf; https://tinyurl.com/mu5yy6z6; Last accessed 3 11 22

Bracing for Polio Survivors PA Polio Network, 2018; https://www.papolionetwork.org/uploads/9/9/7/0/99704804/bracing.pdf; https://tinyurl.com/2p84kjse; Last accessed 3 11 22

Breathing and Sleep Problems in Polio Survivors Post-Polio Health International (PHI), 2011; https://www.polioplace.org/living-with-polio/breathing-and-sleep-problems-polio-survivors; https://tinyurl.com/aec5n7ab; Last accessed 3 11 22

Buckling after Total Knee Replacement Complete Orthopedics; https://www.cortho.org/knee/buckling-after-total-knee-replacement/; https://tinyurl.com/mjjjja4d; Last accessed 3 11 22

Capsaicin Mayo Clinic; https://www.mayoclinic.org/drugs-supplements/capsaicin-topical-route/side-effects/drg-20062561; https://tinyurl.com/3pd5kp42; Last accessed 3 11 22

Bibliography

Cardiovascular Disturbances in Poliomyelitis Polio SA, Polio Australia, December 9, 2019; https://www.google.com/search?q=vagal+nerve+damage+and+polio&rlz=1C1V DKB_enUS954US954&oq=vagal+nerve+damage+and+polio&aqs=chrome..69i 57j33i22i29i30.8865j0j7&sourceid=chrome&ie=UTF-8; https://tinyurl.com/4v8sytrk; Last accessed 3 11 22

Constipation in Polio Survivors Post-Polio Health International (PHI), 2011; https://www.polioplace.org/living-with-polio/constipation-polio-survivorshttps://tinyurl.com/387c3s32; Last accessed 3 12 22

Constipation Nation? The Polio Perspective, May 2014; http://postpoliobransongoers.org/wp-content/uploads/2015/01/22-Polio-Perspective-May-2014.pdf; https://tinyurl.com/4vw8f36d; Last accessed 3 12 22

Coping with Post-Polio Problems Post-Polio Health International (PHI), 2011; http://www.polioplace.org/sites/default/files/files/Manging%20Post%20Polio%20Problems%20III%20OCR.pdf; https://tinyurl.com/2p8jsmp5; Last accessed 3 12 22

Correlation between sarcopenia and osteoporosis in patients with post-poliomyelitis syndrome Annals of Physical and Rehabilitation Medicine, July 2018; https://reader.elsevier.com/reader/sd/pii/S187706571830099X?token=574A0A9 740C46142CDE4154BA29F38D3766F9F2267CA7D836F1A9C7F1A692DB61 038E243DF8423EEF0DB35EFF3E2CC41&originRegion=us-east-1&originCreation=20220118233020; https://tinyurl.com/bdst62sd; Last accessed 3 12 22

Currents issues in cardiorespiratory care of patients with post-polio syndrome Archives of Neuropsychiatry, April,2016; https://www.scielo.br/j/anp/a/ZnRBtk4rLpHW44PMHF6GdBJ/?lang=en&format=pdf; https://tinyurl.com/4svwnjeh; Last accessed 3 12 22

Custom rotating hinge total knee arthroplasty in patients with poliomyelitis affected limbs International Orthopaedics, 2015; https://link.springer.com/article/10.1007%2Fs00264-014-2572-y; https://tinyurl.com/57wva7j7; Last accessed 3 12 22

DEXA (DXA) Scan: Bone Density Test Cleveland Clinic; https://my.clevelandclinic.org/health/diagnostics/10683-dexa-dxa-scan-bone-density-test; https://tinyurl.com/2dvezs9x; Last accessed 3 12 22

Differentiating Post-Polio Syndrome from Myalgic Encephalomyelitis and Chronic Fatigue Syndrome Pub Med Central, 2019; https://www.ncbi.nlm.nih.gov/pmc/articles/PMC7531614/; https://tinyurl.com/33yhs5k8; Last accessed 3 12 22

Disability as a Life Course: Implications of Early Experiences for Later Coping Polio Network News Summer 1996; https://post-polio.org/wp-content/uploads/2020/05/PNN12-3pg3-6.pdf; https://tinyurl.com/2p9f8ebv; Last accessed 3 12 22

Disorders of the lower cranial nerves Journal of Neurosciences in Rural Practice, July-September, 2015; https://www.ncbi.nlm.nih.gov/pmc/articles/PMC4481793/; https://tinyurl.com/3cdcx8wn; Last accessed 3 12 22

Dorothea Lange: Drawing Beauty Out Of Desolation NPR: April 28, 2010; https://www.npr.org/templates/story/story.php?storyId=126289455; https://tinyurl.com/5e5zk93v; Last accessed 3 12 22

Dysphagia and post-polio syndrome: past, present, and future Seminars in Neurology, December, 1996; https://pubmed.ncbi.nlm.nih.gov/9112316/; https://tinyurl.com/yckksj43; Last accessed 3 12 22

Dysphagia in Patients with the Post-Polio Syndrome New England Journal of Medicine, 1991; https://www.nejm.org/doi/full/10.1056/NEJM199104253241703?query=prevarrow; https://tinyurl.com/2p8zv9k5; Last accessed 3 12 22

Early Memories of Having Polio: Survivors' Memories Versus the Official Myths First Australian International Post-Polio Conference, November, 1996; http://www.polioplace.org/sites/default/files/files/EarlyMemoriesofHavingPolio-Westbrook.pdf; https://tinyurl.com/2p8955vc; Last accessed 3 12 22

Elderly Norwegian Polio Survivors: Predictors of self-perceived physical and psychological health Edorium Journal of Disability and Rehabilitation, 2018; https://www.ejdisabilityrehabilitation.com/archive/2018-articles/2018100042D05AS-schanke/100042D05AS-full-text.php; https://tinyurl.com/2p8uevxu; Last accessed 3 12 22

Encyclopedia of Polio and Post-Polio Sequelae International Center for Polio Education//The PA Polio survivors Network; http://www.postpolioinfo.com/bruno.php; https://tinyurl.com/2p8ptmw6; Last accessed 3 12 22

Fainting and Fatigue in Polio Survivors The PA Polio Network, 2015; https://www.papolionetwork.org/uploads/9/9/7/0/99704804/fainting_and_fatigue_in_polio_survivors.pdf; https://tinyurl.com/nhpyzw58; Last accessed 3 12 22

Fatigue Post-Polio Health International (PHI), 2011; https://www.polioplace.org/category/blog-tags/fatigue; https://tinyurl.com/cw3ndj9w; Last accessed 3 12 22

Fatigue in polio survivors Spinal Cord, 2001; https://www.nature.com/articles/3101147.pdf?origin=ppub; https://tinyurl.com/ydaf8ux2; Last accessed 3/12/22

Fatigue-It Makes Me Tired, PA Polio Network, March 2022; https://www.papolionetwork.org/uploads/9/9/7/0/99704804/march_2022_news_update.pdf; https://tinyurl.com/8myyn5a9; Last accessed 3 18 22

Gastroesophageal Reflux Disease POST-POLIO HEALTH, Winter, 2007; https://www.polioplace.org/sites/default/files/files/PH23-1pg4-5.pdf; https://tinyurl.com/skt439nj; Last accessed 3 12 22

Gastroparesis Mayo Clinic; https://www.mayoclinic.org/diseases-conditions/gastroparesis/symptoms-causes/syc-20355787; https://tinyurl.com/2p8pnrex; Last accessed 3 12 22

Growing older with post-polio syndrome: Social and quality-of-life implications SAGE Open Medicine, 2007; https://journals.sagepub.com/doi/pdf/10.1177/2050312118793563; https://tinyurl.com/9cskrue5; Last accessed 3 12 22

Growing up with a disability following paralytic poliomyelitis: experiences from persons with late effects of polio Disability and Rehabilitation, 2019; https://www.tandfonline.com/doi/full/10.1080/09638288.2019.1647296; https://tinyurl.com/2cr4r476; Last accessed 3 12 22

Heat and Cold Intolerance (Thermoregulation) Polio Australia; https://polio.org.nz/wp-content/uploads/2021/09/Thermoregulation.pdf; https://tinyurl.com/44xjc6jm; Last accessed 3 12 22

Help Wanted in 2030: TJR Needs will Soar, Severe Surgeon Shortage Possible Orthopedics Today, May 2006; https://www.healio.com/news/orthopedics/20120325/help-wanted-in-2030-tjr-needs-will-soar-severe-surgeon-shortage-possible; https://tinyurl.com/3xjrbr3n; Last accessed 3 12 22

Impact of Nursing on Hospital Patient Mortality: A Focused Review and Related Policy Implications Quality and Safety in Healthcare, February 2006; https://www.ncbi.nlm.nih.gov/pmc/articles/PMC2563988/; https://tinyurl.com/2p8rsuah; Last accessed 3 12 22

Innate host barriers to viral trafficking and population diversity: Lessons learned from poliovirus Advances in Virus Research, 2010; https://www.ncbi.nlm.nih.gov/pmc/articles/PMC3234684/; https://tinyurl.com/2p96dnce; Last accessed 3 12 22

Inverse Relationship Between Polio Incidence in the US and Colorectal Cancer In Vivo, Nov-Dec 2018;https://www.ncbi.nlm.nih.gov/pmc/articles/PMC6365732/; https://tinyurl.com/48zz66ej; Last accessed 3 12 22

KAFO Knee Ankle Foot Orthosis Anatomical Concepts, Inc. https://www.anatomicalconceptsinc.com/knee-ankle-foot-orthosis#:~:text=What%20is%20KAFO%3F,joints%20and%20assist%20safe%20ambulation; https://tinyurl.com/4xrpnmzw; Last accessed 3 12 22

Knee Replacement Surgery by the Numbers The Center Orthopedic and Neurosurgical Care & Research; https://www.thecenteroregon.com/medical-blog/knee-replacement-surgery-by-the-numbers/; https://tinyurl.com/2vs6mwrn; Last accessed 3 12 22

Let's Talk About the Spine Polio Health International 2014 Conference; https://www.papolionetwork.org/uploads/2/7/7/2/27726699/vandenakker_-_lets_talk_about_the_spine_ppt.pdf; https://tinyurl.com/2p8zb6e7; Last accessed 3 12 22

Long-standing Poliomyelitis and Psychological Health Disability and Rehabilitation, 2015; https://www.tandfonline.com/doi/abs/10.3109/09638288.2015.1019007; https://tinyurl.com/23usmpyr; Last accessed 3 12 22

Long-standing Poliomyelitis and Psychological Health The PA Polio Survivors Network; https://www.papolionetwork.org/uploads/9/9/7/0/99704804/long_standing_polio_and_psychological_health.pdf; https://tinyurl.com/y3ahkx7e; Last accessed 3 12 22

Lower Limb Deformities in Poliomyelitis Sequelae Lower Limb Deformities, 2020; https://link.springer.com/chapter/10.1007/978-981-13-9604-5_5; https://tinyurl.com/v7f4d2kj; Last accessed 3 12 22

Management of Instability after Primary Total Knee Arthroplasty: An Evidence Based Review Journal of Orthopedic Surgery and Research, 2021; https://josr-online.biomedcentral.com/track/pdf/10.1186/s13018-021-02878-5.pdf; https://tinyurl.com/3e2x94w2; Last accessed 3 12 22

Managing postpolio syndrome pain Nursing 2006: https://journals.lww.com/nursing/Fulltext/2006/12000/Managing_postpolio_syndrome_pain.13.aspx; https://tinyurl.com/2p8522cf; Last accessed 3 18 22

Many Polio Survivors Forced to Return to Crutches: Medicine: About half of those who beat the disease in childhood are losing mobility. Los Angeles Times, 1991; https://www.latimes.com/archives/la-xpm-1991-08-18-mn-1354-story.html; https://tinyurl.com/4pfmupnr; Last accessed 3 12 22

Medical-Social Worker's Approach to the Problem of Poliomyelitis American Journal of Public Health, 1948; https://ajph.aphapublications.org/doi/pdf/10.2105/AJPH.38.8.1092; https://tinyurl.com/8pwahzk2; Last accessed 3 12 22

Muscle Cramps and Muscle Spasms The PA Polio Survivors Network, 2017; https://www.papolionetwork.org/uploads/9/9/7/0/99704804/muscle_cramps_and_muscle_spasms___august_2017_.pdf; https://tinyurl.com/mu89u69s; Last accessed 3 12 22

Muscle Vanishing in Poliomyelitis Manifested on F-18 FDG PET/CT: An Interesting Imaging Finding Open Journal of Orthopedics and Rheumatology, 2017; https://www.peertechzpublications.com/articles/OJOR-2-107.php.(no tinyurl.com available); Last accessed 3 12 22

Musculoskeletal Diseases And the Burden They Cause in the United States The Burden of Musculoskeletal Diseases in the United States (BMUS), 2014; http://www.boneandjointburden.org; https://tinyurl.com/28dc7azm; Last accessed 3 12 22

Myalgic Encephalomyelitis/Chronic Fatigue Syndrome (ME/CFS) CDC; https://www.cdc.gov/me-cfs/index.html; https://tinyurl.com/2p98jr8c; Last accessed 3 12 22

Neil Young Wikipedia; https://en.wikipedia.org/wiki/Neil_Young; https://tinyurl.com/2p8vpvv4; Last accessed 3 12 22

Neurological manifestations of the post-polio syndrome, Critical Reviews in Neurobiology, 1987; https://pubmed.ncbi.nlm.nih.gov/3315237/#:~:text=Post%2Dpolio%20neurological%20manifestations%20primarily,a%20very%20slow%2C%20progressive%20nature; https://tinyurl.com/yvm7ef7k; Last accessed 3 12 22

Neurological Symptoms in Danes with a History of Poliomyelitis: Lifelong Follow-Up of Late Symptoms, their Association with Initial Symptoms of Polio, and Presence of Postpolio Syndrome European Neurology, 2018; https://doi.org/10.1159/000497483; https://tinyurl.com/mr29ztc2; Last accessed 3 12 22

NIH Post-Polio Syndrome Fact Sheet National Institute of Neurological Disorders and Stroke; https://www.ninds.nih.gov/Disorders/Patient-Caregiver-Education/Fact-Sheets/Post-Polio-Syndrome-Fact-Sheet; https://tinyurl.com/4fvm63bn; Last accessed 3 12 22

Obesity Is a Disease, Recognize It as Such — Failure to recognize this has led to delays in prevention, treatment, and policy change MEDPAGE TODAY, July 18, 2021; https://www.medpagetoday.com/opinion/second-opinions/93620?xid=nl_secondopinion_2021-07-20&eun=g1807584d0r; https://tinyurl.com/2p86btnb; Last accessed 3 12 22

OLDCART Triaging Common Complaints in the Workplace American Association of Occupational Health Nurses Triaging Common Complaints in the Workplace 2003; https://journals.sagepub.com/doi/pdf/10.1177/216507990305100606; https://tinyurl.com/47nna9sw; Last accessed 3/10/22. Last accessed 3 12 22

Orthopedic Surgery Considerations in Post-Polio Syndrome American Journal of Orthopedics, July 2007; https://cdn.mdedge.com/files/s3fs-public/Document/September-2017/036070348.pdf; https://tinyurl.com/5n78ebre; Last accessed 3 12 22

Orthostatic Problems in CFIDS/FM and Post -Polio Syndrome Massachusetts Myalgic Encephalomyelitis/Chronic Fatigue Syndrome (ME/CFS) & Families Association; https://www.massmecfs.org/more-resources-for-me-cfs/60-orthostatic-problems-in-cfidsfm-and-post-polio-syndrome; https://tinyurl.com/7m84ajd9; Last accessed 3 12 22

Osteoporosis Polio Network News Summer 1993; http://www.polioplace.org/sites/default/files/files/Polio%20Network%20News%20Vol_%209%20No_%203%20Summer%201993.pdf; https://tinyurl.com/2p93yy46; Last accessed 3 12 22

Osteoporosis in a Postpolio Clinic Population Archives of Physical Medicine and Rehabilitation, August 2007; https://www.archives-pmr.org/article/S0003-9993(07)00353-X/pdf; https://tinyurl.com/yc45dwp7; Last accessed 3 12 22

Bibliography

Outcome after cementless total hip arthroplasty for arthritic hip in patients with residual poliomyelitis: a case series HIP International, September, 2016; https://pubmed.ncbi.nlm.nih.gov/27229169/; https://tinyurl.com/2p84bvm9; Last accessed 3 12 22

Outcome of total knee arthroplasty in patients with poliomyelitis. A systematic review EFORT Open Reviews, June, 2018; https://www.ncbi.nlm.nih.gov/pmc/articles/PMC6026880/; https://tinyurl.com/2t2fxr7e; Last accessed 3 12 22

Pain in Persons With Postpolio Syndrome: Frequency, Intensity, and Impact Archives of Physical Medicine and Rehabilitation, October 2008; https://www.ncbi.nlm.nih.gov/pmc/articles/PMC2651567/; https://tinyurl.com/ymafvy86; Last accessed 3 12 22

Painful Polio Science Reporter, January 2010; http://nopr.niscair.res.in/bitstream/123456789/7427/1/SR%2047%281%29%2019-24.pdf; https://tinyurl.com/2p88zny8; Last accessed 3 12 22

Paralysis Resource Guide Christopher & Dana Reeve Foundation, 5th Edition, 2020; https://s3.amazonaws.com/reeve-assets-production/English-PRG-2020_Smaller.pdf; https://tinyurl.com/2p9akp57; Last accessed 3 12 22

Parasympathetic Abnormalities as Post-Polio Sequelae: Vagus Caveat The PA Polio Survivors Network, 2018; https://www.papolionetwork.org/uploads/9/9/7/0/99704804/parasympathetic_abnormalities_as_post-polio_sequelae_-_vagus_caveat__1_.pdf; https://tinyurl.com/32kwvyay; Last accessed 3 12 22

Parenting stress: What causes it, and how does it change us? Parenting Science, 2020; https://parentingscience.com/parenting-stress/; https://tinyurl.com/ytwyprty; Last accessed 3 12 22

Part I — Opening the Door; PART II—The Rest of the Story Post-Polio Health International (PHI), 2011; https://www.polioplace.org/living-with-polio/part-i-%E2%80%94-opening-door-part-ii%E2%80%94-rest-story#:~:text=Those%20with%20post%2Dpolio%20weakness,increasing%20the%20possibility%20for%20accidents; https://tinyurl.com/3jdrxumn; Last accessed 3 12 22

Patients with post-polio syndrome are more likely to have subclinical involvement as compared to polio survivors without new symptoms Annals of Indian Academy of Neurology, January – March, 2016; https://www.ncbi.nlm.nih.gov/pmc/articles/PMC4782551/; https://tinyurl.com/2p8pmwrm; Last accessed 3 12 22

Polio Cleveland Clinic; https://my.clevelandclinic.org/health/diseases/15655-polio; https://tinyurl.com/bdd99y8d; Last accessed 3 12 22

Polio & chronic fatigue syndrome Polio Australia; https://www.poliosa.org.au/news/2019/polio-amp-chronic-fatigue-syndrome; https://tinyurl.com/uvnmnjk5; Last accessed 3 12 22

Polio and the Late Effects of Polio Better Health Channel; https://www.betterhealth.vic.gov.au/health/conditionsandtreatments/polio-and-post-polio-syndrome; https://tinyurl.com/4w8upamx; Last accessed 3 12 22

Polio Pioneer Helps Survivors Hold On To Strength NPR May 11, 2009; https://www.npr.org/templates/story/story.php?storyId=103892252#:~:text=Lauro%20Halstead.,is%20a%20polio%20survivor%2C%20too; https://tinyurl.com/3mdbkndt; Last accessed 3 12 22

Polio Survivors Living with Disease's Lasting Effects Fear Some Might Not Even Know Due to Past Stigma, Secrecy ABC News November 12, 2021; https://www.abc.net.au/news/2021-11-13/polio-survivors-living-with-disease-lasting-effects/100568596; https://tinyurl.com/3hn2j76t; Last accessed 3 12 22

Polio Survivors' Perceptions of the Meaning of Quality of Life and Strategies Used to Promote Participation in Everyday Activities Health Expectations October, 2015; https://www.ncbi.nlm.nih.gov/pmc/articles/PMC5060821/; https://tinyurl.com/ae9ka7dk; Last accessed 3 12 22

Polio Survivors Serving Each Other: Bruno Bytes: On the Topic of Muscle Pain The PA Polio Survivors Network; https://www.papolionetwork.org/bruno-bytes.html; https://tinyurl.com/2p8c9bjr; Last accessed 3 12 22

Post-Polio Breathing and Sleep Problems Revisited Post-Polio Health International (PHI); https://post-polio.org/wp-content/uploads/2021/04/BreathingArticlesSalk.pdf; https://tinyurl.com/2286hmfm; Last accessed 3 12 22

Post-Polio Protein Power: Eat Well, Be Well The PA Polio survivors Network; www.papolionetwork.org/uploads/9/9/7/0/99704804/eat_well_be_well_protein_diet.pdf; https://tinyurl.com/4v8uz6fm; Last accessed 3 12 22

Post-Polio sequelae and sleep-related disordered breathing Mayo Clinic Proceedings, March 1998; https://pubmed.ncbi.nlm.nih.gov/9511778/; https://tinyurl.com/34w4yydk; Last accessed 3 12 22

Post-polio syndrome CDC; https://www.cdc.gov/polio/what-is-polio/pps.html; https://tinyurl.com/2p9p65vz; Last accessed 3 12 22

Bibliography

Post-Polio Syndrome Christopher & Dana Reeve Foundation; https://www.christopherreeve.org/living-with-paralysis/health/causes-of-paralysis/post-polio-syndrome-poliomyelitis; https://tinyurl.com/3btc4ces; Last accessed 3 12 22

Post-polio Syndrome MAYO CLINIC; https://www.mayoclinic.org/diseases-conditions/post-polio-syndrome/symptoms-causes/syc-20355669; https://tinyurl.com/4hcc2kwn; Last accessed 3 12 22

Post-polio syndrome CDC; https://www.cdc.gov/polio/what-is-polio/pps.html; https://tinyurl.com/2p9p65vz; Last accessed 3 12 22

Post-Polio Syndrome Fact Sheet National Institute of Neurological Disorders and Stroke; https://www.ninds.nih.gov/Disorders/Patient-Caregiver-Education/Fact-Sheets/Post-Polio-Syndrome-Fact-Sheet; https://tinyurl.com/4fvm63bn; Last accessed 3 12 22

Post-Polio Syndrome Kentucky Neuroscience Institute; https://ukhealthcare.uky.edu/kentucky-neuroscience-institute/conditions/neuromuscular-disorders/post-polio-syndrome; https://tinyurl.com/pt544xd5; Last accessed 3 12 22

Post-Polio-Syndrome Medscape https://emedicine.medscape.com/article/306920-overview; https://tinyurl.com/4bhpjs7z; Last accessed 3 12 22

Post -Polio Syndrome National Organization for Rare Disorders; https://rarediseases.org/rare-diseases/post-polio-syndrome/; https://tinyurl.com/3985jy6x; Last accessed 3 12 22

Post-Polio Syndrome and Anesthesia Anesthesiology September, 2005; https://pubs.asahq.org/anesthesiology/article/103/3/638/8686/Postpolio-Syndrome-and-Anesthesia; https://tinyurl.com/ywm9hpjv; Last accessed 3 12 22

Post-polio Syndrome: More Than Just a Lower Motor Neuron Disease. Frontiers in Neurology, July, 2019; https://www.frontiersin.org/articles/10.3389/fneur.2019.00773/full; https://tinyurl.com/yursuuaf; Last accessed 3 12 22

Post-polio syndrome – polio's legacy Clinical Medicine Journal, June, 2010; https://www.rcpjournals.org/content/clinmedicine/10/3/213; https://tinyurl.com/y8pkh6r2; Last accessed 3 12 22

Post-Poliomyelitis Syndrome Dovepress, August 2019; https://doi.org/10.2147/IMCRJ.S219481; https://tinyurl.com/mp5smuec; Last accessed 3 12 22

Postpolio Syndrome: A Review of Lived Experiences of Patients; https://pubmed.ncbi.nlm.nih.gov/31392174/; https://tinyurl.com/9muhxntu; Last accessed 3 12 22

Pregnancy, delivery, and perinatal outcome in female survivors of polio Journal of the Neurological Sciences, July, 2007; https://pubmed.ncbi.nlm.nih.gov/17395208/; https://tinyurl.com/bdfew44n; Last accessed 3 12 22

Preventing Complications in Polio Survivors Undergoing Surgery (or) Receiving Anesthesia International Center for Polio Education; http://www.postpolioinfo.com/library/surg.pdf; https://tinyurl.com/26zztkud; Last accessed 3 12 22

Prolonged benefit in post-polio syndrome from comprehensive rehabilitation: A pilot study Disability and Rehabilitation July, 2009; https://www.tandfonline.com/doi/abs/10.1080/09638280801973206; https://tinyurl.com/2p97d238; Last accessed 3 12 22

Psychological Resilience and Depressive Symptoms in Older Adults Diagnosed with Post-polio Syndrome Rehabilitation Nursing, July-August 2010; https://www.ncbi.nlm.nih.gov/pmc/articles/PMC3432643/; https://tinyurl.com/bdw7d4kv; Last accessed 3 12 22

Resilience Center on the Developing Child Harvard University; https://developingchild.harvard.edu/science/key-concepts/resilience/; https://tinyurl.com/yc8kzxpp; Last accessed 3 12 22

Resilience: How to Build it in Children 3-8 Years Old Raising Children: The Australian Parenting Website; https://raisingchildren.net.au/school-age/behaviour/understanding-behaviour/resilience-how-to-build-it-in-children-3-8-years#:~:text=Resilience%20is%20the%20ability%20to,the%20foundation%20of%20children's%20resilience; https://tinyurl.com/2p8umsts; Last accessed 3 12 22

Separation Anxiety and School Refusal Medscape; https://emedicine.medscape.com/article/916737-overview; https://tinyurl.com/2492823z; Last accessed 3 12 22

Separation Anxiety Disorder MAYO CLINIC; https://www.mayoclinic.org/diseases-conditions/separation-anxiety-disorder/symptoms-causes/syc-20377455#:~:text=Separation%20anxiety%20disorder%20usually%20won,or%20other%20health%20care%20provider; https://tinyurl.com/mu6ak6dm; Last accessed 3 12 22

Bibliography

Separation Anxiety Disorder Management News Medical Life Sciences; https://www.news-medical.net/health/Separation-Anxiety-Disorder-Management.aspx; https://tinyurl.com/aubvkhwb; Last accessed 3 12 22

Sleep Apnoea (sic) – personal story Polio Survivors Ireland; https://polio.ie/about-polio/personal-stories/; https://tinyurl.com/yckstbyx; Last accessed 3 13 22

Sleep disorders in aging polio survivors: A systematic review; Annals of Physical and Rehabilitation Medicine, November, 2020; https://www.sciencedirect.com/science/article/pii/S1877065719301800; https://tinyurl.com/y97dp7ey; Last accessed 3 12 22

Slow Guts and Polio Survivors The PA Polio Survivors Network; https://www.papolionetwork.org/uploads/9/9/7/0/99704804/slow_guts_and_polio_survivors.pdf; https://tinyurl.com/2p8eure5; Last accessed 3 12 22

Slow Guts and Polio Survivors International Center for Polio Education; http://postpolioinfo.com/library/SlowGuts.pdf; https://tinyurl.com/yc8awmvn; Last accessed 3 13 22

Special Considerations for Treating Dental Patients Exhibiting the "Post-Polio Syndrome" Special Care in Dentistry, September-October, 2001; https://pubmed.ncbi.nlm.nih.gov/11803639/; https://tinyurl.com/v7ujv5ah; Last accessed 3 13 22

Surviving in a post-polio world; Social Science and Medicine, April, 2014; https://pubmed.ncbi.nlm.nih.gov/24607679/; https://tinyurl.com/2p983m6y; Last accessed 3 12 22

Suspect post-polio syndrome in older patients with OSA Clinical Advisor, June 27, 2012; https://www.clinicaladvisor.com/home/the-waiting-room/suspect-post-polio-syndrome-in-older-patients-with-osa/; https://tinyurl.com/3e97aftw; Last accessed 3 12 22

Swallowing Difficulties and Medications The PA Polio Survivors Network; https://www.papolionetwork.org/uploads/9/9/7/0/99704804/swallowing_issues_and_medications.pdf; https://tinyurl.com/mr2uvnbn; Last accessed 3 13 22

Swallowing Difficulties and Polio The PA Polio Survivors Network; https://www.papolionetwork.org/uploads/9/9/7/0/99704804/swallowing_difficulties_and_polio.pdf; https://tinyurl.com/bdevhhhv; Last accessed 3 13 22

Swallowing Problems The Lighthouse Coastal Empire Polio Survivors Association, Inc. Newsletter April, 2011; https://www.coastalempirepoliosurvivors.org/content/April2011Newslettter.htm ; https://tinyurl.com/3a7p7ra7; Last accessed 3 13 22

Symptoms Post-Polio Syndrome National Health Service; https://www.nhs.uk/conditions/post-polio-syndrome/symptoms/#:~:text=Muscle%20weakness&text=Weakness%20can%20occur%20in%20muscles,affected%20muscles%2C%20known%20as%20atrophy ; https://tinyurl.com/ytez8k6w; Last accessed 3 13 22

Symptoms Predictive of Sleep Disordered Breathing in Post-Polio Syndrome https://thorax.bmj.com/content/76/Suppl_2/A73.2; https://tinyurl.com/bdm8mffp; Last accessed 3 13 22

Tests for Breathing Problems If You Have a Neuromuscular Condition IVUN International Ventilator Users Network; www.ventusers.org; https://tinyurl.com/4vskjfzd; Last accessed 3 13 22

The Effects of Cold on Polio Survivors The PA Polio Survivors Network; https://www.papolionetwork.org/uploads/9/9/7/0/99704804/effects_of_cold_on_polio_survivors.pdf; https://tinyurl.com/5ed8nvw7; Last accessed 3 13 22

The Fight Against Polio NPR, May 11, 2009: www.npr.org/templates/story/story.php?storyId=103892252; https://tinyurl.com/2p9bzpbr; Last accessed 3 13 22

THE HASSLES OF LIVING WITH POST-POLIO: SOME SURVIVAL STRATEGIES 12th World Congress of the International Federation of Physical Medicine and Rehabilitation, Sydney, March 1995; http://www.polioplace.org/sites/default/files/files/Hassles%20of%20Living%20w%20PP-Survival%20Strategies.pdf; https://tinyurl.com/3as6mbp3; Last accessed 3 13 22

The Late Effects of Polio: Introduction to Clinical Practice Polo NZ (New Zealand); https://www.healthnavigator.org.nz/media/7516/the-late-effects-of-polio-introduction-to-clinical-practice.pdf; https://tinyurl.com/5yjc4nky; Last accessed 3 13 22

The Polio Narratives: Dialogues with FDR Bulletin of the History of Medicine, (John Hopkins)2001; https://doi.org/10.1353/bhm.2001.0115; https://tinyurl.com/2p97tchr; Last accessed 3 13 22

The Polio Paradox Chronic Neuroimmune Diseases January 1, 2014: http://www.anapsid.org/cnd/diffdx/polioparadox.html; https://tinyurl.com/2p8cjcxw; Last accessed 3 13 22

Bibliography

The Post-Polio Roller Coaster The PA Polio Survivors Network; https://www.papolionetwork.org/uploads/9/9/7/0/99704804/the_pps_roller_coaster.pdf; https://tinyurl.com/2vhee9hh; Last accessed 3 13 22

The Psychological Aspects of Polio Survivors Through their Life Experience Annals of Physical and Rehabilitation Medicine, February, 2010; https://www.sciencedirect.com/science/article/pii/S1877065709002826?via%3Dihub; https://tinyurl.com/4u9fzyd7; Last accessed 3 13 22

The Resilience Scale for Adults: Construct Validity and Measurement in a Belgian Sample International Journal of Testing; https://www.tandfonline.com/doi/abs/10.1080/15305058.2010.508570; https://tinyurl.com/rtt57uch; Last accessed 3 13 22

The Vagus Nerve The PA Polio Survivors Network; https://www.papolionetwork.org/uploads/2/7/7/2/27726699/conference_booklet_articles__complete_.pdf; https:/; https://tinyurl.com/yeypm8n2; Last accessed 3 13

Total hip Arthroplasty in Patients Affected by Poliomyelitis The Bone & Joint Journal, June, 2018; https://pubmed.ncbi.nlm.nih.gov/29855245/; https://tinyurl.com/2k6xju4j; Last accessed 3 13 22

Total Hip Arthroplasty in Patients of Post Polio Residual Paralysis: A Retrospective Case Series Indian Journal of Orthopaedics (sic), July-August 2017; https://www.ncbi.nlm.nih.gov/pmc/articles/PMC5525524/; https://tinyurl.com/2p9xc2ac; Last accessed 3 13 22

Total Hip Arthroplasty for Patients with Residual Poliomyelitis at a Mean Eight Years of Follow-up Acta Medica Okayama, February 2018;https://pubmed.ncbi.nlm.nih.gov/29463934/; https://tinyurl.com/6r5k5nyr; Last accessed 3 13 22

Total Hip Arthroplasty Performed in Patients with Residual Poliomyelitis: Does It Work? Clinical Orthopaedics (sic) and Related Research, March 2014; https://pubmed.ncbi.nlm.nih.gov/24203163/; https://tinyurl.com/2p89bf34; Last accessed 3 13 22

Total Hip Replacement OrthoInfo; https://orthoinfo.aaos.org/en/treatment/total-hip-replacement/; https://tinyurl.com/mr442s9h; Last accessed 3 13 22

Total Knee Arthroplasty in Limbs Affected by Poliomyelitis The Journal of Bone and Joint Surgery, 2002; https://citeseerx.ist.psu.edu/viewdoc/download?doi=10.1.1.910.8971&rep=rep1&type=pdf; https://tinyurl.com/2p9bhemd; Last accessed 3 13 22

Total knee replacement in a polio patient with prior extension osteotomy: a case report Journal of Surgical Case Reports, 2022; https://academic.oup.com/jscr/article/2022/1/rjab575/6507821; https://tinyurl.com/mw3jnffv; Last accessed 3 13 22

Transformer Man: An Exploration of Disability in Neil Young's Life and Music (Beyond) Popular Culture; https://scholarspace.manoa.hawaii.edu/bitstream/10125/58349/809.pdf; https://tinyurl.com/bdhbsdp7; Last accessed 3 13 22

Understanding Fatigue for Post Polio Syndrome (PPS) and Late Effects of Polio (LEOP) Patients DUNCAN Foundation; http://duncanfoundation.org/wp-content/uploads/2018/03/DUNCF-Fatigue-Doc.pdf; https://tinyurl.com/3k9tpa97; Last accessed 3 13 22

Uses of Braces and Orthotics for Conservative Management of Foot and Ankle Disorders Foot and Ankle Orthotics, 2018; file:///C:/Users/susan/Downloads/Uses_of_Braces_and_Orthotics_for_Conservative_Mana.pdf; https://tinyurl.com/3v7km9ry; Last accessed 3 13 22

Vagus nerve Wikipedia; https://en.wikipedia.org/wiki/Vagus_nerve; https://tinyurl.com/2p9a2tzz.

What is Hypoventilation? Ventilatory Assisted Living, Spring 2003; https://www.polioplace.org/sites/default/files/files/IVUN%20News%20Vol%2017%20No%201.pdf; https://tinyurl.com/2wwrutnz; Last accessed 3 13 22

What is the difference between a syndrome and a disorder? Igenomix; https://www.igenomix.net/blog/what-is-the-difference-between-a-syndrome-and-a-disorder/; https://tinyurl.com/bdhajkvt; Last accessed 3 13 22

What is the ICD-10 Code for Post-Polio Syndrome? Quantum Rehab; https://www.quantumrehab.com/quantum-rehab-clinicians/icd-10-codes-post-polio-syndrome.asp#:~:text=About%20the%20ICD%2D10%20Code,effective%20on%20October%201%2C%202017; https://tinyurl.com/yckhs5e8; Last accessed 3 13 22

Why Neil Young has good reason to know the value of vaccines Edinburgh Evening News, 2/2/2022; https://www.edinburghnews.scotsman.com/news/opinion/columnists/covid-vaccines-why-neil-young-has-good-reason-to-know-the-value-of-vaccines-steve-cardownie-3550590; https://tinyurl.com/yben2kks; Last accessed 3 13 22

Bibliography

Southview Isolation Hospital

Southview Hospital (historical), Wisconsin, Placekeeper; https://www.placekeeper.com/Wisconsin/Southview_Hospital-1574510.html; https://tinyurl.com/uxwv8s6e; Last accessed 3 13 22

Southview Isolation Hospital, Pinterest; https://www.pinterest.com/pin/533395149617684322/; https://tinyurl.com/yckkk4cz; Last accessed 3 13 22

Surgical Glove Use

How Does Autoclave Sterilization Work? Grainger KnowHow;https://www.grainger.com/know-how/equipment-information/kh-how-does-autoclave-sterilization-work#:~:text=An%20autoclave%20is%20used%20in,such%20as%20bacteria%20and%20spores; https://tinyurl.com/bmja2twp; Last accessed 3 13 22

The Dangers of Powder in Surgical Gloves Molynlycke; https://www.molnlycke.com/our-knowledge/the-dangers-of-powder-in-surgical-gloves/; https://tinyurl.com/5n6vubxd; Last accessed 3 13 22

The History of Disposable Gloves AMMEX, December 12, 2016; https://blog.ammex.com/the-history-of-disposable-gloves/#.YN4_NOhKhdg; https://tinyurl.com/2p9c7wfm; Last accessed 3 13 22

The History of Surgical Gloves, Past Medical History; https://www.pastmedicalhistory.co.uk/the-history-of-surgical-gloves/; https://tinyurl.com/yckpjv5p; Last accessed 3 13 22

Survivorship Guilt and Shame

CONSIDERING PTSD FOR DSM-5 Depression and Anxiety, 2010; https://www.ptsd.va.gov/professional/articles/article-pdf/id35490.pdf; https://tinyurl.com/3twsamrp; Last accessed 3 13 22

Don't Tell Anyone About Your Polio Post-Polio Health International (PHI), 2011; https://www.polioplace.org/living-with-polio/dont-tell-anyone-about-your-polio; https://tinyurl.com/295b3cck; Last accessed 3 13 22

Public Health Campaigns and the 'Threat' of Disability Welcome Collection, September 2020; https://wellcomecollection.org/articles/X1YhrRAAAEt_izkW; https://tinyurl.com/49p68fbn.

What is survivor's guilt? MedicalNewsToday, June 27, 2019; https://www.medicalnewstoday.com/articles/325578; https://tinyurl.com/3nzc27fw; Last accessed 3 13 22

What Is Survivor's Guilt? Verywellmind, February 20, 2021; https://www.verywellmind.com/survivors-guilt-4688743; https://tinyurl.com/3mepy3hc; Last accessed 3 13 22

The Birth Control Pill: A History

FDA approves "the pill" HISTORY, May 9, 1960; https://www.history.com/this-day-in-history/fda-approves-the-pill; https://tinyurl.com/zmfc29nd; Last accessed 3 13 22

The Birth Control Pill A History Planned Parenthood, 2015; https://www.plannedparenthood.org/files/1514/3518/7100/Pill_History_FactSheet.pdf; https://tinyurl.com/5bbwwptw; Last accessed 3 13 22

Type A Behavior Pattern

Chasing Ernst L Wynder: 40 years of Philip Morris' efforts to influence a leading scientist Journal of Epidemiology and Community Health, 2003; https://jech.bmj.com/content/jech/57/8/571.full.pdf; https://tinyurl.com/3bakmcnb; Last accessed 3 13 22

Does personality explain social inequalities in mortality? The French GAZEL cohort study International Journal of Epidemiology, June, 2008; https://pubmed.ncbi.nlm.nih.gov/18276626/; https://tinyurl.com/2ywe7jps; Last accessed 3 13 22

Modifying Type A Behavior Pattern Journal of Psychosomatic Research, 1977; https://www.sciencedirect.com/science/article/abs/pii/0022399977900150; https://tinyurl.com/ms2f5n5s; Last accessed 3 13 22

Phillip Morris USA INTER-OFFICE CORRESPONDENCE TRUTH TOBACCO INDUSTRY DOCUMENTS, July 1, 1991; https://www.industrydocuments.ucsf.edu/tobacco/docs/#id=nzwf0128; https://tinyurl.com/2p8kzsju; Last accessed 3 13 22

"Stress" and coronary heart disease: psychosocial risk factors The Medical Journal of Australia, March 2003; https://pubmed.ncbi.nlm.nih.gov/12633484/; https://tinyurl.com/m554nr6d; Last accessed 3 13 22

Bibliography

Type A Behavior Pattern and Coronary Heart Disease: Philip Morris's "Crown Jewel" American Journal of Public Health, November, 2012; https://www.ncbi.nlm.nih.gov/pmc/articles/PMC3477961/; https://tinyurl.com/2p9f2cyk; Last accessed 3 13 22

TYPE A BEHAVIOR PATTERN: SOME OF ITS PATHOPHYSIOLOGICAL COMPONENTS BULLETIN OF THE NEW YORK ACADEMY OF MEDICINE, September 1977; https://www.ncbi.nlm.nih.gov/pmc/articles/PMC1807381/pdf/bullnyacadmed00143-0005.pdf; https://tinyurl.com/y7vssu7e; Last accessed 3 13 22

Vaccination

Africa battles out-of-control polio outbreaks Science, March 3, 2022; https://www.science.org/content/article/africa-battles-out-of-control-polio-outbreaks; https://tinyurl.com/2p95bpe2; Last accessed 3 14 22

American healthcare's racist history helped fuel a fear of vaccines, Quartz, July 30, 2020; https://qz.com/1886133/us-healthcares-racist-history-helped-fuel-a-fear-of-vaccines/; https://tinyurl.com/nsbuc6mu; Last accessed 3 14 22

An Anti-Vaccine Film Targeted To Black Americans Spreads False Information, NPR, June 8, 2021; https://www.npr.org/sections/health-shots/2021/06/08/1004214189/anti-vaccine-film-targeted-to-black-americans-spreads-false-information; https://tinyurl.com/yc4mnaz3; Last accessed 3 14 22

Anti-Vaccination Leaders Fuel Black Mistrust of Medical Establishment as Covid-19 kills people of Color The Washington Post, July 17, 2020; https://www.washingtonpost.com/dc-md-va/2020/07/17/black-anti-vaccine-coronavirus-tuskegee-syphilis/; https://tinyurl.com/yc6nm9bb; Last accessed 3 14 22

Cutter Laboratories Wikipedia; https://en.wikipedia.org/wiki/Cutter_Laboratories; https://tinyurl.com/5amfw3cn; Last accessed 3 14 22

Defeating Polio, The Disease That Paralyzed America NPR, April 10, 2015; https://www.npr.org/sections/npr-history-dept/2015/04/10/398515228/defeating-the-disease-that-paralyzed-america; https://tinyurl.com/yvx5bwtr; Last accessed 3 14 22

Development of the Polio Vaccine: A Historical Perspective of Tuskegee University's Role in Mass Production and Distribution of HeLa Cells Journal for Healthcare for Poor and Underserved, November 2012; https://www.ncbi.nlm.nih.gov/pmc/articles/PMC4458465/; https://tinyurl.com/y24758x3; Last accessed 3 14 22

Diseases You Almost Forgot About (Thanks to Vaccines) CDC; https://www.cdc.gov/vaccines/parents/diseases/forgot-14-diseases.html; https://tinyurl.com/3cfxfnts; Last accessed 3 14 22

Doctors warn of polio 'outbreak' threat as 2 new preliminary positive cases found The Times of Israel, March 11, 2022; https://www.timesofisrael.com/doctors-warn-of-polio-outbreak-threat-as-2-new-preliminary-positive-cases-found/; https://tinyurl.com/4f86d7bp; Last accessed 3 14 22

Edward Jenner and the history of smallpox and vaccination Baylor University Medical Proceedings, January 2005; https://www.ncbi.nlm.nih.gov/pmc/articles/PMC1200696/; https://tinyurl.com/9mwt4n7c; Last accessed 3 14 22

How Robert F. Kennedy Jr. Became the Anti-vaxxer Icon of America's Nightmares Vanity Fair, May 13, 2021; https://www.vanityfair.com/news/2021/05/how-robert-f-kennedy-jr-became-anti-vaxxer-icon-nightmare; https://tinyurl.com/4n4s25v3; Last accessed 3 14 22

Israel finds first case of polio in over 30 years in three year old girl who was NOT vaccinated against the virus; Daily Mail, March 8, 2022; https://www.dailymail.co.uk/health/article-10591567/Israel-finds-case-polio-30-years-four-year-old-girl.html; https://tinyurl.com/57kjyfhm; Last accessed 3 14 22

Jonas Salk and the Polio Vaccine National Archives Dwight D. Eisenhower Presidential Library; https://www.eisenhowerlibrary.gov/research/online-documents/jonas-salk-and-polio-vaccine; https://tinyurl.com/4c7nfkm4; Last accessed 3 28 22

Living with a Pandemic: Polio in the 1940s North Caroline Public Health, February 11, 2021; http://mediahub.unc.edu/living-with-a-pandemic-polio-in-the-1940s/; https://tinyurl.com/bz46za5; Last accessed 3 14 22

Louis Pasteur Wikipedia https://en.wikipedia.org/wiki/Louis_Pasteur; https://tinyurl.com/2p82jykv; Last accessed 3 14 22

Malawi declares polio outbreak WHO; https://www.afro.who.int/news/malawi-declares-polio-outbreak; https://tinyurl.com/2p83cxrn; Last accessed 3 14 22

National Participation Trends 1955-6 in the Polio Vaccination Program Journal Storage,1962; https://www.jstor.org/stable/4591594; https://tinyurl.com/28x8eumy; Last accessed 3 14 22

Bibliography

Patients in Afghanistan Face Growing Obstacles to Care Journal of the American Medical Association, July 20, 2021; https://jamanetwork.com/journals/jama/fullarticle/2782174; https://tinyurl.com/mr3hx33z; Last accessed 3 14 22

Photos Salk Labs Google Images: https://www.google.com/search?q=jonas+salk+laboratory&hl=EN&tbm=isch&s xsrf=ALeKk02Pp6sxd08qgEDcyR7l1iEZJOG9hA%3A1629208969547&source =hp&biw=1280&bih=600&ei=icEbYeSwH5rB0PEPiPC6uAQ&iflsig=AINFCb YAAAAAYRvPmZDwbc6ShaavA1rWxf49kvFEG1kl&oq=jonas+salk+laborat ory&gs_lcp=CgNpbWcQDDoECCMQJzoFCAAQgAQ6CAgAELEDEIMBOgg IABCABBCxAzoLCAAQgAQQsQMQgwE6BggAEAgQHjoECAAQHjoECA AQGFCCCCFi3VGDEZmgAcAB4AIABaIgBjhCSAQQyMS4ymAEAoAEBqgE LZ3dzLXdpei1pbWc&sclient=img&ved=0ahUKEwikmZKvnLjyAhWaIDQIH Qi4DkcQ4dUDCAY#imgrc=1HJu26YK_n3j3M&imgdii=rFAH0_wyUD8GjM; https://tinyurl.com/2p95ke3s; Last accessed 3 14 22

Plagues and People: Infectious and Epidemic Disease in History Department of History University of California, Irvine; http://faculty.humanities.uci.edu/bjbecker/plaguesandpeople/lecture18.html; https://tinyurl.com/yckwa88u; Last accessed 3 14 22

Polio and Swimming Pools: Historical Connections The History of Vaccines, The College of Physicians of Philadelphia; https://www.historyofvaccines.org/content/blog/polio-and-swimming-pools-historical-connections; https://tinyurl.com/2vhhcfuj; Last accessed 3 14 22

Polio Elimination in the United States CDC: https://www.cdc.gov/polio/what-is-polio/polio-us.html; https://tinyurl.com/2p8zhawz; Last accessed 3 14 22

Polio Vaccination CDC; https://www.cdc.gov/vaccines/vpd/polio/index.html; https://tinyurl.com/2njt2szp; Last accessed 3 14 22

Pregnancy and Rubella CDC; https://www.cdc.gov/rubella/pregnancy.html; https://tinyurl.com/ycknsyry; Last accessed 3 14 22

Resurgence of measles or polio outbreaks likely to happen, experts warn Life Sciences, April 24, 2020; https://www.news-medical.net/news/20200424/Resurgence-of-measles-or-polio-outbreaks-likely-to-happen-experts-warn.aspx; https://tinyurl.com/2p8ppcnd; Last accessed 3 14 22

Smallpox CDC; https://www.cdc.gov/smallpox/index.html#:~:text=Thanks%20to%20the%20suc cess%20of,occurring%20smallpox%20have%20happened%20since; https://tinyurl.com/2p9e93mn; Last accessed 3 14 22

Tetralogy of Fallot Nemours Children's Health, May 2017; https://kidshealth.org/en/parents/tetralogy-of-fallot.html; https://tinyurl.com/2kf56452; Last accessed 3 14 22

The Campaign To Wipe Out Polio Was Going Really Well ... Until It Wasn't NPR, October 30, 2020; https://www.npr.org/sections/goatsandsoda/2020/10/30/929080692/the-campaign-to-wipe-out-polio-was-going-really-well-until-it-wasnt; https://tinyurl.com/2p85v5n6; Last accessed 3 14 22

The Cutter Incident: How America's First Polio Vaccine Led to the Growing Vaccine Crisis Nature Medicine, August 2006; https://www.nature.com/articles/nm0806-879; https://tinyurl.com/3h3jzf5t; Last accessed 3 14 22

The Early Years of CDC's Fight Against Polio, CDC; https://www.cdc.gov/polio/why/index.htm#:~:text=The%20Early%20Years%20of%20CDC's%20Fight%20against%20Polio&text=Jonas%20Salk%2C%20of%20the%20University,OPV)%20in%20the%20early%201960s; https://tinyurl.com/y3w4ymkp; Last accessed 3 16 22

The History of Vaccines The History of Vaccines, The College of Physicians of Philadelphia; https://www.historyofvaccines.org/timeline/all; https://tinyurl.com/25rrppbc; Last accessed 3 14 22

The Legacy of Henrietta Lacks John Hopkins Medicine; https://www.hopkinsmedicine.org/henriettalacks/; https://tinyurl.com/y4nd2hks; Last accessed 3 14 22

The Polio Vaccine Assistance Act of 1955 American Journal of Public Health, https://ajph.aphapublications.org/doi/pdf/10.2105/AJPH.45.10.1349; https://tinyurl.com/4fwp5kun; Last accessed 3 14 22

The U.S. Government and Global Polio Efforts, Global Health Policy, Kaiser Family Foundation; Oct 29, 2021; https://www.kff.org/global-health-policy/fact-sheet/the-u-s-government-and-global-polio-efforts/; https://tinyurl.com/ne92n7jn; Last accessed 3 14 22

There is an equity gap in vaccines March of Dimes https://www.marchofdimes.org/vaccines.aspx; https://tinyurl.com/3k3kvrj7; Last accessed 3 26 22

There Was So Little Information: Polio Survivors Offer Pandemic Perspective NPR, May 12, 2020; https://www.npr.org/sections/coronavirus-live-updates/2020/05/12/852376351/there-was-so-little-information-polio-survivors-offer-pandemic-perspective; https://tinyurl.com/2s3jyv3u; Last accessed 3 14 22

Bibliography

Timeliness and coverage of child vaccinations across India International Growth Center, September 27, 2021; https://www.theigc.org/blog/timeliness-and-coverage-of-child-vaccinations-across-india/; https://tinyurl.com/3ejwpryb; Last accessed 3 14 22

To Boldly Remember Where We Have Already Been: Revisiting the Cutter Polio Vaccine Incident during Operation Warp Speed Brill September 28, 2020; https://brill.com/view/journals/joah/2/1-2/article-p17_2.xml?language=en; https://tinyurl.com/3hdwx7tm; Last accessed 3 14 22

Tuskegee Study Leads to COVID-19 Vaccine Mistrust in African American Community; 11 ALIVE, December 11, 2020; https://www.11alive.com/article/news/health/coronavirus/tuskegee-study-leads-to-covid-19-vaccine-mistrust/85-cb941f55-7991-47c6-bd3e-33692a0e158b; https://tinyurl.com/ycydrdn4; Last accessed 3 14 22

Two Vaccines Smithsonian National Museum of History; https://amhistory.si.edu/polio/virusvaccine/vacraces2.htm; https://tinyurl.com/2p8cse8j; Last accessed 3 14 22

Update on Vaccine-Derived Poliovirus Outbreaks — Worldwide, January 2020–June 2021CDC, https://www.cdc.gov/mmwr/volumes/70/wr/mm7049a1.htm; https://tinyurl.com/3jj9r8tx; Last accessed 3 14 22

Vaccine-derived Poliovirus, CDC; https://www.cdc.gov/vaccines/vpd/polio/hcp/vaccine-derived-poliovirus-faq.html; https://tinyurl.com/wj775wbc; Last accessed 3 16 22

Vaccine Safety CDC; https://www.cdc.gov/vaccinesafety/index.html; https://tinyurl.com/3ahat3t5; Last accessed 3 14 22

We Were There- Polio Conquering Polio in America: The Cutter Incident and Beyond CDC; https://www.cdc.gov/os/wewerethere/polio/index.html; https://tinyurl.com/zsts4uns; Last accessed 3 14 22

What are pathogens? MedicalNewsToday, August 21, 2020; https://www.medicalnewstoday.com/articles/pathogens-definition; https://tinyurl.com/yrye6ep4; Last accessed 3 14 22

What is an Anti-Vaccer MedicalNewsToday, November 4, 2020; https://www.medicalnewstoday.com/articles/anti-vaxxer; https://tinyurl.com/2f6d2ntw; Last accessed 3 14 22

When Black People are Wary of Vaccine, It's Important to Listen and Understand Why CNN, December 18, 2020; https://www.cnn.com/2020/12/17/opinions/african-americans-covid-vaccine-sacks/index.html; https://tinyurl.com/y4amcwd9; Last accessed 3 14 22

Why Are We Involved CDC, October 8, 2021; https://www.cdc.gov/polio/why-are-we-involved/index.htm; https://tinyurl.com/ycxm8k9b; Last accessed 3 14 22

Vietnam

Asian Wars and Battles ThoughtCo; https://www.thoughtco.com/napalm-and-agent-orange-in-vietnam-war-195797; https://tinyurl.com/2s2yfv4h; Last accessed 3 14 22

A Turning Point October 1967 University of Wisconsin-Madison, University Communications; https://1967.wisc.edu/timeline/index.html; https://tinyurl.com/2nb84vdf; Last accessed 3 14 22

Dow Chemical Company Wikipedia; https://en.wikipedia.org/wiki/Dow_Chemical_Company; https://tinyurl.com/4utrwfe5; Last accessed 3 14 22

Images Napalm Google Images; https://www.google.com/search?q=napalm+vietnam+war&hl=EN&tbm=isch&sxsrf=ALeKk010YFMZGr7zH7rHByGUDZJMDw8YRg%3A1629756606936&source=hp&biw=1280&bih=657&ei=vhwkYc6LLKGG0Abo_Y4Y&iflsig=AINFCbYAAAAAYSQqzitoRWXDZ0NvsJCzSg9phalXiTNR&oq=napalm&gs_lcp=CgNpbWcQARgDMggIABCABBCxAzIICAAQgAQQsQMyBQgAEIAEMgUIABCABDIFCAAQgAQyBQgAEIAEMgUIABCABDIFCAAQgAQyBQgAEIAEMgUIABCABDoHCCMQ6gIQJzoECCMQJ1DEEVjAG2CXN2gBcAB4AIABZIgBlgSSAQMxLjGYAQCgAQGqAQtnd3Mtd2l6LWltZ7ABCg&sclient=img; Last accessed 3 14 22

WWI

The 32nd 'Red Arrow' Division in World War I: From the 'Iron Jaw Division' to 'Les Terribles' Revised April 26, 2020; http://www.32nd-division.org/history/ww1/32-ww1.html; https://tinyurl.com/yfw98jkv; Last accessed 3 14 22

United States Army 32nd Infantry Division (Red Arrow) Grove Oklahoma; https://www.cityofgroveok.gov/building/page/united-states-army-32nd-infantry-division-red-arrow; https://tinyurl.com/2yfx7dcf; Last accessed 3 14 22

Bibliography

Wartime Milwaukee Encyclopedia of Milwaukee; https://emke.uwm.edu/entry/wartime-milwaukee/; https://tinyurl.com/2u5zsbmm; Last accessed 3 14 22

WWII

Gender on the Home Front The National WWII Museum, New Orleans; https://www.nationalww2museum.org/war/articles/gender-home-front; https://tinyurl.com/mw9btnbt; https://tinyurl.com/y2b9p5ep; Last accessed 3 14 22

Gender, Stress and Alcohol Abuse in Post-War Britain National Center for Biotechnology Information (NCBI).https://www.ncbi.nlm.nih.gov/books/NBK436954/; https://tinyurl.com/2nhmsx7s; Last accessed 3 14 22

Make It Do—Rationing of Butter, Fats & Oils in World War II Sarah Sundin, March 29, 2018; https://www.sarahsundin.com/make-it-do-rationing-of-fats-oils-in-world-war-ii-2/; https://tinyurl.com/yzbvfjdr; Last accessed 3 14 22

More about Soap UC San Diego, 9/19/18; https://pages.ucsd.edu/~dkjordan/cgi-bin/moreabout.pl?tyimuh=sapo; https://tinyurl.com/2p9y427u; Last accessed 3 14 22

Research Starters: The Draft and World War II The National WWII Museum New Orleans; www.nationalww2museum.org/students-teachers/student-resources/research-starters/draft-and-wwii; https://tinyurl.com/2s3t3yy8; Last accessed 3 14 22

When Milwaukee Went to War - War Memorial Center; https://warmemorialcenter.org/events/75th-commemoration/when-milwaukee-went-to-war-part-9/#:~:text=However%2C%20soon%20married%20men%20without,were%20exempted%20from%20; https://tinyurl.com/24cjrj3j; Last accessed 3 14 22

World War II and the American Home Front National Park Service U.S. Department of the Interior National Historic Landmarks Program; https://irma.nps.gov/DataStore/DownloadFile/465955; https://tinyurl.com/2s4f6xh4; Last accessed 3 14 2

About
Susan L. Schoenbeck, MSN, RN

Susan Schoenbeck is a nurse and a writer whose manuscripts have been published in journals that attract the attention of physicians and nurses from around the globe. She has authored books for lay public and a variety of healthcare personnel. Letters from readers reinforce her belief to write using language everyday people can readily understand.

Susan continues to teach nursing students at Walla Walla University, Portland, Oregon campus where she serves as writing mentor. A childhood polio survivor, Schoenbeck volunteers to honor those who inspired her. Visit her website: susanschoenbeck.com for information.

Susan Schoenbeck 2022

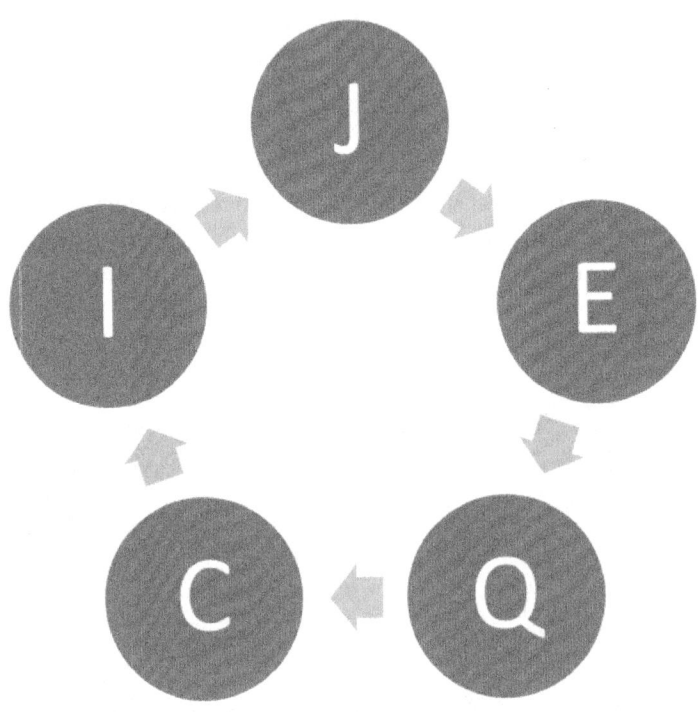

Made in the USA
Monee, IL
26 December 2024

75381673R00236

Edwards Brothers Malloy
Thorofare, NJ USA
October 30, 2014